Additional Praise for Convergence Marketing

"Technology is only the beginning. This book shows how to transform your marketing and business strategies, approaches, structures, and processes—turning technology-enabled opportunities into real profits."

—Mikko Kosonen
CIO and Chief Strategist
Nokia

"*Convergence Marketing Strategy* is a brilliantly conceived blueprint for marketing in the age of the hybrid consumer. Its revelation is timely: success isn't just about hardware and software, but also the 'heartware' and 'spiritware' of the emerging hybrid consumer."

—Y.Y. Wong
Chairman
The WYWY Group, Singapore

"Digital marketing—as dead as the dot-coms? Jerry Wind and Vijay Mahajan x-ray the future customer—a challenging hybrid of cyber- and old eco-animal. Riding the "Centaur" successfully forces the amalgamation of offline marketplace and online marketspace."

—Dr. Ulrich Cartellieri
Member of the Board
Deutsche Bank AG

"Simply thinking about this book's core idea can change your approach to marketing research and strategy—and your tactical decisions about advertising, price, channels, and product development. *This is fundamentally exciting and important.*"

—Russ Winer
J. Gary Shansby Professor of Marketing Strategy
University of California at Berkeley

Additional Praise for Convergence Marketing

"This book is full of must-have tidbits for any marketeer looking to play the game in the post-internet era"

—Mark Goldstein
Former CEO
BlueLight.com

"The future is all about convergence: Dot.coms + not.coms, TV+computer, first world+third world, marketing+finance, and so on. At the center of this future is the centaur—the hybrid consumer who is tech savvy + uniquely human. Wind and Mahajan elucidate the logic+emotion of centaurs and articulate the effective strategies+tactics for marketing to centaurs. This book is a must read for any manager interested in reaching the consumers of today+tomorrow."

—Arvind Rangaswamy
Professor of Marketing
Penn State University

"The concept of the hybrid is *exactly right*. There are no extremes—despite what the media ('out with the old') or those averse to change ('only the old') would have you think."

—Bruce Newman
President
Franklin Mint

"The Web is not replacing old-style marketing with the 'cyber' variety. The Centaur is a neat metaphor for showing how they integrate. I love the way this book debunks today's marketing myths. Whatever you think about post-Web marketing, *buy this book and think again.*"

—Tim Ambler
Senior Fellow
London Business School

CONVERGENCE MARKETING

STRATEGIES FOR REACHING THE NEW HYBRID CONSUMER

ISBN 0-13-065075-7

FINANCIAL TIMES
Prentice Hall

In an increasingly competitive world, it is quality
of thinking that gives an edge. an idea that opens new
doors, a technique that solves a problem, or an insight
that simply helps make sense of it all.

We must work with leading authors in the fields of
management and finance to bring cutting-edge thinking
and best learning practice to a global market.

Under a range of leading imprints, including
Financial Times Prentice Hall, we create world-class
print publications and electronic products giving readers
knowledge and understanding which can then be
applied, whether studying or at work.

To find out more about our business and professional
products, you can visit us at www.phptr.com

CONVERGENCE MARKETING

STRATEGIES FOR REACHING THE NEW HYBRID CONSUMER

Yoram (Jerry) Wind
&
Vijay Mahajan

with Robert E. Gunther

FINANCIAL TIMES
Prentice Hall

Prentice Hall PTR
One Lake Street
Upper Saddle River, NJ 07458
www.phptr.com

A CIP catalogue record for this book can be obtained from the Library of Congress.

Editorial/Production Supervision: KATHLEEN M. CAREN
Acquisitions Editor: TIM MOORE
Marketing Manager: BRYAN GAMBREL
Manufacturing Manager: MAURA ZALDIVAR
Cover Design: ANTHONY GEMMELLARO
Interior Design: WEE DESIGN GROUP

 ©2002 by Prentice Hall
Prentice Hall, Inc.
Upper Saddle River, NJ 07458

Prentice Hall books are widely used by corporations and government agencies for training, marketing, and resale.

The publisher offers discounts on this book when ordered in bulk quantities. For more information, contact: Corporate Sales Department, Phone: 800-382-3419; Fax: 201-236-7141; E-mail: corpsales@prenhall.com; or write: Prentice Hall PTR, Corp. Sales Dept., One Lake Street, Upper Saddle River, NJ 07458.

Printed in the United States of America

10 9 8 7 6 5 4 3 2 1

ISBN 0-13-065075-7

Pearson Education LTD.
Pearson Education Australia PTY, Limited
Pearson Education Singapore, Pte. Ltd.
Pearson Education North Asia Ltd.
Pearson Education Canada, Ltd.
Pearson Educación de Mexico, S.A. de C.V.
Pearson Education—Japan
Pearson Education Malaysia, Pte. Ltd.
Pearson Education, Upper Saddle River, New Jersey

FINANCIAL TIMES PRENTICE HALL BOOKS

For more information, please go to www.ft-ph.com

To the many dot-coms,
some courageous and others foolish,
who conducted the experiments
that pointed the way to the centaurs.

TABLE OF CONTENTS

FOREWORD

In many respects, *Convergence Marketing* is a landmark book. Despite many books and articles on the need to build customer-driven businesses, very few of these works undertake a serious examination of the consumer and, in particular, how consumer needs and expectations are evolving. Many works have been published on consumer behavior and segmentation, but these have generally focused on consumers before the adoption of the Internet as a significant channel for commercial activity.

Convergence Marketing provides for the first time an explicit and detailed context for building customer-driven businesses. It does this by analyzing how consumer needs and expectations are in fact evolving. The authors begin by seeking to understand exactly what consumers are doing given new options made available by the Internet. As a result, they generate considerable insight into the implications for business.

This approach is particularly welcome in light of the shift in power that electronic networks are helping to promote. In physical markets, vendors held a strong position of advantage. Limited shelf space and limited information about products and vendors made it difficult for customers to extract more value from vendors.

Now, this is all changing. Electronic networks help to expand the reach of the customer to find vendors wherever they reside and to obtain much more detailed information about vendor offers. In the process, electronic networks are creating "reverse" markets, where the most productive way to think about market behavior is in terms of customers trying to find the appropriate vendor at a relevant time and to extract as much value as possible from vendors.

Of course, all businesses are themselves customers when dealing with suppliers. The ultimate beneficiary of this shift in power, though, is the end consumer. In light of this, *Convergence Marketing* communicates the urgent need to understand in some detail how consumer needs and expectations are evolving as new technology becomes available. In order to understand how businesses must evolve, we must first understand how the consumer is evolving.

Convergence Marketing is a landmark book in a second dimension as well. It represents a significant shift in focus, marking the beginning of a third era of the Internet. The first era involved growing hype about how the Internet would change everything and quickly generate enormous wealth for those (usually new entrants) who harnessed its power. The second era involved the search for the guilty as the investment bubble burst and as it became apparent that harnessing the value of this new technology was much more difficult than anticipated. The backlash became ugly as various candidates for blame were offered to the public: venture capitalists, investment bankers, Wall Street analysts, greedy pseudo-entrepreneurs, consultants, the media—the list grew with each day.

Convergence Marketing takes a different approach. It steps back and seeks to learn from the experiences, both positive and negative, generated by the early adoption of the Internet as a commercial platform. Rather than focusing on the past as in the second era, it seeks to understand the past in order to provide lessons to guide future action. It understands that lessons are not only learned from the successful, but from the failures as well. In the process, it searches for the right balance. The Internet has clearly not changed everything, but it is also clear that it is changing some things, often in very profound ways. The challenge is to distinguish what remains constant and what must evolve.

It is in this context that the authors develop the central theme of the book: convergence driven by technology. In this respect, the book is also a landmark. They challenge the view of the Internet as a world of its own, distinct and separate from the physical world. Instead, the authors focus on integrating these two worlds to provide a holistic view of both consumers and businesses.

As discussed earlier, the authors begin with a compelling analysis of convergence at the consumer level. Rather than falling into the trap of analyzing consumer behavior only on the Internet or only in physical markets, the authors offer an integrated view of a new kind of consumer—one who is just as comfortable on the Internet as in the mall, and one who understands that both have a role to play in delivering value. This integrated view of the consumer has profound implications for business. The authors persuasively develop these implications at multiple levels—marketing, strategy and organizational design.

As we move into the next stage of business activity driven and shaped by the Internet, we must never lose sight of the consumer. We must give much more prominent focus to understanding how consumers are evolving and the lessons that can be learned from those who led the first wave of business activity on the Internet. And above all, we must never fall into the trap of viewing the Internet as a world of its own. *Convergence Marketing* helps to illuminate the path forward.

John Hagel, III, Chief Strategy Officer
12 Entrepreneuring, Inc., August, 2001

PREFACE: *Running with the Centaur*

> *"A businessman is a hybrid of a*
> *dancer and a calculator."*
>
> Paul Valery, French Poet and Philosopher

The Internet revolution didn't turn out to be anything like we thought it would be. At the end of the 1990s, the discussion of many observers, we among them, focused on the rise of the "cyberconsumer" and the emergence of "Internet marketing." At the extreme, the image of this cyberconsumer was humorously caricatured in a series of Sprint commercials introducing its wireless web, in which people hunched over their computers in dark rooms were invited at long last to step out into the sunlit world. The business model designed for the cyberconsumer was the "pure play" Internet firm, either a separate dot-com or a stand-alone division of a larger company. But the cyberconsumer was largely a myth. Consumers didn't behave anything like we thought they would.

Today, we are entering the age of the centaur. Consumers act across multiple channels. They combine timeless human needs and behaviors with new online activities. They are like the centaur of Greek mythology—half human and half horse—running with the rapid feet of new technology, yet carrying the same ancient and unpredictable human heart. This consumer is a combination of traditional and cyber, rational and emotional, wired and physical, as illustrated in Exhibit P–1. This consumer is not either/or, but both.

The authors came to this center from opposite directions. Jerry Wind was an early champion of digital marketing, highlighting the revolutionary changes of the Internet on consumer behavior, marketing and business strategy. He urged executives to consider the potential of this new technology to transform their businesses. Vijay Mahajan pointed out that not everything had changed, and that many aspects of consumer behavior and marketing remained the same. He urged executives to consider the enduring human characteristics that would continue to shape marketing and business strategy. As we discussed the issue from these two viewpoints, working on a series of projects that led to this book, we came to the conclusion that we were both right: the reality was the hybrid consumer.

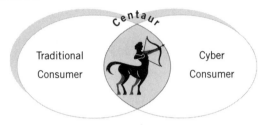

This is *not* to suggest that there are three separate segments (traditional, cyberconsumer and centaur). The reality is convergence. The entire market is becoming centaurs, either directly or indirectly (even if someone is not online, their behavior will still be affected by new technologies, channels and products, and service offerings). This is why we focus so much on the centaur. The centaurs, in turn, are heterogeneous, so there will be many segments among these hybrid consumers.

Even the most tech savvy of U.S. consumers—the 18 to 25 year olds of Generation Y—are not strictly cyberconsumers. A recent survey of more than 600 Gen-Y respondents (51 percent of whom had made online purchases in the past year) found that nearly 40 percent learned about the product online, but bought at a physical store, whereas only 9.3 percent began and ended their search online. When asked where they would prefer to shop, nearly three-quarters chose a store rather than online.[1] Across the spectrum, consumers are combining various channels and approaches, searching online to buy offline, searching offline to buy online—and everything in between (see Exhibit P–2). Charles Schwab found that while about 90 percent of all trades are handled online, 60-70 percent of new accounts are set up in branch offices.[2] People want to be able to see whom they are working with when they turn over their money.

Benefits of Convergence

The power of hybrid models can be seen in the success of Tesco, which raced past pioneers such as Peapod and Webvan to become the largest online grocer in the world. Tesco, using its century-old platform of retail stores in the U.K. as the launching pad for its online service, created a profitable online business that was handling 70,000 orders per week by mid 2001 and had racked up more than $400

68% research online, buy in store

54% research in store, buy online

47% research by catalog, buy online

38% research online, buy over phone

Source: Jupiter Research/NFO, May 2000, *American Demographics*, December 2000.

million in sales the year before. Tesco could set up its online grocery business for a fraction of the investment of Webvan because it was able to build off its existing infrastructure. Tesco has moved into the U.S. market, purchasing a 35 percent investment in Safeway's online grocery service in June 2001, and announcing plans for expansion into South Korea.[3]

The power and profit of the hybrid model can also be seen in the success of Staples.com, which expected to grow online revenues to $1 billion in 2001, nearly 10 percent of company sales. Even more significant, Staples found that the addition of the new channel is not cannibalistic, but synergistic. Overall, customers who shop in the store and catalog spend twice as much as those who shop in the store alone,

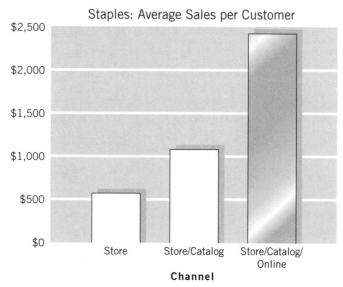

Staples: Average Sales per Customer

Source: *New York Times*, June 25, 2001.

and customers that shop using the store, catalog, and online channels spend an average of $2,500, nearly four times as much as store shoppers, as shown in Exhibit P–3.[4]

The results achieved by Staples and other firms offer a sense of the potential return on investment from meeting the centaur. Convergence strategies offer a variety of opportunities for generating new revenues, reducing costs and creating valuable options for the future, as summarized in Exhibit P–4.

Changing Mind Sets

There is emerging evidence of the immediate benefits of convergence strategies, if investments are made strategically, but these short-term gains are not the only opportunity. Our focus is to look at the opportunities, both short- and long-term, created by the emergence of the hybrid consumer and how companies can capitalize on these opportunities.[5] The last category in Exhibit P–4 may be the most important: the options that convergence strategies create for the future. This book takes a broader view of the strategic impact of the centaur for marketing and business strategy, and the architecture of the organization.

If you believe, as we do, that the centaur is the future of our markets, then the ability to succeed in the future depends on understanding

Potential to Increase Revenue	• Reaches both cyber and traditional segments • Achieves synergies between the online and offline businesses that promote sales • Increases access to the business, anytime, anywhere • Premium services such as customization, home delivery and choice tools increase the stickiness and allow companies to charge a premium price
Potential to Reduce Costs	• Builds on a common inventory, information and logistics base • Reduces cost of contacting customers and other interaction costs • Virtual communities can help reduce the cost of company supplied information and support • Involves customers as co-producers, reduces R&D and marketing costs
Creating Options	• Allows the company to preserve future options • Creates opportunities to move into the most profitable segments or strategies online or offline as the technology and consumers continue to evolve

and "running with" the centaur. Failure to understand these changes creates the risk of significant lost opportunities. What can the integration of the offline *marketplace* and the online *marketspace* do for consumers that neither can do alone? What business principles will guide the integration? How is marketing changing? How do these shifts affect short-term and long-term profitability and growth?

What Is Converging

Convergence, as we discuss it here, means more than the fusion of different technologies (television, computers, wireless, PDAs) or the combination of channels (such as Tesco's or Staple's bricks-and-clicks model). We focus on a more basic convergence within the consumer— the new possibilities created by the technology and the enduring behaviors of human beings. This convergence will shape how the Internet and other new technologies unfold, and the opportunities created for companies. What can consumers do with the technology that they could not do in the past? When will they continue to do things in the way they always have?

Although most of the focus in this book is on business-to-consumer interactions, many of the insights apply equally to business-to-business strategy. The line between B2B and B2C is already blurring. In an environment in which Sun Microsystems is selling products on eBay, is this B2B or B2C? In an environment in which a customer may soon be able to click an order button for an automobile and set in motion a global supply chain to deliver that car, where does B2C end and B2B begin?

Lessons from the Dot-Coms

This book examines the practices of a variety of companies, but we must stress at the outset that these firms are not held up as ultimate models. They all have something to teach us, but many of the successful companies of a year or two ago are now fighting for their lives. And some companies that were all but written off are back in force. We suspect the same unpredictable dynamic will be seen in the future.

This is a particularly dangerous time to engage in benchmarking or to search for excellence. It is not a time for simple recipes. Instead, it is far more important to gain a deeper understanding of how consumers are changing and how they are remaining the same. The actions of these hybrid consumers will shape the way technology is adopted and, ultimately, the future of your markets.

We should take a balanced view of dot-com failures. Mark Twain once said, "We should be careful to get out of an experience only the wisdom that is in it." Twain gives the example of a cat who sits on a hot stove, and learns not to sit on a hot stove again—but also won't sit on a cold stove. The failures of the first wave of dot-coms offer many lessons about what to do, and what not to do, but we need to be careful in taking lessons from them. Although some of the companies that failed had weak business models, some actually had brilliant marketing strategies and business models. The failure of the business is not necessarily an indictment of the idea. Some may have arrived slightly ahead of their time. Some may have suffered from poor execution. It may be that the time is now right for these ideas to flourish.

During the Internet bubble, we have engaged in one of the most extensive, investor-financed experiments in new business models and paradigms. There has been an explosion of experimentation. Although many of these experiments proved to be unprofitable, many new ideas were developed and tested. Incumbent companies and startups that are still alive can benefit greatly from the acceleration of knowledge from this dot-com "school of hard knocks." Pick through the wreckage and look carefully at what happened. Then take away the lessons that you can use.

The Implications of the Centaur

In this book, we offer insights to top executives and key organizational change agents on the characteristics and behavior of these hybrid centaurs and how we need to reshape our marketing and business strategy to meet them. The book explores different intersections between the consumer, technology and company, shown in Exhibit P–5, and their implications for marketing and business strategy and organizational design.

 **AREAS OF CONVERGENCE**

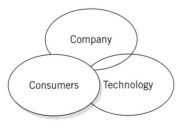

We examine the emergence of the centaur, and the marketing, business and organizational challenges and opportunities created, as illustrated in Exhibit P–6.

Part I offers a portrait of this centaur, what has changed and what remains the same. We also discuss how the focus on the customer has often been lost in the emphasis on technology. These centaurs are complex beings, with a love-hate relationship with the technology, buying books from Amazon.com one day and relaxing in an armchair sipping cappuccino at Barnes & Noble the next.

Part II explores issues at the intersection between the consumer and technology. We consider five key issues at the core of addressing these new hybrid consumers—customerization, communities, channel options, new competitive value propositions, and choice tools. Although these issues have been discussed in the context of the cyber-consumer, they are quite different from the perspective of the centaur. Sometimes consumers want customerization (customized products and services as well as customized marketing), but other times they want to pull standard products off the shelf and receive mass marketing messages. Consumers are members of both physical *and* virtual communities. The hybrid consumers want to be able—in the words of Fidelity—to "call, click, or visit." They are redefining the traditional sources of value, buying products by auction or fixed price or name-your-own price depending on their mood and purchase situation, creating a new value equation. Finally, the Internet offers powerful tools to find information, make decisions, and manage one's life. These tools empower consumers, changing the way they interact with the company. How can you create convergence strategies to address these interrelated issues?

Part III examines the impact of the centaur on marketing and business strategies. As the consumer connects much more directly to companies, marketing has a deeper role to play. Marketing creates new opportunities for growth and rethinking the company's offering, pricing and market boundaries. The centaur has also transformed the traditional 4 Ps of marketing, along with strategies for segmentation, positioning, customer relationships, branding, and marketing research.

As these changes send shockwaves through the organization, another type of convergence is called for—in organizational design. Part IV explores some of the fundamental transformations established organizations need to undergo to meet the centaur. To navigate the whitewater rapids of convergence and change, organizations need new organizational architectures. They need to change their architectures,

 OUR
AIM

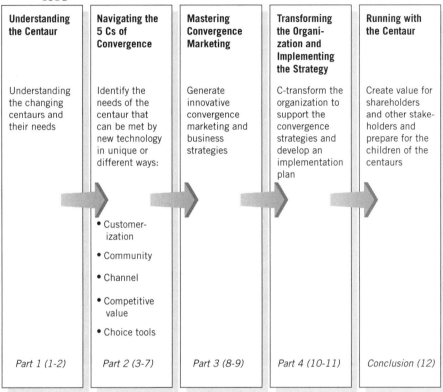

Understanding the Centaur	Navigating the 5 Cs of Convergence	Mastering Convergence Marketing	Transforming the Organization and Implementing the Strategy	Running with the Centaur
Understanding the changing centaurs and their needs	Identify the needs of the centaur that can be met by new technology in unique or different ways:	Generate innovative convergence marketing and business strategies	C-transform the organization to support the convergence strategies and develop an implementation plan	Create value for shareholders and other stake-holders and prepare for the children of the centaurs
	• Customer-ization			
	• Community			
	• Channel			
	• Competitive value			
	• Choice tools			
Part 1 (1-2)	*Part 2 (3-7)*	*Part 3 (8-9)*	*Part 4 (10-11)*	*Conclusion (12)*

creating a broader "c-change" to facilitate convergence across the organization and its ecosystem.

The overall objective is to suggest a new consumer-centric mental model through which to examine the entire business. The kind of shift we are talking about is what Bill Gates describes in the transformation of Microsoft's original mission of "a PC on every desk" to its current mission to "empower people through great software, any time, any place and on any device." The focus is on the convergence of technology and consumer needs.[6]

This book is designed to be an interactive experience. Each chapter begins with a dialogue representing different viewpoints on convergence. Callouts highlight key convergence questions that you can use to challenge yourself and to assess your company's progress. Finally, the close of every chapter offers an "action memo," a set of illustrative hands-on experiments for exploring and applying convergence strategies. We have found the only way to master these new technologies and strategies is to actually experience them and apply them to your own business. These "action memos" are not intended to be exhaustive or to summarize key themes of the chapter, but represent a starting point for your own experiments. We encourage you to share those experiments with us, and other readers, at the Convergence Marketing Forum (convergencemarketingforum.com).

The Relentless March of the Centaur

As Internet penetration increases—and new technologies emerge—we are seeing a relentless march of these new hybrid centaurs. We cannot judge the potential of the Internet and other technologies by their current primitive level of development. John Hagel, author of *Net Gain* and *Net Worth*, says if we compare the Internet to a ballgame, we are still waiting for the national anthem to finish. Michael Nelson, Director of Internet Technology and Strategy at IBM, estimated in 2000 that we were maybe 3 percent of the way into the Internet revolution. He also points out that increased speed of connection, which has been a central focus of attention in the evolution of the Internet, is only a small part of the power of the emerging online world. In addition to raw speed, the fact that the Internet will be always on, everywhere, natural, intelligent, easy, and trusted, will deepen the role of the Internet in our lives.

Nelson compares the development of the Internet to the early days of the electric grid. "The Internet right now is at the light bulb stage," Nelson said. "The light bulb is very useful, but it is only one of thousands of uses of electricity. Similarly, when the next-generation Internet is fully deployed, we will use it in thousands of different ways, many of which we can't even imagine now. It will just be part of everyday life—like electricity or plumbing is today. We'll know we've achieved this when we stop talking about 'going on the Internet.' When you blow dry your hair, you don't talk about 'going on' the electric grid."[7]

There will be naysayers who will use the limitations of the current state of technology as a reason for inaction. Customization is often neither cheap nor simple. Early interfaces with online sites were clunky at best and many home connections remain slow. Throughout this book, we look at the current and future potential of technology and explore how the consumer will interact with it. We won't waste your time giving you a repair manual for a Model T, but instead explore how motor vehicles (particularly newer, more reliable versions) create opportunities for activities such as commerce and family vacations by car. While we must be realistic, we cannot become too mired in the past when the future is so rapidly emerging.

Children of Centaurs: In the Forests of the North

It is clear that we are just getting started with the Internet, and we are even earlier on the learning curve for the new wireless consumers beginning to emerge. Even as businesses are scurrying to absorb the revolution of the Internet, teenagers in Europe and Asia are already shaping the next revolution in mobile communication and commerce. This revolution will play out differently in different parts of the world, and it will probably play out differently than we expect, unless we truly understand the new hybrid consumer. It poses new convergence challenges, but raises the same timeless questions: How will consumers interact with the technology?

Again, this interaction between people and technology will not always be as businesses anticipated. Helsinki teenager Lauri Tähtinen, speaking on a panel of Finnish teenagers at the Wharton Fellows in e-Business Program, said that when he goes out on a Friday night, he doesn't make plans anymore. Instead the 19-year-old goes downtown and starts sending short messages on his mobile phone, pinging his friends to see who's out there. They connect by cell phone and then decide where they want to go for the evening. While companies are excited about developing mobile *information* services that might help customers identify night clubs or order fast food, Tähtinen and his peers are more interested in *connection*. In an environment in which virtually every teenager carries a mobile phone (Finnish market penetration of 78 percent means almost every citizen above the age of 10 carries at least one mobile phone), the mobile conversation is continuous and ubiquitous. Among U.K. teens, short messages outnumber phone conversations three to one, and the parallel phenomenon of instant messaging is one of the most popular applications of teenagers on the PC in the United States and other parts of the world.

The very fact that short messages (SMS) are the top application of mobile phones in Finland is, at first, a surprising thing. The handsets, designed for voice, are not friendly to the process of messaging. Users tap out their 160-word messages on numeric keyboards through complex, rapid-fire keystrokes, smart systems, and creative workarounds. With users paying a charge to send each message on most systems, it would seem unlikely that SMS would be a central part of the mobile phone business. But these young centaurs want to communicate, and they don't let the technology get in their way. It was only in the interaction between consumers and technology that that power of short messages became apparent. Just as email has been the killer application of the Internet, mobile technology is being bent to the human desire to communicate and connect.

"People don't want to be entertained," Tähtinen bluntly states. "They don't want information. If you go into Internet cafés, you see people are not reading the news; they are all sending email or chatting online. They are willing to pay for social interaction. People want to belong to something."

Enduring Lessons

While communications and information technology may be ephemeral and uncertain, there are at least two enduring lessons: The first is that the new technologies, as much as their proponents may want them to, do not replace the old. They live side by side, and they converge. The second is that people are complex, retaining the same enduring human needs even as they adapt to new technologies and behaviors. These may seem like fairly obvious, even simplistic, statements. But they have been overlooked more often than recognized in the mad rush to adopt new technology.

These realities have fundamental implications for marketing and business strategy. What they mean is that there needs to be a convergence of the old technology and the new to create a portfolio of technologies and channels. The storefront and catalog don't go away when you add the Internet. And, even more important, there is an interaction between humans and technology that changes both. There is a convergence of old consumer behaviors and new behaviors that affects the trajectory of technology, the strategies for marketing and, ultimately, the design of the business.

More Human

The wonderful thing about our interactions with machines is not in the ways machines can be made to behave in more human ways, but in the way these interactions make it easier for us to see what distinguishes us as humans. The more we move to machine-mediated interactions, the more we see the fundamental and enduring behaviors that are at the core of marketing and business strategy. It is this interaction between man and machine that is changing us, transforming the practice of marketing and our organizations.

In this book, we examine how we need to transform our thinking about the nature of these emerging consumers. We explore how to reach these centaurs and establish long-lasting relationships with them. We look at the ways that they remain the same and the ways that they are fundamentally different in their expectations and behaviors. And we consider how they have irrevocably changed—and continue to change—the theory and practice of marketing, and the design of our organizations.

Continue the discussion...

Continue the discussion of these concepts with the authors and other readers at the Convergence Marketing Forum (convergencemarketingforum.com).

NOTES

[1] "Is Gen Y Shopping Online?" *Business Week*, June 11, 2001, p. 16. Data from Texas Tech University Institute for Internet Buyer Behavior.

[2] Remarks by Neal Goldstein, Wharton Fellows in e-Business program, San Francisco, January 2001.

[3] "The Lesson from Online Grocery," *The Economist*, June 25, 2001; Stecklow, Steve, "Tesco Sets up Shop in the U.S. with Stake in Grocery Works," *The Wall Street Journal*, June 26, 2001.

[4] Rifkin, Glenn, "New Economy: Re-evaluating Online Strategies," *The New York Times*, June 25, 2001. It does not necessarily imply that the addition of channels is the cause of all or most of the higher revenues from these customers. Staples' most active customers are the ones that will be most likely to utilize multiple channels, so there is a selection bias. While the results are promising, it would be important to explore the overall impact of adding channels.

[5] There are indications that the market also is still banking on the future growth potential of online firms. John Hagel points out that as of July 10, 2001, even after the burst of the bubble, the 37 Internet companies in the Goldman Sachs Internet index had a ratio of market cap to revenue of 8.8 to 1 compared to just 2 to 1 for the Dow. While some of this effect may be

hubris, it also reflects an expectation in the market that these future options will be of value because of the growth potential of these firms. Achieving these gains, however, demands an understanding of the consumers who will shape these markets.

[6] **Bill Gates,** presentation at Microsoft Faculty Summit, July 24, 2001.

[7] Remarks to the Board of the SEI Center for Advanced Studies in Management, The Wharton School, University of Pennsylvania, Philadelphia, September 27, 2000.

Acknowledgments

This book owes a great debt to many people who shared their insights and experiences on this rapidly changing frontier of business. It is these executives and researchers who are living with the challenge of the centaur, thinking about and wrestling with the issues that are pointing the way to the future of convergence marketing. There are too many to fully acknowledge here, although many are noted in the text. In particular, the many people who gave of their time and energy to create and support the Wharton Fellows in e-business. The speakers, faculty and fellows themselves, working on a co-production model, contributed greatly to the insights that inform this book.

We would like to thank our colleagues and reviewers who offered feedback on the manuscript and added so much to the book. We benefited greatly from thoughtful comments by Tim Amber, Steve Andriole, Susane Berger, Jacques Bughin, Candice Carpenter, Colin Crook, Louis Columbus, Peter Drucker, Pete Fader, Neal Goldstein, Mark Goldstein, John Hagel, Mikko Kosonen, Phil Kotler, Malcolm MacDonald, John McGuire, Bruce Newman, Arvind Rangaswamy, Mohanbir Sawhney, Tom Siebel, Russ Weiner, Al West, and YY Wong.

Our editors, Tim Moore and Russ Hall, demonstrated passion, involvement and relentless enthusiasm for the project that helped carry it ever forward and greatly improve the manuscript in the process. Our tremendous thanks to editorial and production supervisor Kathleen Caren and her team for transforming a rapidly changing manuscript into a polished book.

We are grateful for the skilled and indefatigable assistance of Michele Faulls, David Thomas, Mary Kaiser, and Martha Vollmer in our offices for their direct assistance in many aspects of this project, and in keeping the world at bay while we focused on this book. We also are thankful for the research assistance of Archana Vemulapalli.

Finally, this book would never have come into being if it had not been for the enthusiasm of our wives, Dina, Faegheh (Fawn) and Cindie, who put up with the "convergence" of this project into our lives, as it intruded into countless nights and weekends. We are very grateful for their partnership and loving support.

—YJW
—VM
—REG

September 2001

PART 1

UNDERSTANDING THE CENTAUR

In this section, we begin to explore the ways the emerging hybrid consumers are using the Internet and new technologies such as wireless communications, and how they have challenged the initial conventional wisdom about online behavior. The future of marketing and business strategies will not be shaped by technology alone, but by the interaction between technology, the consumer, and the company. As illustrated in the exhibit below, in this section, we focus on the consumer.

In Chapter 1, we offer a brief profile of an emerging hybrid consumer and begin to explore what the centaur means for companies that were designed for an era of offline business, mass messages and markets. How do these centaurs behave? What new segments are emerging? What did the dot-coms fail to see? What were oldline companies slow to recognize?

In Chapter 2, we examine more broadly the relentless march of the centaurs. We also explore how the common myths about traditional consumers (for example, that they are passive and mostly unconnected to peers) and cyberconsumers (for example, that they don't like to shop) have blinded us to the emerging reality of the centaur. We examine how the myths of the traditional consumer initially caused Merrill Lynch to underestimate the power of online channels. We also look at how the myths of the cyberconsumer contributed to the downfall of Garden.com. Finally, we compare the successful convergence business model of online grocer Tesco to the model of pure-play Webvan.

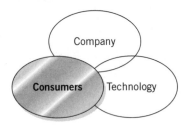

1

THE CENTAUR AWAKENS

"Things do not change, we change."

Henry David Thoreau

TRADITIONAL CONSUMER

"Yes, Henry, but we don't change very quickly. We are pretty set in our ways and once the novelty of the Internet wears off, it will be a bit of a big yawn. People still live in physical homes, go to physical jobs where they eat lunch with physical co-workers, and return to physical families. The online world is, and will be, a small tangent to the real business of life."

CYBERCONSUMER

"We have already changed fundamentally. There are more than 100 million of us online in the U.S. alone and almost all of us are using the Internet for email and to search for information. Things have changed and we have changed. Except for a few people who might be living a life of simplicity out in the wilderness (after throwing their wireless Internet appliances into Walden Pond) most of us have changed in fundamental ways. The Internet is where I have some of my most meaningful interactions, where I can find and buy anything under the sun and meet with people all around the world. My life is completely changed by it."

THE CENTAUR

"In some ways I have changed and in some ways I am the same. I still have the same human needs for interaction, personalization and convenience, but I now have new ways of fulfilling these needs. I will not be boxed in or pinned down. You can think of me as a cyberconsumer, but I am not. You can think of me as a traditional consumer, but I am not. At times, I am one or the other, and both. I will choose from this technology what improves my life and leave behind what doesn't. I will choose when and how I will interact. I will choose when I want to be online and offline. I will go where I want. See if you can keep up."

CONVERGENCE QUESTIONS

>>>*How do your customers combine their online and offline behavior and what does this mean for your business?*

>>>*How can you best meet the needs of these new hybrid consumers?*

>>>*How quickly will they continue to change?*

The Centaur Awakens

The following scenario is not of some distant or unlikely future. It is not some glowing vision of technological utopia or some ode to the old ways of marketing. It is here and now...the complex reality of marketing in an age of rapid change, and a portrait of the emerging centaur. As the centaurs emerge, moving between real and virtual worlds, companies need to develop new convergence strategies to meet them.

Sally Anderson wakes on a Saturday morning in her home outside Philadelphia, Pennsylvania. She fills her coffee maker and fires up her computer. As the coffee drips, she clicks on a link to a web camera focused on a tiny city on the southern coast of Norway. She notes with some satisfaction—and no small amount of longing—that the village square in the city where her grandfather was born is filled with snow. She is a cold-weather person and nothing warms her heart so much as those white drifts. After a long week of work at her own accounting firm, she enjoys leisurely checking her personal email, then reads a joke sent by her cousin in Austin, Texas, with the kind of attention and interest that direct marketers only dream about. She forwards it to a group of friends on her "humor" list. Sally then looks in on the progress of an eBay auction for a ceramic doll that she is within a few hours of winning. She logs out and walks to the curb to retrieve her newspaper from the puddle at the end of the driveway, which her carrier invariably targets. As she peels back the soggy plastic bag, she sits down at the kitchen counter to read the daily headlines, browsing through the newsprint in the same way her grandfather did a century before.

After driving her 12-year-old daughter to soccer practice at the Y, she pulls into the Fresh Fields supermarket. She carefully selects a dozen oranges, squeezing them to make sure they are not overripe. She tries a sample of a new coffee offered at a small table at the end of the aisle. It is quite good, and the peel-off 50-cent-off promotional coupon on the front of the package clinches the deal. She drops a bag in her cart and walks into the personal products aisle where she picks up a bottle of discount shampoo for her husband. She doesn't buy her own shampoo at the store anymore, but instead purchases "Sally's Own" shampoo and personal products through Reflect.com, a customized beauty products site. But her husband, with typical masculine indifference, prefers to use whatever is cheapest. Sally bumps into a friend at the checkout and they exchange a few words as she enjoys the relative freedom of standing in a supermarket aisle without the pull of children or work. Her friend recommends a new book she has been reading, Mary Karr's memoir *Cherry*, and Sally makes a note of the title on her Palm Pilot.

After putting her groceries in the van, Sally goes ten minutes down the road to Nordstrom, where she needs to pick up a dress for a dinner she is attending with her husband Sunday night. She returns a pair of Nine West shoes at the store that she had bought at the Nordstrom.com website. They didn't look as good in real life as they did on the screen. She walks through the dress department, running her hands across the fabric as piano music drifts through the aisles. She still has an hour before she needs to retrieve her daughter. She tries on several dresses before taking a particularly flattering one to the checkout and is snagged by the allure of the perfume counter, where she picks up a new fragrance.

Sally picks up her daughter and goes home to make lunch. After lunch, she logs in to Amazon.com and orders the book *Cherry* with one-click purchasing. While she enjoys an afternoon sipping cappuccino at Barnes & Noble, those days have been few and far between since she started her business. There is no quicker way to send a book speeding to her doorstep than a visit to Amazon.

She receives an email from Peapod asking her if she'd like to renew the regular care package she sends to her 19-year-old son who is studying at the University of Chicago. She sends the care package of his favorite foods every two weeks to his dorm room. She asks for delivery after 7 p.m. that evening. It is a way of showing that she cares and also assuring that the kid won't subsist on chips and soda. The message jogs her memory that she needs to book an airline flight back to Philadelphia for him during winter break in three weeks. She checks prices on Hotwire.com and finds a ticket for just $149. It is a good price, but she decides to go to Priceline.com and submit a slightly lower bid to see if she might beat it.

Sally receives an email from her older cousin in California, who shares a recent photo from a family reunion. Sally forwards the photo to her mother, and would love to pass the photo along to her grandmother, now in her 80s, but the older woman has never touched a computer keyboard. Sally had seen an advertisement for a digital picture frame, and since her grandmother's birthday is coming up in a month, Sally decides to look into it. She goes to MySimon.com and types in a search for "digital picture frame," finding a comparison of vendors that sell the Ceiva frame she is looking for. The same frame that costs $284.99 at Amazon is only $279.95 at a company called Smile Photo

Video and just $224.57 at AccessMicro. Amazon has a three-star merchant rating while AccessMicro only shows two stars, but for a $60 saving, she's willing to take her chances. She clicks through and buys. She can't wait to tell her family they can post photos to the site that will be downloaded automatically to her grandmother's frame.

Anxious about a visit to the doctor on Monday to discuss her problems with carpal tunnel syndrome, she goes to iVillage.com and reads an answer from a doctor about paraffin and vitamin B-6 treatments. The doctor on the site also discusses a variety of other treatments from acupuncture to enzymes. Sally enters the iVillage chatroom on carpal tunnel syndrome, where she reads a post by a woman about a new type of therapy. Sally posts a question to the woman about the treatment, and without waiting for a reply, does a search. She finds an Australian website with information on the therapy and prints out articles to take

How do you combine online and offline behavior in your own life? How do your customers interact with your company online and offline? Why do they choose one channel over another?

with her to her doctor. Her doctor hadn't told her about many of these approaches on her last visit. He's supposed to be an expert in the field, but she now begins to have her doubts.

After finishing some housework and making dinner, she curls up with her husband in front of the television for a little down time. She and her husband laugh at a Pepsi commercial featuring Bob Dole that they saw during the Super Bowl. It is just as funny the second time. Their only difficult decision is which of the hundred or so channels they want to watch.

MEANWHILE, BACK AT MISSION CONTROL...

In a command center deep in the heart of a modern corporation, the marketing department is worried. Sally Anderson and many other consumers who have responded well to mass media advertising appear to be slipping away. The very channels used to connect to them are disintegrating, first into hundreds of television channels and now—even worse—into billions of whizzing packets jettisoned around the planet. These customers were once passengers on large segmented ships on clear trajectories. Now they are exploding into atomistic markets of one, rocketing out to the farthest fringes of the universe. These customers are connecting with the company and with other people in a free-form, self-organizing, organic way. In other words, in a way that the marketers can't directly control. And this has them worried.

Sally and other centaurs—half wired, half not—are living intertwined lives. Sally divides her shopping cart and information gathering between the online and offline world (as illustrated in Exhibit 1–1). She picks up her paper at the curb and her milk at the grocery store, but she also looks to the Net for

EXHIBIT 1–1 SALLY'S TWO WORLDS

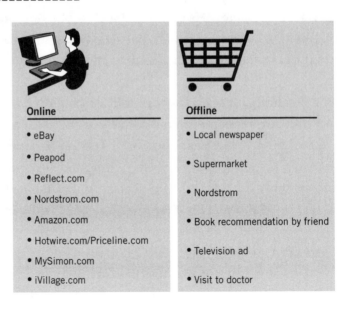

Online	Offline
• eBay	• Local newspaper
• Peapod	• Supermarket
• Reflect.com	
• Nordstrom.com	• Nordstrom
• Amazon.com	• Book recommendation by friend
• Hotwire.com/Priceline.com	
• MySimon.com	• Television ad
• iVillage.com	• Visit to doctor

information and sends her son groceries through Peapod. In some ways, traditional approaches and conventional wisdom about marketing continue to hold. In other ways, this consumer acts quite differently. She acts differently in various situations and there are huge differences across people—even if they appear to be in the same demographic segments.

This marketspace (as opposed to the traditional "marketplace") is more than a new location or new channel, as the marketing department had originally thought. It turns out to be something far more insidious. Now the marketers—at both manufacturing and retail firms—are trapped in some sci fi movie in which the customers are beginning to mutate, a business version of *Invasion of the Body Snatchers*. The marketers at Mission Control never had to ask *permission* to market.[1] They never worried about creating a "community." They focused on segments of customers, so they didn't need to know what was going on inside Sally Anderson's head. When their predecessors offered a new washing machine or box of Tide to Sally's mother, they focused on market segments, not individuals. (Of course, Sally's mother, like many of her peers, is now online, receiving photos of her grandchildren and passing along recipes to Sally.) In those days, all marketers needed to know was that the consumer was part of a herd. Markets were broadcasts, definitely *not* "conversations." Now something is changing, but the change is also not as absolute as some initially thought it would be. Instead, a new consumer, a hybrid, a centaur, is emerging—and this requires new approaches to marketing.

How do you need to rethink your approach to marketing in light of the new hybrid consumer?

THE CHALLENGE OF THE CENTAUR

Sally Anderson probably doesn't know it, but she is changing the discipline of marketing. The most radical shift of marketing in the digital age is not merely the emergence of new technology or channels, but transformations deep inside the consumer.

The new technologies have changed the way customers behave—what they expect and how they view their relationship to corporations—online and offline. Sally Anderson probably would not consider herself a cyberconsumer, the term used to refer to consumers who purchase online, but she leads a very different life than her mother or grandmother did at her age. She and the other emerging centaurs—and even more so, her children—are radically transforming the practice of marketing.

The Internet and other technologies allow Sally to do things that she could never do before. They permit her to fulfill basic human demands and desires in new ways (as summarized in Exhibit 1–2). While these capabilities—for customerization (customized products and services and marketing), community, channel options, competitive value, and choice tools—are now widely recognized, they have often been considered in isolation. This view tends to overemphasize how the world will be changed by the technology rather than how the technology will be changed by the world. For example, customization technologies allow Sally to have tailor-made products, marketing messages, and experience, yet she often chooses instead off-the-shelf products, mass messages and standard shopping experience. Why? She can be part of a vast array of virtual communities, but spends her life moving between online and offline communities. Why? She will sometimes buy online, sometimes by phone, and sometimes at a physical store. Why? She can choose a wide range of pricing models and in a single day might buy from an auction, fixed price, or name-your-own-price system. Why? She will sometimes accept the marketing messages of companies and sometimes seek out third-party information. Why?

We selected these five areas—customerization, community, channel options, competitive value, and choice tools—because they represent important intersections between the potential of the new technology and the enduring patterns of human behavior. How consumers and technology interact in these areas has implications for marketing and business strategy. For each of these "5 Cs," there is a convergence between the traditional behaviors of consumers and new behaviors. Now that we know

EXHIBIT 1-2 CHALLENGES OF THE EMERGING HYBRID CONSUMER

The Demands of the Centaur	Illustrative Convergence Challenges for Marketing
Desire for uniqueness, personalization, and customization Sally buys customized products from Reflect.com and a customized care package on Peapod, yet also purchases off-the-shelf products in Nordstrom's and the grocery store.	*Customerization* How can companies offer the right mix of standard and customized products? How do they need to rethink their approaches to new product development? How can companies offer the right balance of personalization and mass marketing messages?
Desire for social interaction Sally enjoys meeting friends in the store—getting book recommendations from her physical community—but goes to iVillage to discuss her medical problems with experts and other women.	*Virtual communities* How can companies combine real-world communities and virtual communities in a way that leads to profit? Should companies create their own communities? Given that consumers are participating in a number of communities already, how can companies tap into them?
Desire for convenience and channel options Sally wants to walk in or log in, interacting where and when she desires, anytime and anyplace. She wants the company to be accessible and responsive—on her schedule not the company's.	*Channel options* How can companies combine multiple channels into a seamless interface? How can they anticipate how consumers will interact with them? How can they add new channels to existing systems and assure high levels of service and quality across phone, clicks and visits?

EXHIBIT 1–2 **CONTINUED**

The Demands of the Centaur	Illustrative Convergence Challenges for Marketing
Desire for value	*Competitive value equation*
Sally mixes purchases in physical stores with online markets throughout the day. She buys shoes at Nordstrom online and returns them in a physical store. In purchasing her airline tickets, she actively names her own price but then buys at a discount, and she also purchases through auctions on eBay.	How do companies need to reshape their pricing strategies in an environment in which customers have many more pricing options (auctions, name your own price, etc.)? How can companies address the higher expectations of customers for value and service? How do information, education, and entainment contribute to value?
Desire to make better decisions Sally goes to MySimon to compare prices for a digital photo frame, yet Hotwire and Priceline keep their sophisticated pricing tools hidden from the customer.	*Choice tools* Given that customers have access to more search engines and decision-making tools, how do companies need to transform their strategies? How can companies put more tools into the hands of customers, to simplify their lives, without giving away their business or driving customers to rivals? How can they best balance company-initiated messages with unbiased information?

what consumers *can* do with the technology, we have to look more carefully at what they are likely to *want* to do.

The challenge for organizations is to understand what these underlying desires and complex behaviors mean for marketing and how to meet these needs. Which traditional marketing concepts still work, and which ones do they need to eliminate or change? Which new marketing approaches do they need to add?

This emerging centaur has enduring human needs and desires, but these have been sharpened and attenuated by the promise of technology. These needs and desires include:

- *Desire for uniqueness, personalization, and customization:* Sally now expects the world to revolve around her. Large corporations are expected to know her likes and dislikes. Sally and her peers, and even more so her children, don't even want to have to ask for what they want. ("You should know what I am thinking!") Sally might be pleased when Marriott brings a Diet Coke with lime to her table anywhere in the world without being asked (provided she has not changed her preferences) and she values Amazon's recommendation for a book that proves to be a keeper. But she is very quick to get angry when she calls her phone company about a problem and has to give the same information to three different representatives. ("Why don't they know me? I've had my phone service with them for more than a decade!") At the same time, she does not want to have her privacy compromised in any way, and she reserves the right to change her mind. So companies have a hard time knowing where to draw the line in this personal service. Companies like Amazon or Schwab are personalizing their interactions with customers. More than this, Sally wants customized products and services, like the shampoo she buys from Reflect.com. On the other hand, her husband is happier just to buy something off the shelf, and Sally wants to pick out her oranges personally. Sometimes Sally and her husband just want to curl up in front of the tube and watch the messages that are pumped into their living room. How do companies effectively combine customization with mass production? How can they balance mass messages with personalized interfaces? How can companies provide the right mix of off-the-shelf and customization? How can they create flexible systems to offer options to customers without overwhelming them, and then design their product development systems to deliver those options quickly? How can companies use marketing communications to offer coherent experiences to consumers and build lasting relationships with them?

- *Desire for social interaction:* People have always had a desire for social interaction, but the centaur has more opportunities to participate in online and offline communities. This has created new expectations. Sally goes to iVillage for medical advice because she feels comfortable sharing her challenges with other participants in the chatroom. People can flow in and out of them with a click. On the other hand, these virtual connections can be quite deep. For example, one woman's post on a mother's message board at iVillage read: "This board has become my solace in a hectic day." Another single mother wrote to the pregnancy message board that the community had helped her "get these secrets off my chest and was surprisingly nonjudgmental." As an indication of the bonds formed by these online relationships, the woman said she was surprised to receive baby gifts from women she had only met online.[2] Where the marketing discipline focused on "positioning," encouraging a customer to identify with a certain community (sporty and upscale suburban professionals who buy SUVs, for example) or identifying affinity groups, now the idea of community is much broader and more interactive. People are seeking out others who share their own interests (people who paddle kayaks in the Northeast who happen to own SUVs, for example) or are facing a similar challenge (women preparing to give birth). They are forming communities that are powerful and have a profound impact on their lives. The challenge for companies is to turn these communities into commerce. Even "successful" communities such as iVillage and Turf.com have yet to demonstrate their financial viability. How can companies create a convergence of the economic and social aspects of communities, finding profit without destroying the community in the process? How can companies build communities or tap into existing ones? How can companies leverage the centaur's participation in both real and virtual communities to develop convergence strategies?

- *Desire for convenience and channel options:* Convenience once meant a store on every corner, but now the 24-hour "convenience" store no longer pushes the limits of convenience. Sally can purchase books, electronics products, and airline tickets outside of standard business hours. Consumers can download software and other digital products immediately. Still, convenience is not defined by the company but by the consumer. They want a richer set of relevant channel options, the ability to do what Fidelity Investments has referred to as "click, call or visit" strategy, offering multiple channels that provide seamless access to the company. Companies need to be able to interact with customers in multiple locations and through multiple channels, when and where the customers want to interact. How can com-panies offer multiple channels for interaction and ensure these channels all work together? How can both manufacturers and retailers reshape their strategies for these new channels?

- *Desire for competitive value:* The value equation is being redefined. The technology facilitates the application of pricing models such as auctions or name-your-own price strategies. There is a convergence of buyer-initiated and seller-initiated pricing models. Sally pays fixed prices in the grocery store or Nordstrom, but names her own price on Priceline and participates in an auction on eBay. But pricing changes are just part of how the value equation is changing. The value equation is being reshaped as companies focus on broader definitions of value that include not only product and price, but also factors such as novelty, control, and speed. The underlying product is being redefined as it is increasingly bundled with information, education, and entertainment. These options have changed the way the centaur thinks about pricing and the way companies need to shape their value propositions relative to their competitors. How can companies reshape their approaches to pricing to take advantage of new flexible pricing strategies and still generate a profit? How can companies address the higher expectations of customers for value and service?

- *Desire to make better choices:* People want to make informed decisions, but often the information is not available or it is in the hands of the seller. The Internet offers the opportunity to put more tools in the hands of customers and this has changed the behavior and expectations of the centaur. Sally uses MySimon to get a better deal on the digital picture frame for her grandmother. An increasing array of decision tools are helping customers simplify their process of searching and buying online. Companies like Bizrate provide even evaluations of company performance based on surveys of individual customers. These are only a foreshadowing of more powerful shopping bots that are waiting in the wings. But information changes the balance of power in relationships. Even the physician, who was once viewed as a god, is being dropped a notch or two thanks to abundant medical information that can be found online. After finding medical information online, 15 percent of patients were more likely to question their physician's knowledge and 9 percent said they were considering looking for a new doctor.[3] Companies are understandably reluctant to put all the tools in the hands of consumers. Does Amazon want customers to know that AccessMicro can beat its price on Ceiva photo frames? How can companies offer customers decision tools to simplify their decisions, without driving the customers to competitors? How can tools typically used inside the company be put into the hands of consumers (for example, allowing customers to access their bank or loan information online) to the advantage of both? Given that customers have access to more decision tools, how do companies need to reshape their strategies?

These five interrelated opportunities created by the centaur require companies to rethink their approaches to marketing. What parts of their traditional marketing practices need to be modified or abandoned? Which new capabilities and practices need to be added to their portfolio of tools? Companies need to find new ways to create customerization, build communities, provide relevant channel options, offer competitive value, and provide decision tools to customers. The way companies have creatively met these challenges, and especially the challenge of addressing different combinations of these needs for different segments, will be the focus of the second section of the book.

> **What opportunities are created for your business through the new potential for customerization, communities, channel options, competitive value equations, and choice tools? How can you take advantage of these opportunities?**

RUNNING WITH THE CENTAUR

In addressing the challenge of this hybrid consumer, there are two primary types of mistakes companies make: treating the centaur as a *completely different* phenomenon or treating the centaur as *the same* as the traditional consumer. Both mistakes are equally disastrous.

- *What the dot-coms failed to see:* Many of the early dot-coms made the first mistake. They were so enamored with their hot technology, business models, and hoards of venture cash that they forgot about the customer who was allegedly at the center of their business proposition. Many online companies assumed that making the shopping experience more efficient would be a great plus for consumers. But these companies apparently failed to see that many consumers actually *like* to shop. They may want to run their hands down rows of clothing in Nordstrom, or sip cappuccino in Barnes & Noble. A study of 48 dot-com failures found that many of the failed companies had a flawed understanding of their customers.[4] Companies also neglected to apply fairly simple marketing tools for measuring customer loyalty and other factors that could have provided clear insights into the future challenges they would face in building their markets. Online marketers have often failed to recognize the diverse reasons *why* people buy, and how these motivations affect *how* they buy.[5] These companies have stood at the tail of the centaur and described this consumer from that perspective.

- *What the oldline firms are slow to recognize:* At the same time that many online firms have failed to see how the centaur is similar to the traditional consumer, oldline firms often get into trouble when they fail to recognize how the centaur is different. Companies thought they could just drive their banner ads onto this new medium or publish their brochureware on a website, like billboards on the Information Superhighway. Consumers were not interested. These centaurs needed more interaction, engagement, and individual attention. Companies need to offer multiple channels. The Web also offers opportunities for market expansion, opening new geographic markets or customer segments—but only if companies recognize this and take advantage of it. We must stress that we are not saying that marketing, as we know it, is dead. Far from it. Some of the old marketing tools and models work well in the new environment, but some need to be discarded, modified, or added to. Companies clinging to traditional approaches have stood at the front of the centaur, focusing on the continuity, and fail to recognize sufficiently the differences. Even now, when more firms recognize the potential of the new technologies, many are limited by short-term financial objectives or organizational processes from developing or implementing convergence strategies. They don't have the courage or capacity to change their wheels while they are driving the car, so they fail to undertake the large-scale transformations that companies such as Charles Schwab, General Electric and Enron have made.

Companies that are still standing after the dot-com collapse and have capital to invest have a tremendous opportunity. As Andy Sernovitz, CEO of consulting firm GasPedal Ventures, commented, "We've developed techniques and tools and business processes that never would have been built in a normal economy. How can you steal the stuff that the Internet kids with the earrings invented and apply it to your business? If you have a company and decent business sense, it is a wonderful time to make a lot of money."[6]

As a manager of an established firm, how can you take advantage of the power of the hybrid consumer to transform your marketing strategy? As an online firm, how can you take advantage of the wisdom of traditional marketing to strengthen your strategy?

The key is to be on the leading edge, but not the "bleeding edge." Since no one really knows where this line is, companies need to engage in continuous experimentation to find out what works. This way you can make small investments that enhance your future learning, yet still manage the business for the short-term. Keep your eye on the consumer. By gaining a deeper understanding of consumers, you can stay with the centaurs, instead of getting too far ahead or behind.

The 20/20 Vision of 1-800-CONTACTS

There are tremendous opportunities in addressing the interrelated aspects of the emerging centaurs such as Sally. For example, 1-800-CONTACTS, the world's largest direct marketer of contact lenses, has aggressively migrated its business from the telephone to the Internet. Online orders, which accounted for just 4 percent of its business in 1998, shot to 37 percent in 2001, making it the Internet's largest contact lens store, with online revenue of $53 million. Even more significantly, online sales were driving the future, accounting for a third of new orders. (Of course, its cyberactivity brought the company into greater conflict with its real-world rivals, private optometrists, and national vision chains, who have raised protests.) With a multichannel strategy of accepting orders by "phone, mail, fax and the Internet," the company's overall revenue continued to climb rapidly, to $145 million in 2000 (as shown in Exhibit 1–3).

1-800-CONTACTS also built upon its existing successful business in telephone and mail order sales, leveraging the

EXHIBIT 1–3 SALES BY 1-800-CONTACTS

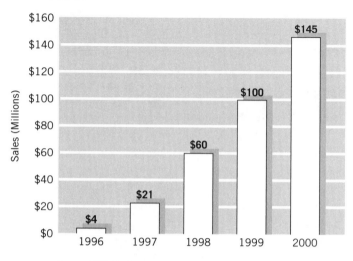

Source: 1-800 CONTACTS

resources of its customer service and warehouse. In a single warehouse in Utah, the company stocked more than 10 million contact lenses, delivering 100,000 (more than two tons) every day to consumers. The inventory of name-brand contacts allows the company to ship 90 percent of its orders within 24 hours of receipt.

What is it about the company that made it so successful in online business? This winner has a somewhat different profile than one would hypothesize. First, the product was physical, not digital as was expected, but it was perfectly suited to online sales. Contact lenses are easy to specify (search goods) and the wearer is accustomed to regular replacement of this disposable product. The purchase price was fairly high and the mailing and inventory costs were low because of the small package size and light weight. People don't select contacts the way they pick up oranges. They don't buy them for gifts or need to research them extensively before making the decision to purchase. More than 60 percent of sales were repeat and replacement purchases, which lowers the amount of information and emotional involvement. The product also was not a "new-to-the-world" product nor was it customized, but rather something that was tried and true. The company also had no alliances, which was counter to expectation and counter to the many alliances of Amazon.com. Yet the key to the success of 1-800-contacts.com is that very few of the reasons why the centaur might shop offline applied in this business.[8]

Convergence Marketing

As 1-800-CONTACTS found, there can be tremendous opportunity in creatively developing a new set of strategies to meet the centaur across multiple channels. There is no simple formula. Not every product or market lends itself to the approach taken by 1-800-CONTACTS. Every company must determine how to best balance the complex demands of the various segments of hybrid consumers. By better understanding these needs of the centaur, companies can better develop online and offline strategies that work to meet these needs. Just as retailers are learning to combine "clicks and bricks," marketers need to combine traditional marketing strategies with emerging online strategies.

On the following pages, we explore approaches to marketing to the centaur. It is not a revolution—with crowds racing through the streets toppling over the statues of the past. It is not the end of marketing as we know it. These revolutionary slogans are focused on the cyberconsumer, but centaurs are not strictly cyberconsumers. Nor is it the continuation of the status quo. These centaurs are not entirely traditional consumers. They are a creative fusion of the two, coming in many shades along the spectrum from cyber to traditional. The centaurs demonstrate that the basic human wiring of customers remains the same—but the software of expectations and interactions running through their heads and hearts is now quite different.

As much as Sally Anderson has already started the transformation of the centaur, her children will be even more immersed in this world. They will be more comfortable with the technology, and will lead the way into wireless m-commerce and m-lifestyles, broadband interconnectivity—and whatever happens next. The certainty is that there will be new technologies and business models and this new generation will find new uses for

Action Memo

- Buy the same book (could be this one) from
  www.Amazon.com and www.bn.com. How is the overall
  customer experience different for the two purchases? Which
  one was quicker and easier? Which cost more? How do you
  feel about that? Which one arrives first? What follow-up
  messages do you receive? Try to come up with hypotheses
  for the difference in marketing strategies.**Can you test these
  hypotheses or apply these approaches in your business?**

- Go into a Barnes & Noble store and observe customers. What
  can they do there that cannot be done online? What are
  behaviors that might be supported online if they were offered?
  What offerings could be made when the Internet is fast, easy and
  always on? What opportunities do you see of the company to
  market to hybrid consumers across channels? **What opportunities are you overlooking in your own business?**

*We invite you to share the results of these activities and
suggest other action memos at the Convergence Marketing
Forum (www.convergencemarketingforum.com).*

them, which their originators and the businesses that rolled
them out never envisioned.

It is a complex picture. Human beings are complex beings–
and even more so now that they have begun to consort with
smart technology. The companies that can understand these
changes will find new ways to connect with their customers.
Companies that don't focus on the centaur will be missing a big
opportunity. To capitalize on the opportunities presented by the
centaurs, companies need to run with them. To meet the new
realities of this converging consumer, companies need to create
convergence of their own marketing approaches, joining old
and new, online and offline. They need to create new strategies
for customerization, communities, channels, delivering competitive value and offering decision tools. In the process, they will
reinvent their companies and the marketing discipline, leading

to the convergence of diverse functions within the organization and a drawing together of internal and external stakeholders. This book and the stories of pace-setting companies discussed herein are designed to help point the way.

NOTES

[1] Seth Godin, *Permission Marketing*, New York: Simon & Schuster, 1999.

[2] Lisa Kraynak, Vice President of Strategic Development, iVillage, Wharton conference on "Virtual Communities and the Internet," April 2000.

[3] Sean Nicholson, Wharton Virtual Test Market, presentation to ICG/Wharton Forum on e-Business, December 5, 2000.

[4] Mahajin, Vijay and Raji Srinivasan and Jerry Wind, "The Dot-Com Retail Failures of 2000: Were There Any Winners?" working paper, McCombs School of Business, University of Texas at Austin, 2001.

[5] Balasubramanian, Sridhar, Vijay Mahajan, and Raj Raghunathan, "How Consumers Buy May Affect the Utility of What they Buy," working paper, McCombs School of Business, University of Texas at Austin, 2001.

[6] Remarks to the Wharton Fellows in e-Business Program, at idealab! New York City, May 9, 2001.

[7] 1-800-CONTACTS Form 10-K, 2000; and www.1800contacts.com.

[8] Mahajin, Srinivasan and Wind, see note 4 above.

2

THE REALITY
OF THE CENTUAR

"All human actions have one or more
of these seven causes:
chance, nature, compulsion, habit,
reason, passion, desire."

Aristotle

TRADITIONAL CONSUMER

"Aristotle is right. The emotions that drive human behavior are the same that they've always been. The Internet doesn't change that. It is nothing more than a new distribution channel. The technology will come and go, but we will keep doing what we have always done. We have seen the weakness of these upstart revolutionary dot-coms. The cyberconsumer is a myth, and I don't believe it."

CYBERCONSUMER

"Aristotle didn't know about the Internet, which has become a new motivation for human actions. The cyberconsumer is a fundamentally new type of wired consumer. Shut down your marketing departments and close your books. This is a revolution. The traditional consumer is a memory. The old rules do not apply here."

THE CENTAUR

"While the motivations for human actions remain the same, the Internet now gives us powerful new ways of realizing our passions and desires. I can connect with a friend on the other side of the world, but also may choose to share lunch with a friend from down the street. You are both right. The cyberconsumer is a myth and the traditional consumer is rapidly becoming a memory. The reality is the centaur."

CONVERGENCE QUESTIONS

>>> *What is the reality of the centaur? What parts of the idea of the cyberconsumer and traditional consumer need to be challenged in this process?*

>>> *What segments of the centaur are most relevant for your business?*

>>> *How quickly is this centaur emerging?*

>>> *How do you need to change your strategies to meet them?*

THE REALITY OF THE CENTAUR

Our views of the traditional consumer and the cyber-consumer are based on myths. The reality is the centaur.

Sipping tea in the kitchen of an old childhood friend on a Saturday afternoon, Joanne Knight mentions with a sigh that she really needs to leave to do the family grocery shopping. Her friend, Ruth Mandalay, just smiles and says she is now using an online grocery service. She never has to leave home to do her grocery shopping. She can shop in her nightgown in the middle of the night when the house is quiet. Ruth calls up the computer program and shows how quickly she can place her order from her existing list. If she wants to, she can see only organic or fat-free items in the store.

Joanne is impressed and, at first, a little envious. But as she thinks about it, Joanne realizes she actually likes the experience of shopping at her favorite store. She likes to try out new flavors of coffee. She likes to taste the samples of new cheeses and breads. She likes to see the oranges she is picking out and let her mind wander as she slips through the aisles and thinks about the culinary possibilities.

The experience on the computer screen, even with pictures of the items, seems rather flat in contrast. And there is the inconvenience of having to be there to receive the delivery in addition to the delay in scheduling. Joanne likes to live her life a little more spontaneously.

"Don't you miss shopping?" Joanne asks her friend. At first, the question catches Ruth off guard. "Miss shopping?" she askes incredulously. "Didn't you just sigh a minute ago as you thought about it?" But as Ruth thinks about it, she realizes she *does* miss shopping. This surprises her more than anything, because she assumed that a busy person like herself would value any time-saving convenience available to make life more efficient. It would be like washing dishes by hand instead of putting them into the dishwasher. But now she begins to wonder.

In the end, both Ruth and Joanne decide that they will shop in the store for the fruit, flowers and other goods but order the boring and bulky staples online. This will allow them to benefit from the efficiency of the online experience and the immersion of the offline experience.

WHERE'S THE CUSTOMER?

As we pick through the wreckage of the dot-com revolution, there is one piece of the puzzle that has been noticeably missing, one empty hole at the heart of it: the consumer. The dot-com debacle is not just the story of "irrational exuberance" and overzealous entrepreneurs and investors, but also the story of a generation so enthusiastic about the *technology* that we often lose sight of the *people* at the center of it.

These houses were built upon the sand of assumptions about people and their behavior that fly in the face of millennia of human experience. On the one hand, some companies assumed consumers would make rapid and fundamental changes in their behavior. Yet we have held onto some of our traits and shopping patterns as stubbornly as a morning cup of coffee. On the other hand, other companies have made the mistake of believing that this powerful new technology would have little or no impact. The lesson of the centaur is that technology does change us, but no matter how fast we gallop ahead, we remain human.

Those who argued that everything would be changed by the Internet are only partially right, as are those that argue that everything would remain the same. In the centaur, there is a mix of aspects that are transformed and those that remain the same, as illustrated in Exhibit 2–1. Each extreme leads to a set of myths about consumers.

What's Changed

- Customerization and personalization
- Participation in virtual communities
- Access anytime, anywhere
- New pricing and value equations
- Desire to make better decisions

What Remains the Same

- Like to shop
- Sometimes value human benefits above efficiency
- Desire for fair price, not best price
- Integrating new channels into existing ones
- Lower transaction costs make it easier to walk away
- Real is sometimes more interesting than virtual

THE INTERNET POPULATION *IS* THE POPULATION

Basic human motivations are more important than ever. More than half the United States is now online[1] and many developed nations are well on their way to crossing this threshold (see Exhibit 2–2).[2] Early Internet users, like most early adopters of any new technology, were a strange breed. These initial netizens were predominantly high-income, tech-savvy, Caucasian young men—in short, "geeky white guys." The broadening of the Internet population means that the online population is increasingly representative of the general population. High concentrations of Web users show up in demographic clusters that range from wealthy suburbanites to low-income rural populations. With rising penetration of personal computers and Internet access, the customer mix on the average online site is looking less like the floor of a Comdex convention and more like the aisles of Wal-Mart. As Lee Rainie, director of the Pew Internet & American Life Project, comments: "Americans online are not a monolithic group anymore. There are so many people using the Internet in so many different ways that it is

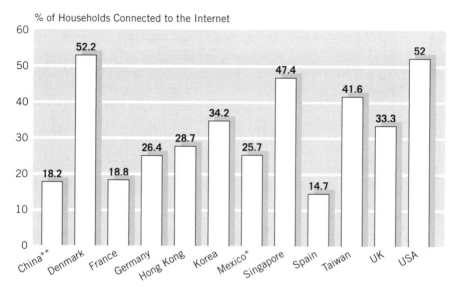

EXHIBIT 2–2 GLOBAL HOUSEHOLD INTERNET CONNECTIONS

% of Households Connected to the Internet

Source: NetValue, November 2000

* Households connected to Internet in Mexico DF, Guadalajara & Monterrey Socio-economic levels A&B, C+, C, D–
November 2000

** China (Beijing, Guangzhou, Shanghai)- November 2000

hard to define the center of gravity."[3] There is not an online and offline consumer. They are one and the same. To paraphrase the oft-quoted cartoon character Pogo: "We have met the Internet and it is us."

The online population, like the offline population, is made of diverse segments. In fact, the Internet introduces additional segments.[4] Studies of the Wharton Virtual Test Market found that the most meaningful online segmentation (relating to purchases and time spent online) is not based upon demographic factors but rather factors such as online experience, a wired lifestyle, time pressure and purchases from catalogs.

As an example of non-demographic segmentation, McKinsey identified a set of online segments based on Internet adoption and behavior(see box).[5] On the Internet, as might be expected, comfort with making purchases increases with experience online, something of vital interest to companies in assessing the revenue potential of their business. New technologies such as the mobile Internet are expected to follow similar adoption curves and companies need to be careful to distinguish the characteristics of early adopters from late followers.

Most approaches to segmentation, however, have focused on either traditional demographic and geographic segments (such as Claritas' Prizm segmentation system), new cyber-segments such as the McKinsey example, or the seven-segment "occasion" system develop by Booz Allen & Hamilton.[6] Some systems are now exploring segmentation of the market based on convergence, the way consumers behave across channels. For example, eBates.com distinguishes among different types of dot-shoppers, including: "hunter-gatherers," Baby Boomers who use the Internet like a consumer magazine to search for information, but buy offline; and "time-sensitive materialists"

An Example of Segmentation of Online Consumers

In a study of more than 6,000 active users, McKinsey and Media Metrix indentified the following segments:

- **Connectors** (26%): These are the new users of the Internet who use it primarily to connect and communicate. They are also more connected to offline brands.
- **Samplers** (26%): These are light users who explore multiple domains.
- **Simplifiers** (20%): They use the Internet to make their lives more efficient, so they require end-to-end convenience.
- **Routiners** (11%): These consumers are light users who go online to look for information and are not primarily interested in shopping.
- **Surfers** (10%): While small, these consumers are the heaviest users, spending the most time online and exploring multiple domains.
- **Bargainers** (4%): These consumers use the Internet for price comparisons, shopping for the best buy online.
- **Funsters** (3%): These consumers are also looking for information, but primarily in a few domains focused on entertainment.

Source: McKinsey/Media Metrix, October 2000

---

who use the Internet as a convenience tool.[7] As the pool of hybrid consumers continues to grow, these and other convergence-based segmentation schemes will become more significant in targeting the right products, services, and channels to different consumers.

For simplicity, we refer to "the centaur" throughout the book to distinguish this consumer from the views

As the Internet becomes faster, easier, and more ubiquitous, how will this change the compostion of your company's online customer base? How will it change your offline customer base?

of the cyberconsumer and traditional consumer. In reality, however, we need to bear in mind that there are many "breeds" (segments) of centaurs with very specific characteristics.

The Relentless March of the Centaurs

The demographic picture of the Internet is changing rapidly. While understanding the different segments is vitally important in shaping strategies, it is also crucial to rise above the fray. Whatever the picture is today, it will change tomorrow. Among the forces driving the proliferation of the Internet are: the increased acceptance of Internet access at work, the acceptability of Internet access in schools, new modes of accessing the Internet without a PC (cell phones, PDAs, television). Moreover, companies such as Ford, Enron, and others are supplying employees with free personal computers and Internet access for their homes. Globally, economic progress and infrastructure development continue to drive growth. The Internet will continue to expand globally with rising GDP per capita and development of enabling infrastructure (such as broadband cable and wireless connections).[8] All of these forces have led various forecasters to estimate that the number of Internet users will reach one billion worldwide somewhere between 2004 and 2008.

Very few of these wired consumers are strictly online. The Pew Internet & American Life study finds that 93 percent of those online use email,[9] but one would expect that almost all of these also use conventional "snail mail" as well. Even more telling is that 65 percent of those on the Internet go online to look for movies, books, and other offline leisure activities. The

EXHIBIT 2-3 **THE RELENTLESS MARCH OF THE CENTAURS**

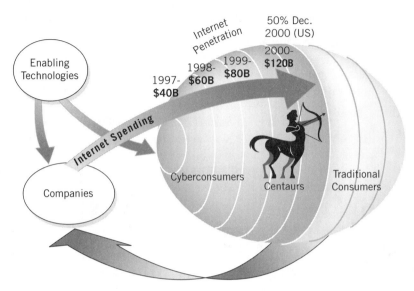

Source: Approximate overall U.S. corporate Internet spending, International Data Corp., 2000.

spread of the Internet continues to expand the group of hybrid consumers in a dynamic, reinforcing cycle, as illustrated in Exhibit 2–3. As companies increase their Internet spending— topping an estimated $120 billion in 2000—they continue to drive the penetration of the Internet to more than half the U.S. population (with similar, or sometimes even more dramatic, advances in other nations). These centaurs will continue to march forward into the decreasing pool of uninitiated, traditional consumers. In the end, the centaur wins.

As shown in the figure, companies actively drive this process of expanding the pool of hybrid consumers. For example, when Kmart launched its online site BlueLight, it offered users a free Internet Service Provider (ISP)

How do your customers combine their online and offline behaviors? How will this change in the future? Why is this important to your business?

with its software. The goal was to encourage shoppers in the stores who had never been online to go onto the Internet, ensuring that their first online experience would be with BlueLight.

Centaur Time

This view of consumer dynamics probably underestimates the advance of the centaurs. In addition to Moore's Law, which states that chip density doubles every 18 months (or faster) for the same cost, there are the network effects that increase the value of having more people online in ways that are not strictly linear. This is recognized by Metcalfe's Law, which states that the value of a network is equivalent to the square of the number of nodes. Further, Gilder's Law indicates that bandwidth doubles every 12 months or less at the same cost. Second, the impact of the Internet on consumer behavior extends far beyond those consumers who actually have a PC wired to the Internet at home or even work. Even people who have never been online are living in a culture in which companies are beginning to shift their strategies to meet the demands of the centaurs. These unwired customers begin to adopt some of the expectations and mindsets of the centaur. They expect more customization, personalization, shopping options and interaction. As indicated by the dotted lines in Exhibit 2–3, the ripple effects of the centaur extend far out in front of the actual physical penetration of the Internet.

We again stress that we cannot judge the potential of the Internet based on its current, primitive level of development anymore than we could understand the Concorde by looking at the Wright Brothers' first plane. These early models can be used to help envision how the technologies might ultimately develop, and how consumers might ultimately use them. We should not, however, be limited in our thinking (at least in the long term) by the current limitations of technology. The transformation of the Internet is moving far more quickly than advances in the aircraft or any technological and social revolution of the past. With similar performance improvements, an automobile that cost $10,000 in 1975 would cost $1 in 2000.[10]

Hundreds of millions of people have been exposed to the Internet for the first time in the past decade. From email to information gathering to creating virtual communities, they can do things more efficiently in terms of time and cost, more effectively, and most importantly, they can do things that they could not have done before. How is this changing their behavior as consumers? Some have envisioned a segment of cyberconsumers who conduct most or all of their business and much of their life online. At the other extreme, some have continued to assume that although this new technology is powerful, consumers are unchanged by it. They will continue to act the way they always have. Both perspectives are based on myths about the consumer. The reality is that consumers are changing in fundamental ways, but not completely. Consumers retain some of the characteristics and needs of the traditional consumers. There are segments that lean more toward the cyberconsumer view and the traditional consumer view, and people's behaviors vary over time and across situations. The reality is the hybrid, the centaur. It is this convergence of old and new that drives the convergence strategies in marketing. In this chapter, we look at some of the myths implied by these extreme views of the consumer to give us a better understanding of what this new consumer is, and is not.

MYTHS OF THE TRADITIONAL CONSUMER

Perhaps it goes without saying that there have been some fundamental changes in the behavior of consumers, but marketing is often driven by residual beliefs about consumers. Among the myths of the traditional consumer that have been challenged by the Internet are:

Myth 1: Only the elite want customization. The mass market, driven by manufacturing constraints, assumed that consumers were willing to trade off customization for price and speed of delivery. They would allow Henry Ford to dictate the color (black) in exchange for a car that could be afforded by everyman. But now, with online ordering and flexible manufacturing, these expectations have changed. Consumers expect to receive a product tailored to their desires without paying extra for it. They not only want any color under the sun, but also distinctive formulations, their names on the labels—and they don't want to have to wait for it. But the mass-market mindset persists, focusing on carving up groups of customers into market segments and viewing personalized **How can you expand the customization of your products, services, marketing messages, and experiences? Do your customers want this customization today? Will they in the future?** messages and customized products and services as the exclusive domain of a small elite.

The concept that customization is a luxury for the elite is a myth of the traditional consumer.

Myth 2: Price is the bait set by the seller. Traditionally, companies have assumed that pricing was a game driven by the seller, with customers as passive recipients. Companies developed complex pricing strategies to attract customers, and they used price promotions to drive traffic. While these prices were designed to elicit a response from consumers, it was more like the way deer come to salt licks. In this Pavlovian view, the consumers did not play an active role in pricing strategy, except in a few cases such as the bazaar where haggling was the norm. Companies developed product line strategies, with lower priced offerings designed to snag lower-end consumers and ultimately migrate them toward the higher end (as GM did in moving customers from Chevys through Buicks to Cadillacs) or to segment out the more price sensitive customers (as supermarkets do with low-priced house brands and use of national brands as "loss-leaders"). The reality today is that consumers want to do the hunting and the pricing.[11] New models such as name-your-own-price (Priceline) and auctions (eBay) have turned the tables. They make the consumer an active partner in developing pricing. As companies create longer-term relationships with customers, they are beginning to look at **How can you use new pricing models to attract and retain customers while increasing profits?** value-based pricing and the total cost of ownership. Pricing strategy is not a matter of finding the right bait, but rather developing a system for dynamic interaction and value-based pricing.

The concept that consumers are passive recipients of pricing is a myth of the traditional consumer.

Myth 3: The consumer is on the couch. Companies have envisioned that consumers sit on the couch and are passively entertained. In this view, consumers separate information, education, and entertainment into different compartments in their lives. The consumer is a passive recipient (or, some might contend, a victim) of messages channeled through the mass media to where he or she is sitting. With a paucity of specific information and channels that connected with everyone or no one, the marketer saw these consumers as broad and blurry segments, and was forced to go after gnats with an elephant gun. The most targeted approach, direct marketing, was still one-way and somewhat scattershot, as witnessed by the number of direct mail pitches that go directly in the circular file. Today, consumers can actively search for information. They expect to have interactive experiences that inform, educate, and entertain. With advances in database marketing and data-mining, the ability to target consumers has increased dramatically. Consumers are searching for the company and the company is searching for the consumers. The consumer is no longer on the couch.

How can you increase your interaction with proactive customers?

The belief that people are passive recipients of information and entertainment is another myth of the traditional consumer.

Myth 4: Location, location, location. The goal in the past was to find a prime location and offer attractive hours to drive the consumer to you. Now, consumers expect to be able to buy anytime (24/7), from anyplace. Location is no longer as important as consumers increasingly can buy quickly and efficiently from home, the road, the beach. Stores are still important (see the myths of the cyberconsumer below), but the most important location is to be where your customer wants to purchase from you at the time the customer wants to make that decision. Companies need to offer integrated experiences across diverse channels, allowing consumers to interact seamlessly in any way they choose.

How can you rethink your location so that you can meet customers wherever they want to interact with the company?

The belief that customers have to come to your place, on your schedule, is another myth of the traditional consumer.

Myth 5: Consumers are islands. Companies also assume that consumers act alone in making their decisions. Marketers traditionally have targeted individual customers, or at most buying centers (such as purchasing agents and end users in business). Except for the relatively minor considerations such as "word of mouth" and opinion leaders, consumers for the most part have been treated as isolated islands in their purchasing decisions. Companies focused more on interacting *with* individual consumers than interactions *among* individuals. In this view, companies could actually benefit through a divide-and-conquer strategy of focusing on isolated consumers who do not share information. The reality is that consumers are now increasingly connected to one another in virtual communities and companies need to build and manage relationships with communities, not just individuals. A word-of-mouth comment that might have affected a handful of other buyers in the past now could influence thousands or millions. With this technology, the butterfly in China really can create a windstorm on the other side of the world. The unit of analysis and dynamics of interaction have changed, increasing the importance of interactive buzz.

The value of the network increases as more people join. One of the reasons that eBay has been so successful in auctions is that it has gathered a critical mass of both buyers and sellers. One of the competitive advantages of Amazon is its large community of customers who are willing to contribute reviews.

This interaction is deepened and accelerated through peer-to-peer technologies such **How can you use social interactions and communities online and offline to benefit your business?** as Napster and Gnutella. Facilitated by the Internet, the interaction among consumers is becoming increasingly important to their interaction with companies.

The idea that consumers are isolated islands is another myth of the traditional consumer.

Myth 6: Customers will accept what you tell them: In a sense, controlling the spin on information was the foundation of most traditional marketing. Segments and variable pricing were based upon one segment being separated from another. Companies made money on information asymmetries, so it was in their interest not to reveal too much information. The companies used powerful decision-making tools to target customers, but did not put these into the hands of consumers. Companies didn't make their costs and pricing transparent, nor did they make it easy for consumers to compare their offerings with those of rivals, unless those comparisons were favorable. Now, consumers are no longer content to be kept in the dark. The Internet is *transparent*. Consumers have a wide variety of independent decision-making tools at their disposal and they are using them to make better decisions. They can go to sites to find price and product comparisons across diverse sellers and they can even get ratings directly from other customers on sites such as Bizrate.com. Companies need to determine how they will respond to this newfound consumer power, even putting the tools for direct comparisons into customers' hands. Companies also have to find new ways to work with these more empowered customers and to find sources of

Can you provide decision-making tools and information to customers in a way that benefits your business?

value that do not depend on keeping the customer in the dark through information asymmetries.

The belief that consumers are willing to be spoon-fed information for making decisions is another myth of the traditional consumer.

Merrill Lynch: Perils of the Myths of the Traditional Consumer

Early on, many traditional companies clung to the myths of the traditional consumer. They did not want to recognize how much had changed. While financial services firm Charles Schwab & Co. was a leader in moving its business online, Merrill Lynch was slow to catch on. When Schwab made the leap to make its online business a centerpiece of its operation rather than a stand-alone business, it was highly uncertain whether consumers would be willing to trade online. Managers were also worried about cannibalizing their high margin brokerage business. But, when consumers proved willing to trade online and Schwab's aggressive strategy moved some 90 percent of its trades online and drove its market cap past the venerable Merrill Lynch by early 1999, Merrill was forced to take notice. It had to abandon its view of the traditional consumer and acknowledge that it had to play in cyberspace.[12]

By early 2000, Schwab had 3.7 million online accounts compared with just 16,000 by Merrill Lynch after its first quarter of operation. Noted analyst Dan Burke for Gomez Inc., has commented, "It's going to take the full-service brokers time to catch up and hit their stride."[13] Many traditional companies such as Merrill were slow to recognize how the traditional consumer had been changed by the Internet (often deluding themselves by thinking *their* customers were different). While the ranks of the companies that cling to the old view of the consumer have been thinning, the burst of the dot-com bubble has led to a resurgence of the belief that companies do not need to radically rethink their view of the consumer or their approaches to marketing. Nothing could be further from the truth. Whatever happens to the Internet startups, the consumer has been changed. People can do things they have never done before and they have new expectations that have tremendous implications for the way companies need to approach marketing. Companies like Schwab that have recognized these fundamental changes may be more in step with the market than those that don't. The reality is the traditional consumer will never be the same.

Since then, however, Merrill and other oldline firms, in part shocked by the success of Schwab, have awoken to the potential of online trading. Merrill rolled out new online trading resources and created a two-tiered pricing structure, matching Schwab's $29.95 price per trade for discount online trading at the low end and offering fee-based, full-service trading at the high end. By the middle of 2000, Merrill was launching more than 200 software products per month. It built a broadcasting studio to send out online interviews and comments from analysts. It segmented its customers based on their potential and matched the level of service to them. Its stock climbed steadily upward, even as Schwab saw its fortunes fall with the dot-

In what ways do you still subscribe to the myths of the traditional consumer?

com failures and a steep drop in trading volumes. While Schwab was innovative in leading the way into the market, it was blinded to the risks by its early success and also, perhaps, fell victim to the myths of the cyberconsumer, which are discussed in the next section.

MYTHS OF THE CYBERCONSUMER

It is clear that the cyberconsumer has changed. But this transformation is not as complete as some have envisioned. The recent dot-com failures have helped to highlight some of the myths of the cyberconsumer. Among these myths are:

Myth 1: People don't want to be troubled with shopping. First and foremost, the Internet was going to be a wonderful world, in which machines would take over the hassle and burden of shopping. With a few clicks, we'd be able to breeze through the tedium of picking out clothing or trudging through grocery aisles. Our shopping would be done in our bedroom slippers, leaving us more time to do the things we really like to do, things like... shopping.

The fact is that human beings like to shop. One only has to observe the phenomenon of the shopping mall on a Saturday afternoon to appreciate that people actually enjoy shopping. We revel in it. In fact, there are a wide range of motivations for buying that have nothing to do with efficiency, as

How can you use the fact that people like to shop in designing your business? When do they like to shop in stores and when do they prefer to shop online?

discussed below. The utility we derive from shopping itself outweighs the transaction costs (including the time and expense of driving to the store, selecting groceries, paying for and carting them home).

The distaste for shopping is a central myth of the cyber-consumer.

Myth 2: Efficiency is all that matters. The second myth of the cyberconsumer is that consumers value transaction efficiency above all else. As Amazon.com CEO Jeff Bezos has commented, "Time is the most precious commodity in the late 20th century."[15] The idea was that the Internet was going to take out all the inefficiencies from the transaction experience. No more wandering around stores looking for products. No more endless visits to multiple retailers to compare prices. No more traffic and crowded mall parking lots. You can get in, get your goods, and get out quickly. (Admittedly, the clunky, Model-T version of the "Worldwide Wait" has yet to fully deliver on the promise of such "frictionless" transactions, but the assumption that this is all people want may be flawed.)

The fact is there are other things human beings value besides efficiency. Stand behind a supermarket patron with packets full of cents-off coupons and you'll see this clearly. When your daughter buys you a tie for Christmas—and she tells you she went to three stores to pick it out—transaction efficiency is the last thing on her mind. The gift is more valuable because of the effort she put into finding it. The *inefficiency* of the process actually adds to its value. Similarly, most small antique stores are jam packed to the rafters with odds and ends without any particular order. But antique shoppers love to wander through them precisely because the stores are inefficient, meandering romps that allow buyers to spot one-of-a-kind furniture they might never have thought to purchase. The inefficiency *is* the value of the experience.

This doesn't mean that we don't want efficiency. Many times efficiency is all we want. If you know the title of a book and don't need it for a few days, in a few clicks at Amazon.com, you can have the book speeding toward your mailbox. Gone are the days when you had to wander through bookshelves, finding the category and shelf where

Is your online business model built around transaction efficiency? When do your potential customers care about transaction efficiency? When are they willing to tradeoff efficiency for other benefits?

this "needle in a haystack" was hidden, if it was on the shelf at all. Efficiency is very important, but it is not the only thing. This is a fact that we must never forget.

The primacy of efficiency is another myth of the cyberconsumer.

Myth 3: Consumers want to get the best price. In addition to transaction efficiency, the assumption of many Internet businesses was that consumers want the cheapest price. The Internet promised information efficiency, allowing prospective customers to look at every company that offers a given product and compare them easily to find the best possible product at the best possible price. But surprisingly, it turned out that people were not always interested in getting the cheapest price. Consumers overall are looking for a *fair* price, but not necessarily the best price. (There are obviously some segments that are willing to go to any lengths to get the cheapest price, but overall this is less important than it might seem.) An MIT study of how consumers use shopping bots to make automatic price comparisons in purchasing books found

What prices are your customers willing to accept? How can you offer a *fair* price without offering the *lowest* price? How important is it to your customers to get the cheapest price?

that consumers don't always choose the cheapest price. In fact, consumers are willing to pay an average of 10 to 15 percent more to buy from a retailer they have visited previously.[16]

The concept that consumers always want to get the cheapest price is another myth of the cyberconsumer.

Myth 4: Consumers are either online or offline. One of the great myths of the cyberconsumer is that there is such a thing as a cyberconsumer. In talking about the cyberconsumer, we sometimes act as if these people are wired from dawn to dust. Even consumers who are "always on" through high-speed, broadband access buy both online and offline. As consumers gain more experience on the Internet, they are beginning to find interesting ways of combining their online and offline behavior.

A number of studies show that consumers value access to multiple channels and actively research and buy products across different channels. A major U.S. study of multichannel shopping found that the majority of consumers want to use more multiple channels when shopping. More than three-quarters preferred to use more than one channel to learn about new products (82 percent) and to search for product information (77 percent).[17]

A major study of multichannel retailers by the National Retail Federation found that 68 percent of any company's catalog shoppers have also shopped in the company's physical stores. The same study found that 59 percent of online retail shoppers have made purchases in the same company's store and 43 percent from catalogs. Jupiter Research estimates that these multichannel shoppers spend about one third more than those shopping through single channels. The opportunity for retailers is that just 4 percent of offline shoppers buy from the same store's online businesses, so the flow from real to virtual stores is far less developed.[18]

Even when they are offline, there is increased use of technology to shape the consumer experience. A recent survey of retail technologies identified a variety of key technologies for retailing, including 3-D virtual stores and online store information. In-store technologies, which may be even more significant in shaping the shopping experience, include product information/ordering kiosks, frequent shopper kiosks, virtual display case, electronic point-of-sale signage, hand-held shopping assistant, body scanning, and self-scanning or self-checkout.[19]

New technologies and new channels are always expected to displace the old. In fact, they very often end up existing side by side. The advent of ballpoint pens did not, as some expected, lead to the end of the fountain pen. The television didn't mean the end of radio, and the VCR didn't shut down the movie theaters. People are surprisingly adept at integrating these new technologies into their lives, and surprisingly resistant to giving up the old even as they adopt the new. This is also true with the Internet.

Consumers have finely coordinated their online and offline behaviors into a seamless whole that serves their needs. Sellers should be as adept at balancing their online and offline businesses. **How can you best combine online and offline channels?**

Sometimes we treat the online and offline consumer as different breeds when they are not only the same breed but often one and the same person.

The concept that all consumers are either wired or offline is a myth of the cyberconsumer.

Myth 5: Ease of visiting stores will lead to more purchasing. The 24-hour, seven days per week accessibility and no-driving-required access to online businesses was expected to make it easy for cyberconsumers to visit and to buy. But companies have found that while consumers can find your site with a mouseclick, it is just as easy for them to leave empty-handed. The browsers have not been converted into buyers. While virtually every visit to a physical grocery store results in a purchase, the Internet shows almost the opposite pattern. In 1999, more than 70 percent of Internet retailers experienced less than a 2 percent conversion rate from browsers to buyers.[20] This led to a

How can you make your online offerings more sticky to turn browsers into buyers?

"fatal attraction" phenomenon, in which web sites attracted a growing number of visitors, at high cost, but were unable to convert those visitors into buyers.[21]

Another myth of the cyberconsumer is that easy access would automatically lead to more purchasing.

Myth 6: The Internet is inherently fascinating and attractive. There was also an assumption that anything online would just be captivating to its audience. This was the age when every company under the sun added a dot-com after its name, before subsequently losing them like a summer tan. (In the first four months of 2000, nine times more companies added dot-com to their name than dropped it. In the subsequent three months, the ratio dropped to one to one.)[22] In fact, people have a love—hate relationship with the technology. After the novelty wears off, they become bored with the Internet. This boredom with the medium, or "online ennui," has been blamed for contributing to the fall of the dot-coms, the failure of online advertising, and the slowing growth of consumer PC sales in early 2001.[23] But the Internet does offer engaging and interactive applications. People will also connect through mobile devices, televisions, and other interfaces that will decrease the downtime and integrate the technology more thoroughly into life.

It is important to recognize that the Internet as it exists today is nothing like it will be in the future. We are at the earliest stages of the evolution of the Internet and the crude tools available to us in the "stone age" period will be nothing like we will have even in the foreseeable future. Faster, more powerful connections with interfaces more integrated into life will increase the "fascination" of the Internet in the future.

Even so, it will be the content that will be fascinating, not merely the novelty of the medium itself. We need to recognize that the real world can be, in many ways, more engaging. The challenge is to find areas in which you can add value online in some way, either through efficiency or other sources of less tangible value. The novelty of the medium alone is not enough to sustain it.

How can you keep your online offerings new and interesting? How much of interest in your online business is driven by novelty and how much will endure when the hype has passed? With the rise of the Internet, how do your offline offerings need to change?

The idea that everyone is fascinated by the Internet is another myth of the cyberconsumer.

Garden.com: Perils of the Myths of the Cyberconsumer

Understanding the emotional complexity of the consumer is a life-and-death issue for any company, online or offline. Consider garden.com. This online gardening site was a brilliant concept, but it was shuttered in part by some of these myths of the cyberconsumer. Garden.com brought a new integrated offering to the highly fragmented, $50 billion gardening industry, in which no company had more than a 1 percent market share. The goal, in the words of founder Cliff Sharples, was to become the "Starbucks" of gardening, creating the first "category killer" in this industry.[24]

Direct mail distribution had already been proven through catalog sales, with 10 percent of gardening products shipped directly to customers. Two of three U.S. households participate in gardening and the demographics of gardeners closely paralleled online profiles. Gardening customers were well educated and wired, representing some 48 percent of online shoppers. Gardening is a passionate, lifetime hobby.

Garden.com built a powerful and efficient interface for customers and an equally powerful supply chain system. It developed an innovative software and logistics system that, in collaboration with Federal Express, carried plants directly from the growers to the customer's door. This allowed it to offer customers 16,000 unique product offerings without holding inventory—far more than even the most super of the gardening super centers. The site also offered value-added content, such as the ability to design a garden with plants tailored to customers' local climate and soil. For example, after the customer enters a zip code and answers a few questions, the site could offer a selection of plants that would thrive in their local climate and do well in a yard that has lots of shade or problems with deer. Garden.com created one of the biggest horticultural databases in the world. A novice gardener could have access to expert advice. Finally, there could be no more of those annoying trips to the nursery.

The company was among the most promising dot-com firms, attracting more than $100 million from venture capitalists and investors. It grew at 300 percent per year, drew more than 4 million visitors and more than $5 million in revenue. Then, after a five-year run, garden.com wilted on the vine, shutting its doors in December 2000. What went wrong? While there are many factors that may have contributed to its failure, there is one glaring issue related to human behavior: Many people actually like to go to nurseries and pick out plants. They like to walk through the greenhouses and see and smell the flowers. They like to get expert advice from the staff at the nursery and chat with other consumers. They like to pack bags of mulch, garden ornaments, and trays of begonias into the backs of their SUVs. It is very time consuming and inefficient, but people like the experience. The transaction cost *is* part of the value of the experience. They like it so much that the promise of perfect information and efficient transactions was no match for it.

Time and again what was missing from the dot-com equation was an understanding of the human behavior of the consumer. There is usually a superficial reference to fulfilling the needs of customers, but usually the needs that are presented are for transaction and

How much of your business is built around the myths of cyberconsumers? How can you challenge these myths?

information efficiency. These are not always the central needs of customers. There are many other reasons for buying or acting that don't emerge from strict logic. We are not rational decision makers. We are not solely rational, economic creatures. We are complex, beings with both rational and emotional sides. Buddhists have a word for this combination: "semba," which has been translated as a cross between "heart" and "mind."[25]

The Human Motivations: Why You Pick Up Toys at the Airport

If it is not just efficiency that motivates the consumer, what is it? As is noted in Aristotle's opening quote for this chapter, there are many timeless causes for human actions. Since Aristotle's day, there has been extensive research on consumer behavior, exploring social, psychological and anthropological explanations of human actions. Although we will not attempt to delve into this rich literature in any detail, we will explore a few illustrative examples of the varied reasons why people buy, beyond the strictly rational economic ones. Many of these motivations, which are part of our hard wiring as human beings, are not changed by the Internet.

For example, consider the business travelers who stop in the airport to buy souvenirs for their young children. These toys could be bought more cheaply and more efficiently online, but their value comes from their symbolic meaning. It shows that mommy or daddy was thinking about the child at that moment. The toy, which very often self-destructs rapidly, is valuable because of its symbolic meaning. This is just one of the "inefficient" reasons that people buy. Among these motivations are:[26]

- **Self affirmation:** People want to do things themselves. They go to the supermarket and they pick out their own tomatoes, carefully testing and selecting them. That the buyer isn't an expert on tomatoes doesn't matter. The buyer feels: "I have done this—it may be bad, but I like it."

- **Symbolic meaning:** We already discussed the symbolic meaning of souvenirs bought by business travelers or gifts bought for family members. The diamond industry also would not exist without symbolic meaning. A diamond is an inanimate object, but when it is part of an engagement or wedding ring, it means far more. The trip to a jeweler to pick out a wedding ring has meaning that extends far beyond the ring itself. Any groom-to-be who would dare to try to make that process an efficient (or inexpensive) one may end up standing alone at the altar.

- **Scripts for shopping:** Some people have standard routines for going shopping. They go out for a walk and stop at the same store every morning and pick up the morning paper, or they go shopping once a week every Wednesday night. These routines are part of the pattern of our life and very often include shopping experiences.

- **Experience:** The reason there are perfume tester bottles and automobile test drives is that people like to experience products. We like to try on clothes and taste food samples in the grocery store. Shopping is a multisensory experience that is greatly reduced online. (And while there are new technologies that work on generating smell and flavors or virtual reality that replicates visual impact, the entire tactile experience of shopping promises to be a distinctly physical phenomenon for many years to come.)

- **Social influences:** Finally, we buy because of social influences. When you try on a new suit or dress and the salesperson says you look great in it, that is a social influence. These are influences we feel directly in offline purchases, but are harder to replicate online. We also follow fads, from stock to beanie babies, where our purchasing behavior is not shaped by cold logic but rather by a desire to keep up with others.

These and similar reasons for buying have nothing to do with transaction efficiency or information efficiency. They don't have to do with logic, but rather that quirky human wiring that makes us all so unique and endearing. This may be something that some companies would like to see go away, but it is here to stay. The reality is the centaur has a warm and beating human heart.

Of course, even for these behaviors that appear to have a very strong human reason for being inefficient, Internet companies are developing creative ways to take these experiences online. In the case of travelers buying souvenirs discussed above, a company called GuesswhatIbroughtyou.com offers time-constrained travelers the option of shopping online and having the souvenirs delivered directly to their hotel rooms by 7 A.M. the next morning.[27]

> How do human motivations such as self-affirmation, symbolism, buying scripts, experience, and social influences affect the way consumers approach your products and services?

While the human motivations for bringing home souvenirs remain the same, this new business model offers a new way to fulfill them.

MOVING TO THE CENTAUR

The views of the traditional consumer and the cyberconsumer present a bifurcated view of the world. The two types of consumers are seen as separate and independent, when in fact they are clearly overlapping. The reality is that there is substantial fusion of the two, and this convergence is where we find the hybrid consumer, the centaur.

This centaur is where companies can find tremendous opportunities in transforming their businesses. Even small bricks-and-mortar businesses, which once seemed destined to be wiped out by online competitors, have found ways to benefit from the Internet. A survey of 1,500 small town retailers by the National Trust for Historic Preservation found that they derived more than 14 percent of their total sales from the Internet. They thrive by serving existing customers or offering specialized products that fill distinct niches.[28] Nowhere is the importance of the Internet for small businesses more evident than in the numerous professional sellers on eBay. Every company needs to figure out how it can work across all three segments.

Webvan and Tesco: A Tale of Two Grocers

The story of two cybergrocers illustrates the power of taking a broader view of the consumer. Tesco, the largest supermarket chain in the U.K. launched an online shopping service in England that built upon its existing brand and infrastructure and focused on traditional customers, cyberconsumers, and centaurs. Webvan offered strictly online ordering and delivery in the United States, focusing on the cyberconsumer. By February 2001, Tesco was the largest home grocery shopping business in the world, doing £300 million of business with 90 percent coverage in the U.K. and plans for international expansion in Europe and Asia. The business was already profitable, generating more than £6 million in weekly sales. Webvan was on the ropes, losing $600 million in 2000, postponing expansion plans and shutting down its Dallas, Texas, operation. In July 2001, Webvan shut down its operations and filed for Chapter 11.

Tesco had an obvious advantage in not having to add warehouses, because it could build off its existing network of stores and its process capabilities. But Tesco also recognized the need to sell to traditional consumers, cyberconsumers, and the new c-consumers. Tesco not only drove customers from its stores to the Web business as expected, but also found that online customers were making their way into physical stores for the first time as a result of their electronic connections. Over half the sales are new to Tesco. These consumers could not easily be pinned down as traditional or cyberconsumers.

The overlaps between its offline and online businesses offer significant marketing advantages to Tesco. "I have almost no customer acquisition costs," said John Browett, CEO of Tesco.com. "I just bolt onto the existing infrastructure and away I go. We put all our focus on making sure the delivery is perfect." For example, the company launched its electrical products business for $1 million whereas a competitor spent $50 million on a similar launch. If the business earns $10 million in the first year, Tesco is banking profits while the competitor is still recouping losses.[29]

Tesco is also adding a wide range of other products, from books to CDs to baby clothes, home furnishings and electronics. Not only that, but Tesco offers an ISP that customers can use to connect to its web site and financial services they can use to pay for them.

This is not a U.K. phenomenon. As noted in the preface, Tesco is exporting its online grocery revolution to the U.S. (with a stake in Safeway's e-grocery business) and South Korea. Another company, Caprabo, a major traditional supermarket retailer in Spain provides another example of how a traditional supermarket can transform itself into an online grocer. By following the Tesco model of using its existing stores as a base for delivery, Caprabo has created a successful online grocery service at the very modest cost of less than opening one small physical store. It is already planning to break even within the first year of operations.

How can you apply the insights of Tesco (building an online offering on the foundation of an offline organization) to your own business?

For Webvan, which focused on cyberconsumers alone, it has been the worst of times. For Tesco, focusing across all three segments, it has been the best of times.

A Spectrum of Convergence:
Beyond the Simple Answer of Bricks and Clicks

The moral of the story of the centaur is *not* that every business needs to move to a "bricks and clicks" strategy. This is the simplistic conclusion that some have drawn from the failures of pure-play Internet businesses. Even the term "bricks and clicks" implies you put the two sides together, and this is how many companies have approached this challenge. They have set their bricks next to their clicks. Convergence is something different. It is not the two strategies placed side by side, but a fusion of the two that creates a new entity, new value proposition, new business and revenue models, new strategies and new organizational architecture. Convergence is like mixing yellow and red to create orange. Online and offline are combined to create a new convergent color. In the process, both original colors are transformed into something different.

The exact mix of the two depends on the business and there are many variations in the spectrum of convergence strategies. Every business needs to understand the changing centaurs and design its business strategy around them. This may lead to a "bricks and clicks" strategy, but not always. The right balance depends on the type of business and customer.

How can your business benefit from a digital strategy? What parts of your business need to remain physical? What is the optimal convergence strategy for your business?

Every company needs to determine the right balance between the physical business and cyberbusiness to meet the demands of the centaur and continue to evolve this balance as technology and consumers change.

Start with an understanding of the complex behavior and motivations of the consumer, and then design the products and services that can best meet these needs. Only then can you develop the necessary marketing, business, and organizational strategies. The consumer is at the center, as illustrated in Exhibit 2–4. You cannot answer the question of what to do in marketing without first asking the question of whom you are marketing to. The second part of the book explores some of the key characteristics of the centaur and their implications for marketing strategy.

In addition to placing the consumer at the center of the process, we also need to understand what consumers can do now that they couldn't do before. At the same time, we need to recognize the enduring principles of the consumer. Rather than

EXHIBIT 2–4 **PUTTING THE CONSUMER AT THE CENTER**

What organizational architecture and processes are needed to support these strategies?

What business and marketing strategies are needed to develop these solutions?

What product & service solutions can meet these needs?

Consumer Who are the centaurs and what do they need?

Offline

Online

one perspective or the other, it is this twin view that provides the deepest insights on the emerging consumer. This consumer is a mix of old and new, wired and unplugged. This is a being adapted to the new realities of this digital age, yet with the psychological and genetic programming of millennia of experience: a true centaur.

NOTES

[1] "New Internet Users: What They Do Online, What They Don't and Implications for the Net's Future," Pew Internet & American Life Project, September 25, 2000, http://www.pewinternet.org/reports.

[2] Nielsen/Net Ratings reports in September 2000 that there are 269 million people across 20 countries with Internet access from a home PC.

[3] Weiss, Michael J., "Online America," *American Demographics*, March 2001.

[4] Bughin, Jacques, "Buying on-line: Tenure versus sociodemographics," Digital Economy Lab, McKinsey.

[5] McKinsey & Company and Media Metrix, October 4, 2000, based on a U.S. sample of 6,006 users spending more than 180 minutes online in three months.

Action Memo

- Imagine your offline interaction with consumers ceased to exist. All your physical stores evaporated. Your physical salesforce was wiped off the face of the Earth. Consumers *only* have online access to your business. What would your have to give up? How could you creatively replace these parts of the business online? How would your customers react? **What insights can you apply from this thought experiment to your business today?**

- Now, imagine the opposite. The Internet is destroyed overnight. What do you give up? How do you replace it?
- Which segments of your customers are most like "cyberconsumers"? Which segments of your customers are most like traditional consumers? Study each of these extreme segments. **What can they teach you about reaching the larger population of hybrid consumers?**

We invite you to share the results of these activities and suggest other action memos at the Convergence Marketing Forum (www.convergencemarketingforum.com).

---

[6] Rozanski, Horacio D., Gerry Bollman and Martin Lipman, "Seize the Occasion: The Seven-Segment System for Online Marketing," *Strategy & Competition*, issue 24 (Third Quarter 2001), pp. 42–51.

[7] Weiss, Michael J., "Online America," *American Demographics*, March 2001.

[8] Suárez Sandra L. and Mauro Guillén, "Developing the Internet: Entrepreneurship and Public Policy in Comparative Perspective," Working Paper, November 2000, Wharton e-Business Initiative; Bughin, Jacques, "Macrodrivers of Internet connectivity within and outside OECD," Digital Economy Lab, 2001.

[9] Pew Internet & American Life Project Survey, November-December 2000. http://www.pewinternet.org/reports/.

[10] Mark Myers, Wharton Fellows in e-Business, Silicon Valley, July 10, 2001.

[11] Sawhney, Mohan and Philip Kotler, "Marketing in the Age of Information Democracy," *Kellogg on Marketing*, Dawn Iacobucci, ed., New York: John Wiley & Sons, 2000.

[12] Green, Heather, Leah Nathans Spiro, et al. "A Bull in the Online Shop," *Business Week*, February 8, 2001, p. 6.

[13] Schwartz, Jeffrey, "Schwab Reaps Benefits of Early Net Investments," *Internetweek* June 12, 2000, p. 61.

[14] "Merrill Lynch: A Reluctant Success," *The Economist*, June 9, 2001, pp. 79–80; Gasparino, Charles and Ken Brown, "Schwab Sees Its Stock Suffer from Move into Online Trading," *The Wall Street Journal*, June 19, 2001, p. A-1.

[15] Hof, Robert D. "Bricks-and-Mortar Blockheads," *Business Week e.biz*, December 13, 1999, p. EB104.

[16] Brynjolfsson, Erik, and Michael Smith, "The Great Equalizer? Consumer Choice at Internet Shopbots," Working paper, MIT Sloan School of Management (July 2000).

[17] "Creating the Ideal Shopping Experience," Indiana University-KPMG, survey was conducted in May–June 2000.

[18] Lipke, David J. "Mystery Shoppers," *American Demographics*, December 2000, p. 41.

[19] "Retail Technology in the Next Century," *An Indiana University-KPMG Study*, 1999.

[20] Forrester 1999, quoted in Wendy W. Moe and Peter S. Fader, "Capturing Evolving Visitor Behavior in Clickstream Data," The Wharton School, Department of Marketing working paper, March 2000.

[21] Agrawal, Vikas, Luis D. Arjona, and Ron Lemmens, "E-Performance: The Path to Rational Exuberance," *McKinsey Quarterly*, 2001, No. 1, p. 31.

[22] Brubaker, Harold, "Company names shedding dot-com," *Austin American Statesman*, September 4, 2000, p. D-3.

[23] Schlender, Brent, "Online Ennui," *The Economist*, March 19, 2001, p. 84.

[24] Cliff Sharples, remarks at the 1999 board meeting of the SEI Center for Advanced Studies in Management, Philadelphia, September 1999.

[25] Norberg-Hodge, Helena. *Ancient Futures*, Delhi: Oxford University Press, 1991, p 82.

[26] Sridhar Balasubramanian, Vijay Mahajan and Raj Raghunathan, "How You Buy May Influence the Utility of What You Buy," Working Paper, University of Texas, 2001.

[27] "GuesswhatIbroughtyou.com," *American Way*, May 15, 2001, p. 17.

[28] Kaufman, Leslie, "The Opposite of Amazon.com," *The New York Times*, September 22, 2000, p. c-1.

[29] John Browett, remarks to the Wharton Fellows in e-Business program, Barcelona, February 2001.

PART 2

NAVIGATING THE FIVE Cs OF CONVERGENCE

With new technologies, consumers can do things they could never do before. They can create customized products and services that were once only available to the elite. They can participate in virtual communities that stretch around the globe. Consumers can interact with companies online and even download products almost instantly. They can engage in interactive pricing models such as auctions and participate in new online experiences. Finally, they can use powerful tools to search for information, make decisions, and manage their lives.

With all these new options at their disposal, how are consumers changing? How are they combining their traditional behaviors with the constantly advancing possibilities of the technology? In this section, we explore the convergence of the consumer with the

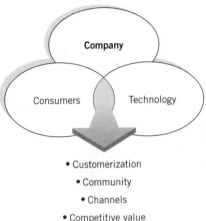

- Customerization
  - Community
    - Channels
- Competitive value
  - Choice tools

technology. In particular, we examine five areas where this convergence is taking place:

- Customerization
- Communities
- Channels
- Competitive value, and
- Choice tools

We chose these five areas for several reasons. As noted above, these represent areas where technology allows consumers to do things they couldn't do before. Most of the discussion of these topics in the past few years has focused on this issue of what consumers can do now with the new technology. Our focus in this book is to ask the next question. Once we know what consumers *can* do, what *are* they doing and what *will* they do in the future? How are they combining new behaviors with old?

That leads to the second reason why we chose these five areas. They are applications where there are significant convergence challenges and opportunities. For example, consumers want both customized *and* standardized products, are part of physical *and* virtual communities and want access through online *and* offline channels. The third reason these areas were selected is because they represent important consumer needs. Finally, all these areas have significant implications for marketing and business strategy.
In the following five chapters, we examine each of these "5 Cs," exploring key challenges and opportunities. We also offer sets of strategies in each area that can be used to promote convergence.

3

CONVERGING ON CUSTOMERIZATION

MAKE IT MINE

"You can have any color you want, as long as it's black."

Henry Ford

TRADITIONAL CONSUMER

"I agree with Henry. Give me a break with all these options already. I've got places to go. I just want to walk into the dealer and pick out a car I like. There are enough standard offerings to satisfy me. Besides, I happen to like black."

CYBERCONSUMER

"Get with it, Henry. I'd like to design my own car from the ground up, mix my own color so it matches my eyes and have my name and family coat of arms on the hood instead of your family name and corporate logo. By the way, I want it now. Got it?"

THE CENTAUR

"The answer is not black and white. Sometimes I want to roll up my sleeves and design the product and other times I want you to recommend a set of options. Like a diner in an expensive restaurant, I'd like to see the menu and wine list, but then ask the waiter what he recommends. I want customization when I know what I want and when it is important to me. Otherwise, I'll keep buying off the shelf. I want both customized and standardized products."

CONVERGENCE QUESTIONS

>>>*Should you customize your products and services and marketing messages? What types of products and services lend themselves to customization and which ones to standardization?*

>>>*What is the right mix of customized and standardized offerings?*

>>>*What are the limits of customization (technological and human)?*

CONVERGING ON CUSTOMERIZATION:
Make it Mine[1]

Companies can offer customized products, marketing messages, and experiences, and this combination, referred to as "customerization," is transforming interactions with customers. Yet, with all the options in the world, hybrid consumers in some situations still buy standardized products off the shelf and respond to mass market messages.

Over the years, John Randolph, an avid reader of *Prevention* magazine, has gradually added about a dozen vitamins and nutritional supplements to his daily routine. Each morning, he spends ten minutes rationing out his set of capsules and tablets from a row of bottles in his kitchen cabinet.

So when he reads about a new service offered by a company named Acumins to give him a custom-made supplement, tailor-made to his own personal formula, it seems made to order. He goes online, and while he is there, he is even more pleasantly surprised to find a tool called "SmartSelect." It asks him several dozen questions about his lifestyle and health to develop a personalized nutritional supplement designed to meet his needs. He is pleased to see that the recommended mix of supplements includes many of the ones he had selected on his own, as well as some he hadn't thought of. It also leaves out several that he has become particularly attached to from his own reading. He modifies the recommendation to include them.

He receives his customized vitamins and revels in the ability to open only one bottle in the morning. But the next week, while browsing through the aisles of the health food store, he notices a blue-green algae supplement advertised at the end of the aisle. He reads a brochure next to the display and decides to try a bottle. He seems to have more energy, so he keeps taking it. A few weeks later, he reads a fascinating study in the newspaper about the benefits of concentrated Omega 3 capsules, made from fish oil. He adds those as well to his daily routine. Soon, he is once again taking a varying mixture of pills, including the core supplement from Acumins. He realizes that while he likes the convenience of single pill, he also values the flexibility of exploring new supplements in the store. He has never felt that his health could be boiled down to a single formula. It is a lifelong quest, continually changing as new studies are done, and new formulas are created or discovered. This is not something to be traded for efficiency. John Randolph is much more complex than even he suspects. Even though he has the option of mass customization, it does not completely satisfy his needs.

FROM MASS PRODUCTION TO CUSTOMERIZATION

In the industrial age, consumers shaped their expectations around the limits of technology. They were willing to accept a few basic mass-produced models of cars in a single color for a lower cost and quicker turnaround. When the choice was between a horse and buggy on the farm and a new Model T, they were happy to have the car, no matter what the color. Tailor-made products and services were far more expensive and took much longer to deliver. They were generally the province of the elite who could afford the time involved in creating them and the cost involved in purchasing them.

But people are individuals and they want a car that reflects their personality. Led by General Motors, companies began addressing this desire by developing product lines tailored to certain segments. Companies produced a limited variety of styles and colors. This made production and inventory more complex, but once customers began to expect this type of variety, it was impossible for a company to survive by making a single model in a single color. Even so, customers were not completely satisfied. They spent days looking for just the right car and finally settled for something that might satisfy them on a few dimensions even if it failed on others. Variety also drove up inventory costs for manufacturers, with General Motors holding about $40 billion in inventory.[2] Companies bore the costs of returns and price discounting owing to overproduction of unpopular designs and missed opportunities because of underproduction. Because the company didn't know exactly what people wanted (and often the customers themselves didn't even know), companies were forced to throw a lot of things out there and see what sticks.

Companies tried to gain a better understanding of their customers. In the world of mass production, customer-focused companies used marketing research to guide new product development. They did their best to understand the customers in a broad sense, using powerful tools such as conjoint analysis and its associated simulation and optimization models,[3] but the best they could hope for was to gain a glimpse into what certain segments of customers preferred. And even with these advances in understanding customer desires, technologists pointed out that some of the most successful ideas such as the Sony Walkman or Chrysler minivan were not suggested by customers but developed through creative leaps by managers who understood the power of the technology and its potential to meet customer needs.[4]

Customers are also sometimes overwhelmed with the options all this variety presents. Consumer product makers launched 31,000 new products in the U.S. in 2000. This can lead to an option glut. A study by Stanford University psychology professor Mark Lepper found that less is sometimes more. Lepper set up sample tables with jars of jam and gave customers who stopped for a sample a coupon for their next jam purchase. One group of subjects was presented with 30 jars of jam while the other saw a table with just six jams. In the first group, apparently overwhelmed with choices, only 3 percent used their coupons to buy jam while 30 percent of the shoppers with six choices purchased the jam.[5]

Benefits of Mass Customization

The technology of mass customization seemed designed to reduce or eliminate the tradeoffs between the consumer demand for more options and the corporation's demand for more efficiency. It offered customers the opportunity to purchase tailor-made products that were once available to only the elite, if they were available at all, for a price only slightly above mass-produced items. Just as Henry Ford's mass production had promised to put the luxury of an automobile in every garage, the new technology of mass customization promised to put the luxury of customized products in the hands of everyone.

Customers like John Randolph gain many benefits from this process. There is experimental evidence that customization increases satisfaction—customers allowed to specify their preferences in selecting products were more satisfied.[6] It opens many more choices. While the average physical store carries just 130 ready-to-wear pairs of Levi's jeans for any given waist and inseam on its shelves, the company's customized Original Spin could offer nearly 1.7 million variations to meet customer tastes for about $10 over the price of a mass-produced item.[7]

Among the most significant direct benefits to the firm are substantial reductions in inventory, the opportunity to enhance customer loyalty, avoid pitfalls of commoditization, and gain ongoing insight into customer preferences that can help guide the made-for-inventory products. Acumins reported that its customers were three **What are the opportunities for your business presented by customization?** times more loyal than those buying generic products, even though the custom vitamins were sold at a premium.[8]

The Move Toward "Customerization"

Most of the focus in mass customization has been on the manufacturing technology and not on the customization of marketing. At the same time that operations managers have been retooling their factories for flexible manufacturing, marketers have been targeting and customizing their messages. This

EXHIBIT 3–1 CONVERGING ON CUSTOMERIZATION

Customized Operations / Customized Marketing

customization of marketing replaces anonymous transaction with deeper, more interactive relationships with consumers that are built over time.

The concept of *customerization* goes beyond simply customizing the operations to customize both manufacturing and marketing interactions, as illustrated in Exhibit 3–1. In essence, the customer is invited into the R&D lab and the marketing design center and asked to be an active collaborator in developing the product and services, marketing messages and experiences. This is not merely creating the ability for the company to customize products for customers, but also the ability for customers to customize products, services, positioning, pricing, marketing communications and experiences for themselves.

The customization of both the operations and marketing leads to a variety of different strategies, as illustrated in Exhibit 3–2. Where product or manufacturing customization is high but marketing is low, there are mass-customized products. When both of them are low, then it is standardized. Where products are standardized but marketing messages are customized, we see strategies of personalization or 1-to-1 marketing. Where both product and marketing messages are customized, we create the highly interactive and flexible approach of "customerization."

There is an important distinction between personalization and customization. Personalization is what the company does to try to tailor the product or service to the customer. For example, Amazon might offer a personalized opening web page with recommendations for a specific user based on past purchases (using collaborative filtering). This is more of a passive process on the part of the consumer. Customerization is something the consumers do for themselves. For example, MyYahoo offers a number of elements that can be combined

EXHIBIT 3-2 **CUSTOMIZATION OPTIONS**

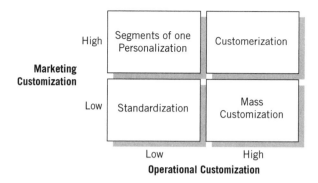

into a personal web page or Dell allows customers to put together various components into a computer system. This is an active process on the part of the consumer. There are many opportunities for expanding personalization and customerization on the Net.

Consumers can have very different reactions to personalization and customerization. Despite the extra effort to self-customize, this consumer-directed approach is sometimes valued more highly than personalization created by the company. For example, a study of 300 online consumers by Paul Nunes and Ajit Kambil found that visitors would rather customize a site themselves than have the company automatically personalize it. For a grocery site, 55 percent of online consumers said they'd like the ability to customize it while only less than 6 percent preferred personalization.[9] Many customers are far more interested in what they can do *with* the company rather than what the company can do *for* them. The essence of customerization is "co-production" between the company and the customer.

It should be noted that while technology continues to evolve, even manufacturing customization is still not free or easy. Brad Oberwager, founder of Acumins customized vitamins business, found that at the start of the business as much as 50 percent of the customized orders had to be mixed in small batches by hand by teams of pharmacists. This was done at a loss. Through improving production technology and making subtle adjustments to customer offerings, the company was able to reduce the hand-made orders to a few percentage points. Acumins also charged about three times the cost of a standardized vitamin supplement for the customized formulations, so the customization was not entirely free for the customers. In many customized businesses, primitive customer interfaces and decision-making tools also mean that customers have to invest a significant amount of time and effort to undertake customization (at least initially). These transaction costs raise the bar for customization. Repeat purchasing, however, is far faster and easier.

These tradeoffs will very likely be resolved with continuous improvement in technology, narrowing the cost in time and dollars between customized and mass-produced offerings. Smarter decision-making tools and agents (discussed in Chapter 7) will already know customers' preferences and will help find and design products for them, reducing the time customers have to spend designing and searching. The technology could also adjust for the fact that our choices vary over time and with purchase occasions. But even if customized products were just as easy to develop and cost exactly the same as mass-produced offerings, does it naturally follow that customers will want to customize all their products and services? Given the reality of the centaur, maybe not.

The move toward customerization has many benefits for consumers and their organizations. For consumers, it provides products, services, messages, and experiences that better meet their needs. For the company, it can protect against commoditization, reduce inventory, help redesign operations and planning, encourage customers to spend more on premium products and services, build relationships with customers, improve channel management, and create a platform for innovation.

Customerization changes many aspects of marketing, as illustrated in Exhibit 3–3. Customized operations and marketing create a more interactive relationship with customers, more targeted segmentation,

How can you profitably combine standardization, mass customization, personalization, and customerization in your business?

 **THE SHIFT OF CUSTOMERIZATION**

	Old Model—Mass and Segmented Marketing	New Model—Marketing Customerization
Relationship with customers	Customer is a passive participant in the exchange	Customer is an active co-producer
Customer Needs	Articulated	Articulated and unarticulated
Segmentation	Mass market & target segments	Customization segments and "segments of one"
Product and service offerings	Line extensions and modifications	Customized products, services, and marketing
New Product Development	Marketing and R&D drive new product development	Customer interactions drive new product development, and R&D focuses on developing the platforms that allow customerization
Communication	Advertising and PR	Integrated, interactive, and customized marketing communication, education, and entertainment
Distribution	Traditional retailing and direct marketing	Direct (online) distribution and rise of third party logistics services
Branding	Traditional branding & co-branding	The customer's name as the brand; My Brand or Brand 4 ME
Basis of competitive advantage	Marketing power	Marketing finesse and "capturing" the customer as "partner" while integrating marketing, operations, R&D, and information

and individualized branding. Instead of focusing on building market power in established markets, customerization focuses on the "finesse" of partnering with the customer while integrating marketing, operations, R&D, and information.

WHY THE CENTAUR SOMETIMES PREFERS STANDARDIZATION

There are times when the consumer prefers to sit back and relax, to not have to wade through a menu of options, but rather pick up the lunch plate on the cafeteria line or purchase the combo meal from the fast-food restaurant drive through. There are times when it may be simpler or more fulfilling for the centaur to live like a peasant rather than have the options for customization of a king. The more involved the consumer is in the purchase, and the more time they have, the more they may like to be engaged in shaping the product and marketing.

On the other hand, there are a number of reasons why standardized products and messages may endure, including:

- *Fitting in with the crowd:* One has only to view the dress and hairstyles of a set of teens, or how casual dress has swept through the workplace, to know that very often there is more value in being part of the crowd. People wear Rolexes or drive Mercedes to make a statement, and the statement is that they fit in with a certain crowd and not with another. (Of course, customization can be offered within a common brand.) The "fit" of the product is not as important as the "fit" with peers. Oberwager points out that, ironically, sometimes luxury items such a top-of-the-line Jaguar offer fewer opportunities for customization than moderately priced cars. (Does anyone want a luxury without air conditioning or power windows?) Similarly, shared mass marketing messages can create a sense of connection, as shown by ad messages such as, "Where's the beef?" that work their way into the popular language and culture.

- *Experience:* Early experiments with customized movies found that people often did not want to choose their own ending of the movie. They may want to experience the surprise of discovering the end of the movie or to be engaged in the artist's vision. Some segments at certain times will want to customize their experience, however, as shown by the rising popularity of "Sims," large-scale online simulations in which participants take on virtual alter egos and live in simulated cities with thousands of other participants. Even here, many of the same people who inhabit these self-directed online fantasies also choose to engage at other times in more passive experiences such as movies and television. In addition to experiences such as movies, for many consumers the experience of visual artwork or the experience of shopping, touching, and selecting clothing, is not the same online. Very few customers are willing to purchase an automobile without a test drive, but a completely customized automobile is impossible to test drive until it is built. Online simulations can offer virtual experiences, such as eyeglass retailer Paris Miki's ability to show customers how a set of frames might look on their face, but right now these experiences are a pale imitation of the original.

- *The need for fit:* One of the reasons for the failure of Custom Foot, which offered mass customized footwear online, is the subjective nature of fitting shoes.[10] Two customers might be measured for a size 10 shoe, but one might prefer a tight fit whereas the other might prefer a loose one. Some aspects of the styling and feel of the fit may not be captured by current technology by simply measuring foot size. In a shoe store, the customer tries on several pairs to find the right "feel," using measurements only as a starting point.

- *Uncertainty:* When you buy something off the shelf, you know exactly what you are getting. It may not be exactly what you *want,* but when you put the jeans on, you know how they fit, look, and feel. When you design something from scratch, you have created a prototype and like all prototypes it may or may not be exactly as you envisioned it.

- *The complexity of choice:* Making decisions is hard work. There is a limit to the amount of time and energy customers want to put into designing their own products and services. Some customers who are buying a box of tissues may not want to have to answer a dozen questions to do so. (On the other hand, some may be intrigued by the opportunity to design their own patterns and choose their own features.) For some products, customization is just not worth the effort, although which products warrant this attention will depend upon the individual. The time and energy involved in making choices is greatly reduced on repeat purchases. The first purchase may be time consuming to set up, but subsequent purchases are usually much faster. New technologies also will help reduce the time and cost involved.

- *Unarticulated needs:* Sometimes customers don't know what they want until they see it. When preferences are not explicit, companies can infer them from other information. For example, a customized coffee maker inferred the customers' preferences for coffee by a series of questions such as how they liked their steaks cooked or what type of chocolate they preferred. But often consumers don't know they want something until they actually see it and they find what they want by experimenting, hands on, with a variety of different variations of the product.

- *The right to change one's mind:* In addition to unarticulated needs, consumers may engage in "variety seeking" behavior, experimenting with new choices. In most product categories, consumers develop a consideration set of products that reflects their preference for variety. They may rotate choices within this set or even expand the set to satisfy their individual needs for variety. Customization often assumes that customers have a predictable set of preferences, but in fact preferences change over time and based on the situation. Offering a simple customized product that can be repurchased may not meet this demand to change one's mind.

• *Integration:* While changing a zipper fly to a button fly in jeans is relatively straightforward, products such as automobiles are more than a collection of components. The components need to fit together in a way that ensures performance, safety, reliability, and a smooth ride. In an article on automotive customization by John Paul MacDuffie and Susan Helper, they conclude that a true mix-and-match automobile (a Honda engine in a GM chassis) will probably not be possible unless auto companies create standardized interfaces, if it is possible at all.[11] The need for components to fit together into an integrated whole means that there are limits to customization. Although we may be able to select an orange dash board with three cup holders and a eyeglass case (assuming you'd want to), it is unlikely that customers will be invited to design their own engines anytime soon.

• *Repair and reselling:* The more specialized the product you create, the harder it will be to repair or resell. If you have a home that is so customized to your distinctive tastes, it might be difficult to find another buyer with the same set of tastes or one willing to invest the time or money to make it their own. It may be that you create a work of art that has value because of its uniqueness, but the more customized a product is, the more narrow will be the secondary market for it. Also, the more customized the product, the more difficult it often will be to repair.

What are the factors that might make your customers prefer standardized over customized products and services?

These concerns (and the limits of current technology) are reflected in some negative reaction to customization initiatives. *Business Week* columnist Ann Therese Palmer was annoyed by all the questions asked by Reflect.com, an online beauty site launched by Procter & Gamble. The questions are used to create customized products for hair or skin. But Palmer just wanted to buy a standardized product. "If you're a game-show aficionado and love answering pointless questions about yourself, you'll love Reflect.com. But if you just want some lipstick, you might think about going somewhere else...This incessant question-asking delivers the opposite of the Internet's promise: time-consuming shopping that's no fun... As a result, buying the shampoo takes 35 minutes, one tube of lipstick takes 40 minutes, and the moisturizer 40 minutes. For your information, guys: This normally takes about 10 minutes in a drugstore or department store—with in-person guidance on how to apply the product and free product samples tested on my skin to see how they look."[12]

What she doesn't fully appreciate are the facts that some women actually enjoy the experience, some find the customized results worth the effort, and all benefit repurchasing efficiency—once the customized lipsticks or shampoos are developed, they can be repurchased in seconds. But her comment that the experience is "no fun" is an indication that she enjoys a shopping experience that is more experiential and less cognitive. The experience of testing perfume at the cosmetics counter is fundamentally different than answering questions online about perfume. Of course, there are technologies under development to reduce the dependency on questions (through games and other interfaces) and to add touch, smell, and engage the other senses online, so the virtual perfume counter may not be so far off.

Because of the value of standardization discussed above, companies (at the very least in the short term) will have to offer both customized and off-the-shelf products. Palmer's gripe about Reflect.com would be muted if she could have skipped over the questions and bought a standardized product with a single mouseclick. The most powerful business models will not be either standardized/mass market offerings or customerized, but rather the combination that the centaur wants at any given time. Some customers will want customized offerings while others will want to buy them off-the-shelf. Centaurs will want

CONVERGING ON CUSTOMERIZATION: MAKE IT MINE   Chapter 3

customization for some products (a car), but not for others (detergent). Moreover, they may want standardized products on certain occasions (for example, when they are in a hurry) and customized offerings for the same products on other occasions (when they have more time to deliberate).

The companies that can effectively combine standardization and customerization will best be able to meet this need. As illustrated in Exhibit 3–2, the convergence challenge for companies is not merely to develop capabilities for customerization, as important as this is. It is to find the right way to balance and capture the synergies between customerization and mass marketing/standardization.

CONVERGENCE STRATEGIES FOR CUSTOMERIZATION AND STANDARDIZATION

Both customerization and standardization add value for companies and consumers in different ways. Given the strong interdependencies between operations and marketing in designing and implementing any customerization strategy, the discussion of strategies in this section combines both dimensions of customerization. How can companies effectively and creatively combine mass production and customerization strategies? How can they combine standardized and customized marketing messages and experiences? There are a variety of strategies:

- *Integrate online and offline customization:* Visitors to Paul Allen's Electronic Music Project (EMP) museum in Seattle are given a pointing device that provides stories, commentary, and song tracks related to the photos of famous musicians, instruments, and other items on display. By pointing the device at a particular exhibit, the visitor receives a customized guided tour. Though the quality of the content may be better, this is not too different from the systems for self-guided tours at many museums. But there is something quite different happening there. While the visitor is pointing to exhibits, the device has the capacity to create a customized sets of "bookmarks" of the experience. At the end of the physical tour, the device is docked into a network and the bookmarks are uploaded online. The visitors then can return to the virtual music collection, enter a ticket number, and enter a customized digital museum where they can revisit only the exhibits that interested them and explore them in greater depth. At the same time, the museum has an opportunity to see firsthand which exhibits are of greatest interest to its visitors and could conceivably add more detail either online or offline to the exhibits of most interest. The online and offline experiences are seamlessly customized and the standardized museum experience has become customized.

This is a model that companies might look at closely. Visitors to Amazon.com can checkout in seconds with "one-click" purchasing tailored to their customized settings for mailing and billing or receive customized recommendations for books. But visitors to physical bookstores don't have these options (although Mobil's Speedpass, which allows customers to pay for purchases with the swipe of a key ring, or the automated toll systems such as E-ZPass, are steps in this direction). What would happen if visitors to a physical bookstore were directed to books they might like based on their last purchases? Or what if they could point a device at actual books on the shelves and create an online list of potential books to purchase or explore in the future, and then enter a web site with customized information about those books and those authors? There are many opportunities for integrating customization online and offline, capturing buyer preferences in the store and moving them online or using online information to shape the store experience.

- *Ask the next question:* Southwest Airlines has created one of the most user friendly and powerful travel sites (southwestairlines.com) by continuing to ask the next question. If you book a ticket, it asks you if you want a rental car and hotel room. But since it already knows where you are landing, it immediately presents you with a set of options for that destination. This not only reduces steps for the user, but it means the company is thinking one step ahead of the customer, which is the essence of personalized service. Instead of stopping with its own tickets, it thinks about what else the customer might need. As you offer customized products, what are the complementary offerings that should be added to the package? How can you integrate them seamlessly? How can you tailor your marketing messages as part of the interaction with customers?

- *Invite the customer into the lab:* To take full advantage of customerization for product design, companies need to give R&D a direct pipeline into the market and invite customers (figuratively speaking) into the laboratory. For example, Texas Instruments (TI) posted the design specs for a new calculator (TI-92) on its web site. This product is designed for use in schools and is targeted at school teachers as the primary purchase influencers. TI engineers then invited customer participation and feedback by sending email to chat groups where high school teachers congregate on the Web. Thousands of teachers responded. A week later, TI posted a revised prototype based on the responses. The design specifications were finalized only after several rounds of such interactions. Selling this product was much easier because it was tailored to customer needs and was "pre-sold" to customers who had played a role in creating it. Not only the product was customized, but also the marketing message, because the teachers had a personal involvement in the process. The product went on to become one of the most successful calculators sold by TI. Interestingly, when a competitor quickly came out with a copycat product, many customers were incensed that a "competitor stole *our* ideas." The market owned the product, and therefore, the product owned the market!

In addition to this sense of ownership, companies benefit directly from the time customers invest in product design. Michael Schrage, author of *Serious Play*, estimates that Microsoft beta testers contributed an estimated $1 billion to the effort of launching Windows 95. These customers spent hours working out bugs and improving the software at no cost to Microsoft. As Schrage notes, "Microsoft spent less on development of Windows 95 than its customers did."[13]

- *Use the customized choices to inform mass production:* By combining customer configuration with a mass production strategy, companies can use the insights from the customized products to shape their mass-produced line. Customer design choices may portend emerging trends. For example, P&G's Reflect.com web site for customized cosmetics might provide real-time insights on the preferred product characteristics of consumers that can be incorporated into its mass-produced cosmetics.

- *Understand the value chain of your brand:* You have to understand the customer and the competitive dynamics of the network. Even if U.S. car companies want to create build-to-order models, they still have to decide how to deal with their existing dealer network. What type of customization platform is needed to support the consumer and the dealer? What user interface is needed to make it easy and understandable by all members of the value network?

- *Understand your segments:* Different consumer segments may have different attitudes toward customization, and some consumers may prefer to finish the process face-to-face. *Consumer Reports* found that even among those attempting to buy online, only about a third of potential buyers actually complete the deal. Most preferred to finish their negotiations at the dealer or did not think they were getting the best price online.[14] Some of this reluctance to complete the deal online, however, may be due to the poor development of processes and technologies.

A 2000 survey by J. D. Power and Associates found that 17 percent of North American car buyers would purchase a build-to-order vehicle the next time they bought a car—provided they didn't need to pay more for it or wait longer than eight weeks.[15] BMW sold 15 percent of its U.S. vehicles made-to-order in 1998 (and some 60 percent in Europe) and the company was looking for ways to increase the U.S. percentage of those orders, each of which saves dealers an average of $450 in inventory costs.[16]

- *Increase digital content:* By increasing the digital content of offerings, companies can make it easier to customize at low cost. For purely digital products (e.g., music, news, etc.) and services (e.g., online stock trading), this is easy to do. For digital products, there are inherently innumerable options for customers to choose from and customerization improves the fit between what the customer wants and what the firm can offer profitably. Companies need to think creatively about ways to increase the digital content of even products that don't appear to lend themselves to digitization. Consider two diverse products—an automobile and a hot cup of cappuccino. It is now conceivable that we can digitize some elements of these products or their shopping and consumption experiences. Mercedes Benz recently introduced an online customizer—you can now build your own E300 Turbo Diesel. The company is trying to digitize parts of the shopping experience. How about a cup of cappuccino? It is conceivable that a cappuccino machine could be designed to take into account the type of coffee beans, type and amount of milk, temperature, brewing time, etc. to adjust to different tastes, leading to a customized cup of cappuccino. Eventually, the cappuccino machine could become an Internet appliance that downloads the appropriate brewing instructions from the Internet, or is activated remotely over the Internet so that the coffee is ready when the customer comes home.

- *Grab the low-hanging fruit of superficial customization:* Sometimes even superficial customization can create greater customer choice (or at least the impression of it) without significantly changing underlying products and processes. Companies like GM and Ford, instead of creating true build-to-order systems (or perhaps as a precursor to them) are developing what Forrester has referred to as a "locate to order" system. Consumers put in their preferences and the system locates a vehicle at a nearby dealer that most closely matches those characteristics.[17] Canada has offered customized postage stamps that allow customers to design stamps with their own pictures and VO Whiskey.com offers customized bottles of whiskey, an easy process of changing the label, without tampering with the formula for the product inside the bottle. Volkswagen offered limited-edition colors for its new Beetle. The fundamental functionality of the product is not radically changed, so the complexity of this type of customization is reduced for both the buyer and the seller, while the perceived benefit of customization is greatly enhanced. The key is to understand the customizable features that have the greatest value to the consumer.

- *Keep standardized offerings a click or step away:* Matt Calkins, CEO of personalization technology company Appian, says that they try to develop sites that ensure a standardized page is always a click away.[18] That way if customers get tired out or lost in the complexity of customerization, they can always quickly return to predictable world of standardized offerings. It is important to keep standard and customized offerings within easy reach of one another. In addition to doing this online, companies also do this in physical stores. The terminals in Barnes & Noble that allow for rapid searching and ordering of books are right next to the standard selections that allows for leisurely browsing. Making it easy to switch from customized to standardized interfaces and experiences, and vice versa, is vital to meeting the demands of a centaur who sometimes may want customized products, but other times wants to browse from a fixed set of options.

- *Design for future customization:* Some toys are designed to be upgraded after the sale through the Interent. For example, Neurosmith developed a cartridge system that will allow parents to change the tune that plays on the company's Music Blocks for infants. Hasbro's e-Specially My Barney allowed parents to log onto a web site and provide information about the child's birthday and favorite colors, and download new songs and stories through the site.[19]

Lego, whose name has long been synonymous with low-tech customization, is extending its customization through high-tech additions. Its sets of plastic building blocks are not only infinitely reconfigurable, but they can be expanded through new product lines such as the Legos Studio line that allows children to use a PC camera, editing software, and Lego blocks to put together movies that can be shared with other children over the Internet. The company also has developed a variety of games that it offers on its website and through popular video game systems. It also has developed a Lego Mindstorms system that allows youngsters to build and program robots to do tricks such as climbing towers or greeting visitors.[20] Clearly, the customization of any product before it leaves the factory is just the beginning. Creating products and services that can be customized on an ongoing basis is a powerful way of interacting with customers and building continuing revenue streams.

- *Limit complexity by offering the right selection:* The temptation in the customerization of both products and messages is to give consumers too many options, but this may lead to psychological shut down. The key is to offer just the right choice set so customers are presented with variety without being overwhelmed. When CDNow (now part of Bertelsmann eCommerce Group) first introduced its "Supersonic Boom," offering customized CDs that can be assembled by selecting single tracks from a library, it provided customers with a search engine. Consumers were overwhelmed by the choices. The company had better success when it offered a customized Christmas CD during the holiday season, with a preset selection of song titles. Sales took off when customers could select from a more manageable set of options. A smaller set of options is often more valuable than an infinite variety that becomes very complex. Similarly, offering customer products in limited increments can reduce the manufacturing complexity without significantly interfering with choice. For example, Acumins found that it could reduce the complexity of its vitamin manufacturing by offering customers the option of adding a vitamin in 10 mg increments rather than by odd amounts.

Companies need to find the right balance between the consumer desire for options and the manufacturing considerations (complexity, safety, and performance).

Another way to limit the number of options is to present standardized options packages, as is common in the automotive and computer industries, as the starting point in developing more customized products.

- *Personalize messages and products based on careful observation:* Careful observation of clickstreams can help tailor messages to specific segments or to consumers at specific stages of the buying process. "Biometric" software developed by Predictive Networks can infer whether a mom, dad, or children are using a shared household computer based on their clicking patterns. Advertising and other messages could then be tailored to specific users.[21] Similarly, studies of online behavior can offer insights into whether visitors are casual browsers, seeking information or closing in on a purchase. Companies can use these insights to tailor their messages and approaches to buyers at different stages in the purchase process.[22]

- *Simplify customerization:* Obtaining customer input through a game or interactive design can make it easier for customers to interact than by answering questions. The goal is not to gather complete information, but rather to provide the best overall customer experience and simplify the customerization task. Today, most of the interface is done through questions, but it is conceivable that in the future, the interface could be designed as games or through powerful inferences about behavior.

- *Understand the level of attention customers want:* Some customers in a physical store will welcome the attention of a salesperson, whereas others prefer to shop anonymously. Astute salespeople will recognize this and adapt their behavior accordingly. Similarly, online, some customers will happily provide the needed information whereas others resent this intrusion. Since the cutoff between gathering information and intrusion varies customer by customer, the customization experience itself needs to be customizable. This ensures that the process of customization is an interactive and enjoyable experience. Databases and data-mining techniques can help in gathering information without asking.[23] Firms such as net.genesis and e.piphany have developed software systems that combine data-mining technologies with customization strategies.[24]

- **Create an integrated view of the customer:** Companies need to develop an integrated view of customers and deliver consistent messages across different channels. These marketing messages should not only be personalized, but they should be part of an ongoing dialogue. The customer who files a mortgage application online should be offered an update on its status on her next phone call to the company, or her next withdraw from the ATM.

Most companies do not have systems that are well designed to deliver this seamless integration, as we will explore in more detail in Chapter 10. These information systems are often designed around accounts or transactions rather than customers. Systems may be divided by separate divisions or geographic regions. Companies need to create unified databases and integrating platforms for managing customer relationships, to deliver a coherent experience across customers and across channels.

How can you best combine customerization and standardization in your business and which of these strategies can you apply?

THE CUSTOMERIZED FUTURE

The technology for customerization, as noted above, is in a fairly primitive state and will continue to become easier and faster. Similarly, as data-mining has evolved and tools for discerning customer preferences have been developed, the technology for customized and personalized marketing messages and experiences is becoming increasingly sophisticated. We cannot judge the future of customerization by looking at today's technology anymore than we could have anticipated the modern music market by listening to the first scratchy Edison recording. The technology is rapidly changing and improving.

Although consumer expectations appear to be advancing even faster than the technology itself, the technology is catching up. A personal fabricator developed at MIT will allow customers to "print" their dinnerware and other synthetic objects. Increasingly small metal presses may allow more localized production of metal components. Nanotechnology, while still years away, could create even more possibilities for fluid local production. In this way, the "product" would be the design for the dinnerware, as all products become increasingly digital and infinitely customizable.

As companies continue to struggle to find ways to spark innovation in new product development, greater involvement by customers in the process may be the best approach. Studies by Von Hippel and others found that open architecture systems lead to more innovations than closed systems.[25] Since there is value in open systems, the world will very likely continue to move in that direction, and a key focus will be using these systems to create new products tailored to individual customers. This will create new opportunities for customization—beyond selecting from a set of preexisting options. But not for all customers, and not for customers at all times. So companies will need to provide the centaurs with a mix of customized and standardized products and services. They will need to move the isolated experiments and separate operations focusing on customization into the mainstream, creating an integrated whole that provides customers with both the unlimited options of customization *and* the option of "not having so many options" provided by mass production. This is the range of choices the centaurs want and need.

NOTES

[1] This chapter is based in part upon the paper "Customerization: The Next Revolution in Mass Customization," by Jerry Wind and Arvind Rangaswamy, *Journal of Interactive Marketing*, Vol. 15, No. 1 (Winter 2001), pp. 13–32.

Action Memo

- Place an order at Reflect.com. What do you like about the experience of designing your own product? What do you dislike? What would you like to be able to do that you can't? How would you change the approach to customerization if you were designing the site? What kind of personalized messages do you receive as follow-up?

- Visit a cosmetics counter at a department store. How is the experience of making a purchase customized or personlized for you? In what ways is this customerization superior to what you experience online? **How can you apply these insights to your own business?**

- Visit Ford Direct (www.forddirect.com) and go through the process of designing a car. What do you like about the experience? What are the limitations of customerization through this model?

- Visit an automobile dealer. What are the opportunities for customization? How is the customization process different than online? How can you use these insights in your business? **How can you use these insights in designing customized offerings in your business?**

We invite you to share the results of these activities and suggest other action memos at the Convergence Marketing Forum (www.convergencemarketingforum.com).

[2] Mark Hogan, President eGM, "Hotwiring GM," remarks at the "Internet, e-Strategies and Virtual Communities Conference," April 6, 2001, Wharton School.

[3] Green, Paul E., Abba M. Krieger and Yoram (Jerry) Wind, "Thirty Years of Conjoint Analysis: Reflections and Prospects," *Interfaces* vol. 31, no. 3 (May-June 2001), pp. 556–573.

[4] Mahajan, Vijay and Jerry Wind, "Rx for Marketing Research," *Marketing Research*, Fall 1999, pp7–13.

[5] Nelson, Emily, "Too Many Choices: Nine Kinds of Kleenex Tissue, Eggo Waffles in 16 Flavors; Blame Brand Managers," *The Wall Street Journal*, April 20, 2001, p. B-1.

[6] Huffman, Cynthia and Barbara E. Kahn (1998), "Variety for sale: Mass customization or mass confusion?" *Journal of Retailing*, Vol. 74, No. 4 (Fall), 491–513.

[7] Schonfeld, Eric, "The customized, digitized, have-it-your-way economy," *Fortune*, September 29, 1998, 114.

[8] "Customizing for the Masses: Digital technology lets you order exactly what you want," *Business Week Online*, March 20, 2000.

[9] Nunes, Paul F. and Ajit Kambil, "Personalization? No Thanks," *Harvard Business Review*, April 2001, pp. 33–34.

[10] Wind and Rangaswamy, see note #1.

[11] Helper, Susan and John Paul MacDuffie, "Evolving the Auto Industry: E-Commerce Effects on Consumer and Supplier Relationships," working paper, April 2000, Reginald H. Jones Center, The Wharton School.

[12] Palmer, Ann Therese, "A Beauty Site Marred by Endless Questions," *BusinessWeek Online, e.Biz* , May 5, 2000.

[13] Schrage, Michael, *Serious Play*, Boston: Harvard Business School Press, 2000, pp. 30–31, and remarks to Wharton Fellows in e-Business program, Philadelphia, November 26, 2000.

[14] "A Flat for Car Buying," *Austin American Statesman*, May 5, 2000, p. G1.

[15] Agrawal, Mani, T. V. Kumaresh, and Glenn A. Mercer, "The False Promise of Mass Customization," *McKinsey Quarterly*, 2001 Number 3.

[16] Schonfeld, Erick, "The customized, digitized, have-it-your-way economy," *Fortune*, September 28, 1998, Vol. 138, issue 6, September 28, 1998, p. 114.

[17] Agrawal, Kumaresh, and Mercer, see note #15.

[18] Matt Calkins, interview Archana Vemulapalli, March 1, 2001.

[19] Wilson, David, "New Toys Come with Software Updates Required," *San Jose Mercury News*, February 20, 2000.

[20] McCauley, Dennis, "Lego: No Tech Meets New Tech," *Wired*, May 18, 2001.

[21] Bulkeley, William, "Software Uses Clicking Patterns to Customize Ads," *The Wall Street Journal*, May 25, 2001, p. B-1.

[22] "Turning Browsers into Buyers," Wendy Moe, University of Texas at Austin, presentation at the Wharton School, May 30, 2001

[23] Zahavi, Jacob, "Data Mining" in Wind and Mahajan, eds., Digital Marketing, New York: John Wiley & Sons, 2000.

[24] Seybold, Patricia and Ronni T. Marshak, *Customers.com*, Times Business, Random House, 1999.

[25] Von Hippel, Eric. *The Sources of Innovation*, (New York: Oxford University Press, 1988).

4

CONVERGING ON COMMUNITIES

LET ME BE A PART OF IT

"Man is...a social animal."

Aristotle

TRADITIONAL CONSUMER

"Man is a social animal, but a virtual community is an oxymoron. The communities I care about are the ones where I live and work, where I have enough skin in the game to affect the community and be affected by it. A community is a social and cultural phenomenon, not something to be used for economic gain. Doing that destroys the essence of the community."

CYBERCONSUMER

"Some of my most meaningful interactions are with online communities. These communities allow me to connect with people around the world who share my interests. They allow me the anonymity to share my deepest concerns and to find products and services related to those interests. The Internet provides new ways to help us be social animals."

THE CENTAUR

"I belong to both worlds. I value the personal interaction of my physical communities and I value the reach and focus of my online communities. I want to be able to move from physical to virtual and back again. I want to make connections with others any way I can. I want my communities to make sense socially and economically, to have the right balance between personal values and profit. I will be a social animal wherever and whenever I want to."

CONVERGENCE QUESTIONS

>>>*How can you build communities online and offline that are synergistic and coherent?*

>>>*How can you balance the social and economic aspects of communities to strengthen both?*

>>>*How can you develop marketing strategies based on the community?*

CONVERGING ON COMMUNITIES:
Let Me Be a Part of It[1]

The emergence of the virtual community, knitting together people with common interests from around the globe, is one of the most significant innovations of the interconnected world. But these virtual communities have to be considered in a broader context. This chapter considers how these virtual communities converge with physical communities and how the economic and social purposes of communities can be drawn together.

On her way home from work, Asha goes to the local Indian grocery store in her Austin, Texas neighborhood and picks up beans, rice, and spice for *rajma* and *palaou*. Asha, who graduated from the University of Pennsylvania and is now working as a programmer at a high-tech firm, starts dinner for her husband who is working late. After placing a pot of rice to boil on the stove and soaking the *rajma* for cooking, she flips on her computer and, thanks to her recently installed DSL line, immediately sees a site called Sulekha.com, which she has set as her home page.

She reviews the latest India-related news stories drawn from publications ranging from the *Boston Globe* to the *Hindustan Times*. She shares her thoughts in a discussion of an *Economist* story about the growing political clout of Indians in the U.S. She reads with equal interest the story of the day, contributed by a fellow Indian living in the Middle East, and fashion trends among Indian teens in the United States. She comes across yet another glowing review for the new movie *Lagaan* and decides she has to see it. She places a one-click order for the DVD from *eshakti.com,* an alliance partner of Sulekha.

Asha then checks out breathtaking photos from a Himalayan expedition posted by a trekker who writes: "We saw the Sunset after 12 days from Cheerbasa and it was a welcome sight. We were still 9 km away from Ganotri and it was going to be some time before we went and slept somewhere, but we were not complaining." She also browses through a series of diverse amateur photos posted by community members and thinks about a photo that she would like to share (if she could dig it out of the closet and scan it). She turns to a forum on the topic: "When was the last time you were filled with a sense of awe and why?" Respondents write about sunsets, the birth of a child, and amusement rides. "Trigger_My_Passion" from Tampa, U.S., recalls a visit to India:

"I was literally dumbfounded when I got down from the car and stood in front of Buland Darwaza. I felt like a tiny atom in front of a giant. I still have its picture registered in my mind after nearly 6 yrs."

As she thinks about plans for the weekend ahead, she browses through local events on the site and notes with interest a local classical Indian music concert. It is one of her husband's favorite performers. Since they don't have plans, she purchases tickets online and then emails the information to another couple they met through Sulekha to invite them to come along.

Asha then clicks on a button that says "Baby Name Search." She and her husband have been married for a year, but they've only talked about children as an abstract, distant prospect. Even so, she often asks her husband what he thinks of certain names, and he generally pretends to be interested. It may be a long way off, but still she can dream. She scrolls down through the lists of Sanskrit baby names and imagines what life would be like with a little Sachi or Sagaar running around the house.

THE POWER OF COMMUNITY

Sulekha.com is the largest Indian online community. The site has posted more than 100 percent growth per quarter purely by word of mouth, with no advertising spending. It is exponentially increasing visitors and usage. The content, almost all of which is contributed by members (eliminating the cost of producing the site while engaging members at the same time), is increasing at a parallel rate. Sulekha.com reaches 20 million people of Indian heritage in 70 countries around the world, and over a quarter million pages of content. The site includes news, discussions, photographs, articles, opinions, cartoons, movie reviews, event information, and website recommendations.

The idea for Sulekha came from a monthly letter—*Letter from Austin*—that Dr. Arun Kumar used to email to buddies from his alma mater (Indian Institute of Management) in Calcutta and other friends around the world. This small group evolved into the *Dakghar* (meaning "post office") mailing list of roughly 75 members. The list became a focal point for connection to the Indian community and excellent writing. In 1988, Satya Prabhkar and his wife Sangeeta Kshettry, members of Dakghar, saw the need for a website on a much larger scale, reconnecting Indians worldwide. "Sulekha" was born. Its title, reflecting the site's roots, means "good writing" in Sanskrit.

Sulekha.com is extraordinarily sticky—some visitors call it "addictive"—and enjoys what its founders call "Harley Davidson-ish" emotional loyalty. It has a 60 to 70 percent repeat visitor rate. Its site has won rare acclaim from the Indian media.

But now it faces the challenges of many online communities that have grown organically. As a business, how can it convert the social energy of the site into profitable enterprises without destroying it? How can Sulekha continue to build and strengthen its online community through physical interactions? In the process, Sulekha has published a book, is creating new business models, and building connections in local communities. As Satya Prabhkar commented in an interview, "I don't think we can remain a pure

What role do communities online and offline play in your business? What role could they play?

online company."[2] At the same time that they make the transition, they need to be careful to remain true to the spirit of the community. "As head of the company, my number one responsibility is to understand what the identity of Sulekha is and to ensure our strategies fit that identity."

The Potential of Virtual Communities

As "social animals," we all desire a personal connection with other people. This connection has traditionally been found in physical communities, in a family, a neighborhood, a church, or a work-focused community of practice. These communities have balanced social and economic value, with the town square serving as both a meeting place and a marketplace. These communities could form around ethnic or religious groups, local towns and cities, or interest groups. They could even form around products, such as the "cult brands" of Harley Davidson motorcycles or Apple computers.[3]

As a medium for connection and interaction, the Internet offers an entirely new channel for communities. These virtual communities have the potential for a greater geographic scope (connecting people around the world) and narrower focus (connecting people with very specific interests) than most offline communities. John Hagel III and Arthur G. Armstrong point out that these communities offer benefits to both members and companies. Company gains include: reduced search costs in finding customers, increased propensity for customers to buy, enhanced ability to target and greater ability to tailor and add value to existing products and services. As the critical mass of members grows, with the low costs of virtual interaction, companies have the potential to generate increasing returns from the dynamic interaction of these communities.[4]

Lisa Kraynak, former VP of Strategic Development of iVillage, a leading online site for women, calls community "one of the killer applications of the Internet."[5] Bruce Brownstein of eBay refers to the virtual community of eBay users as the online auction site's "secret sauce." While eBay has been very successful in capitalizing on the economic potential of its community, other companies have faced much greater challenges in the

EXHIBIT 4-1 ILLUSTRATIVE CHARACTERISTICS OF ONLINE AND OFFLINE COMMUNITIES

	Offline	Online
Geographical scope	Geographically bound	Boundless and global
Temporal scope	Specific meeting times	Anytime
Reachability	Expensive and complex	Cheap and simple
Speed of communication	Slow	Instantaneous
Ability to change	Difficult	Easy
Potential for engagement	Somewhat limited	Greater
Identity & Anonymity	More fixed	More fluid and anonymous
Experience	Face-to-face	Virtual

turning the commitment and buzz of their communities into profits.

The members of these virtual communities also derive many benefits, but these benefits are both social and economic. The communities give them the power to engage in passionate discussions on topics of interest and interact with people around the world. Sulekha reaches people of Indian heritage anytime, anyplace, who don't need passports, visas, tickets or reservations to interact "socially." Members of communities also can gain access to a broader group of vendors or information about products and services.

Virtual and physical communities have strengths and weaknesses that are often complementary. The potential face-to-face intimacy of physical community can be enhanced by the benefits offered by online community, as illustrated in Exhibit 4–1. While virtual communities have unmatched geographic scope and focus, they allow for anonymous interaction that can raise issues of credibility or commitment. On the other hand, although roots in a physical community may increase commitment, it does not ensure interaction and some participants in both virtual and physical communities have a greater investment in their online connections than in their physical neighborhoods.

Convergence Challenges

The emergence of virtual communities creates several opportunities for convergence, as illustrated in Exhibit 4–2. The first is the convergence of physical and virtual communities. The second is the convergence of economic and social elements of communities. Sulekha, for example, created an anthology of some of its best writing in a book called *Sulekha Select*. This project has created a physical product to build its offline presence from the virtual interaction of the community. Sales of the book turn the social energy of the community into economic returns.

The reality of centaurs is that they are members of both virtual and physical communities. Asha shares ideas and photos with her virtual community online, then joins with her husband and other friends to go to a concert offline, and then reviews the concert online. How do these two communities intersect? In the past, because virtual communities have been a new phenomenon, they have been considered more or less in isolation. The first convergence challenge posed by the centaur is to look at the overlap and interaction between the physical and virtual communities in which the centaur participates. This offers more powerful perspectives on reinforcing these communities

EXHIBIT 4–2 **CONVERGING ON COMMUNITIES**

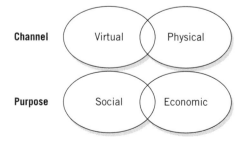

than we gain by looking at either one in isolation. How can companies build interactions and bridges between virtual and physical communities?

The second convergence challenge for companies is to balance the social and economic elements of community. Many successful online communities like Sulekha have grown out of a desire for social interaction without any significant economic objective. Even those that began with a business goal were often organized around a magazine-like advertising model in which the community was gathered through fairly independent content and then advertisements were directed to these targeted eyeballs. The lack of integration of this economic element in the social fabric made it very easy to ignore, and visitors to sites easily passed over it. On the other hand, without a viable economic base, the resources needed to build and sustain the online community (like a physical community) will not be there. One of the key convergence challenges as virtual communities develop is to give them viable economic foundations without eroding their social fabric. This is not a new challenge. When communities are exploited for economic gain, it undermines their social strength. Many early virtual communities that have been successful socially have yet to become profitable. How can companies balance the economic and social objectives of the community to create social and economic aspects that are well integrated and synergistic? How can communities be of benefit to the company and help the company create value?

Are there opportunities for convergence in the physical and virtual communities in which your customers participate? Are their opportunities for convergence of their social and economic goals?

STRATEGIES FOR CONVERGENCE OF PHYSICAL AND VIRTUAL COMMUNITIES

Although 20 percent of the world population is Moslem, there are a limited number of respected centers and universities in the world where Moslems can receive religious education. Not everyone who desires this training can come to these centers.

EXHIBIT 4–3 CONVERGENCE OF PHYSICAL AND
VIRTUAL COMMUNITIES

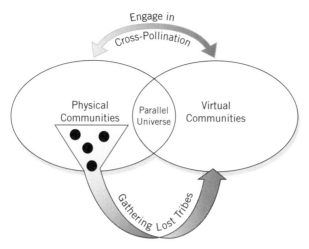

AMIR distance learning Islamic University (www.amir-univer-sity.org) offers an online curriculum in Arabic and English, accredited by world-renowned Abu Nour Institute of Damascus, to Moslems around the world. (The courses also can be delivered by fax and mail.) The physical community of Moslems can be drawn together through the virtual community of this educational program. The programs deepen the spiritual and cultural commitment of students in their local communities and their physical interactions deepen their interest in partici-pating in the virtual community. It is the interaction between the physical and virtual that reinforces the value of both.

Centaurs are active participants in both physical and virtual communities and they use these communities to generate social and economic value. How can companies weave together these physical and virtual communities to increase the value of both? As illustrated in Exhibit 4–3, the strategies for the convergence of physical and virtual communities include:

- *Gather lost tribes:* This strategy takes natural physical communities that are diffused and gives them a place to meet online. Sulekha serves this role in gathering diffused members of the Indian community worldwide. Beautyandsoul.com created the world's largest site focusing on the unmet needs for personal products (including hair and skin care) of people of African heritage worldwide. Online Partners' sites Gay.com and PlanetOut build upon a physical community of 19 million homosexuals in the U.S. and 30 million in Europe, reaching more than 3.5 million people around the world every month. The Internet was a natural center in this case, because it also offers some level of anonymity and a safe haven in an often-hostile world.

- *Create parallel universes:* Sometimes the physical community becomes the basis for the virtual community or the virtual community becomes the foundation for the physical community. In this case, the actual members of each community are the same. For example, subscribers to *Fast Company* magazine join together in local and online communities by geography and interests. The offline community spawns parallel online communities, mirror sites between the physical and virtual worlds. Through Sulekha, members in different cities have formed social clubs and gathered for picnics or to share new books.

- *Engaged in cross-pollination:* Even when parallel universes are not created, the interactions in the physical communities may lead to interactions in virtual communities or vice versa. On the iVillage site, its finance channel "MoneyLife" not only offers content written by financial advisors and interactive tools that allow members to create their own debt reduction planners, but also connects members to resources in their own neighborhoods, such as a 12-step program for debtors. The community of interaction that occurs in virtual space on eBay leads to a physical exchange of goods, and sometimes to personal connections. Sulekha has also carried its online content into offline books and other interaction in physical communities. Similarly, Motley Fool, which

How can you capitalize on the convergence between physical and virtual communities? Which physical communities could be taken online and which online communities can be transferred into physical communities?

began as an online financial site, has carried its work offline with successful print books and other physical products.

- *Take advantage of strengths and weaknesses of virtual and physical communities:* The anonymity offered by virtual communities can be an advantage in allowing community members to share their strong opinions or intimate revelations. Gay communities such as PlanetOut and Gay.com offer members opportunities to gain information and support from the community without giving up their anonymity, something that would be much more difficult in a physical community. In Italy a popular site (www.tradimenti.it, which means "betrayal") focusing on infidelity helps men and women meet and offers them suggestions for holiday getaways. At the same time, it offers strategies for thwarted spouses to win back their partner's attention or extract revenge.[6] The anonymity of the Internet makes it possible to discuss subjects that would be difficult to discuss in physical communities. Some interactions will work best in physical communities and others will work best in virtual communities. As companies craft their convergence strategies, they need to determine when to focus on one side or the other, or both.

STRATEGIES FOR SOCIAL AND ECONOMIC CONVERGENCE

The second convergence challenge is to draw together the overlapping social and economic aspects of communities. When Sulekha began to think about converting its social community into a business, it faced the challenge of converting its social energy into economic wealth. Sulekha is now pursuing a number of options, including selling electronic reports, books, music, travel, and tickets to events.

The experience of the online music-swapping network Napster also illustrates the challenges of transforming a social community into an economic community. Napster built a thriving online community based on individuals swapping music for free online, but the company not only derived no revenue from this activity, but directly threatened the existing revenue streams of major media companies. In late 2000, under pressure from music industry lawsuits, Napster was purchased by German media powerhouse Bertelsmann. As Napster sought to comply with court orders to protect copyright material and to develop a payment system to charge users and pay copyright holders, it saw its online community evaporate. Napster saw monthly music downloads from its site plummet from 2.8 billion in February 2001 to just 360 million in May 2001. In the meantime, users of rival Gnutella quadrupled from March to June of 2001, and a host of other music file-swapping services began to grow rapidly. Many of these new sites, true peer-to-peer systems, may be even harder to regulate than Napster. At the same time, the media giants were rolling out their own subscription services (pressplay and MusicNet) to try to capitalize on the potential for online music that Napster demonstrated.[7]

The centaur desires both social and economic value. A bustling city square with conversations in cafés, speakers on soapboxes, and performers in the street is what attracts people to an active marketplace. The importance of the interaction between the economic and social can be seen in a McKinsey study that found that while transaction-oriented sites convert a mere 2 percent of visitors into repeat customers, online community sites have a 60 percent success rate in converting repeat visitors into members and achieve retention rates as high as 18 percent. Further, the rates of conversion of transaction-oriented sites decline as they grow, but online community conversion rates do not fall with growth.[8] A strong social community strengthens the economic community. Companies need to provide a combination of both *being* and *buying*. Companies have an opportunity to create more value for customers through both social and economic interaction than by either one alone.

As Napster found, the challenge is to integrate the economic element into the community without detracting from a strong social community. Virtual communities can approach this convergence challenge from two directions. Some of the early virtual communities had a purely social nature, supported by corporations that were willing to experiment, advertisers who were learning about online advertising, or volunteers who were passionate about a particular cause. These communities need to discover a way to integrate an economic aspect into the community without diminishing its social value or offending its socially-oriented participants.

Other communities start with a more economic focus and add a social element. For example, eBay's online trading site is ostensibly an economic activity, but it still considers the community as part of the essence of its past success and future potential. Participants are not just transacting business, they are exchanging notes, posting feedback on their transactions, and developing centers of interest around particular collectibles or other auctions. These economic sites can create value by finding ways to integrate deep social connections into their transaction-oriented communities.

How can companies meet the challenge of economic and social convergence? There are a wide range of strategies:

- *Embed the economic in the social:* Embed the revenue streams into the life of the community. For example, imagine an online ethnic community that offers travel services. Now imagine a young Indonesian woman living in New York who is making arrangements for her parents to visit her. It is their first trip abroad. Through the virtual community, she could connect with another community member living in Indonesia who is traveling in the same direction and arrange for this person to accompany her parents on the trip. In addition to booking the actual travel through the online community (the economic interaction), the young woman gains additional value through the social interaction provided by the site. The economic interaction is embedded in the social interaction. This type of service could not be offered by other travel agents, so the woman will not click out of the community to search for better airfares because the value of the social interaction is impossible to price on the open market. The social community is directly integrated into the transaction for travel services and there is both economic and social value created.

- *Tap into the energy of the community through community-generated content:* One of the sources of success of Sulekha is its commitment to let community members create content. This not only produces economic benefits in that it saves the cost of content generation, but it also gives community members a sense of ownership and involvement in the success of the site. The interest and passion of the community members is what gives the community its energy. iVillage uses a network of volunteer moderators to run the site, not only serving its economic ends by saving staffing costs, but, even more important, ensuring strong peer-to-peer interaction by people with a passion for the content. On the other hand, it also has professional content which, while polished, is not directly from the members of the community. Under its "community" button, eBay offers dozens of member chat rooms on specific collectibles and other items, from advertising, antiques and art to movies, toys and trading cards. It also offers community help boards with responses to questions from both members and staff.

- *Create customer communities to enhance customer service and product development:* Customer communities can also take over traditional customer service functions from the company, saving expenses for the company while providing more direct advice to customers. eBay takes this model to the extreme, because sellers directly handle communications with buyers, shipping, financial transactions and any follow-up. eBay doesn't have to maintain inventory or handle customer service complaints related to the merchandise sold on its site. There is an opportunity for companies to achieve substantial savings and improve customer service by nurturing customer communities.

Communities can also play a critical role in new product development. For example, Ford Motors invited women in the iVillage community to help design a minivan tailored to their needs. This not only creates a product tailored to the needs of the target community but also begins marketing the product to a core audience while it is still under development. We also discussed in Chapter 3 how Texas Instruments involved teachers in the design of its new calculator, improving the product and creating a committed group of users.

- **Build bridges to existing communities:** Many virtual communities are already being created without any economic purpose, merely for the social and psychological value of connecting with others. Companies need to ask themselves how they can connect to these communities. For example, Johnson & Johnson created a successful campaign for its teenage skin care product Clean & Clear by tapping into online communities of teenage girls. J&J offered the teens free online audio postcards to send to friends, along with offers of free skin analysis and product samples.[9] MCI did something similar offline with its "Friends and Family" program, tapping into personal, social networks to expand its economic business. There are many opportunities for such "viral marketing" approaches. For example, consumer buying groups (such as Mercata) harness the power of personal networks to obtain lower prices. Firms that want to do this need to be careful not to try to take advantage of the community, and must be sure to interact in ways that create social and economic value for the community members and for the company. J&J's Clean & Clear campaign was successful because the tests and samples were seen as valuable to the recipients. Companies also need to carefully consider how they interact with communities, whether it should be the corporation as a whole or a set of employees that are sincerely interested in the focus of the community.

- **Sustain trust:** The heart of the social and economic fabric of a community is trust. As communities have become a more central focus of business, trust has moved to center stage. In any interaction, trust is crucial, but particularly when making a social community more economically focused. iVillage carefully chooses advertisers for their fit and commitment to building a relationship with the site and its members, and is very cautious about using models and other celebrity endorsers. It wants to set a very different tone than magazines targeted toward women. Says iVillage founder Candice Carpenter, "Women have had magazines blasting perfection at them. Our goal is to let women be focused on themselves."[10]

Part of eBay's success has been based on one of the most stringent privacy policies of any auction site. EBay's leaders considered early on whether they would sell member information to sustain the strength of the community. As eBay Associate General Counsel Brad Handler commented: "We never sell eBay user information. We made the decision early on that we were going to treat our users like a community. Many of our competitors made a different choice. They chose to treat their users as 'wallets' and 'credit cards.' Those competitiors are not around anymore."[11]

- *Balance control with organic growth:* For communities to flourish at all, and particularly to flourish economically, there is a need for some governance and direction. This can be self regulation, but there needs to be a way to sustain the focus and direction of the site without appearing too heavy handed. When community members become disruptive or destructive, there has to be a mechanism for restoring order. On the other hand, communities are organic in their growth. As organic entities, they can be destroyed by overcultivation. The Well, one of the earliest online communities, faltered after it was acquired by a private firm. E-Groups' mailing list for Eritrea (a tiny African country with a population of about 3 million), which connected the Eritrean community around the world, became "the CNN of Eritrea." E-Groups organizers were surprised when they took the server down for a few hours to receive a call from the Eritrean embassy asking what the problem was. "Communities are like mushrooms," comments Jerry Michalski. "They thrive in dark places. A conversation that has 30,000 people is not a conversation."[12] The delicate balance is to provide direction so that the site thrives socially and economically while continuing to capitalize on its organic growth. For example, eBay provides this balance by allowing members to sell virtually any product. When the products reach a critical mass, it creates a category for it. The categories, by focusing attention on a new area such as its automotive sales, help the area to further expand. In this way, the company allows users to set the agenda, but also provides an organizing framework that keeps the community from degenerating into chaos as it expands. This approach combines self-directed with company-directed growth.

- *Use communities for customer feedback:* The downside of organic growth is that disgruntled customers can easily and spontaneously be gathered into communities to attack companies. After failing to receive a reply to a letter he drafted complaining about service on a United flight in 1996, McGill University computer engineering professor Jeremy Cooperstock took his complaints to the Internet. He created a site called "Untied.com" to publish his own gripes as well as those of other United customers. The site gathered more than 3,000 complaints on issues such as rudeness, misinformation, and incompetence.[13] A wide range of similar sites targeting individual companies have been created with names like NorthWorstAir.org, IHateStarbucks.com, and WeHatePacificBell.com. In addition to these company-specific sites, more than a dozen complaint centers have appeared, such as Baddealings.com, Ecomplaints.com, uGetHeard.com, The ComplaintStation.com, and Planet-Feedback.com.[14] Although companies have little control over these sites, except to take legal action against logo or brand use, these online soapboxes actually can be valuable sources of customer feedback. These sites can also provide an independent monitor on the effectiveness of internal customer service. WalMart, for example, monitors a half dozen WalMart complaint sites for damaging accusations and rumors, and it then responds to them.

Communities cannot be manufactured. They have to be discovered and managed. This dance between social and economic, between cultivation and organic growth, is the delicate soil from which successful communities spring.

How can you balance the social and economic aspects of the communities that interact with your business?

DESIGNING COMMUNITIES

Managers need to address a number of issues in developing community-centered strategies that balance physical and virtual, economic and social aspects of communities. Among these design decisions are:

- Should the company create a new community or tap into existing communities? The answer depends both upon the strength of those existing communities and the company's current relationship with different customer segments.

- If the company taps into an existing community, it needs to consider how receptive the community will be. What is in it for the community members? How can the company create a win—win situation that provides value for the community and generates value for the company?

- If the company creates its own community, should it do so as a joint venture with another organization? For example, a company that makes a heart medication might create a community of people suffering from or interested in heart disease in conjunction with an organization like the American Heart Association with an established offline community. The company could also partner with an organization such as iVillage or WebMD that have strong online communities as a way to extend their communities.

- What type of community should be created? What parts should be physical and what parts should be virtual? The more the community can be brought together in a single geographic space, the more it can work as a physical community. The more widely dispersed the community, the more a virtual community is needed. The greater the anonymity that is needed, the more a virtual community may be able to provide it, but when there is a need for face-to-face interaction or participation in an event, the physical community can often be more powerful.

- Finally, how does this design of the community relate to the company's business and marketing strategies? What is the investment and payoff, direct or indirect, for the company?

THE EVOLUTION OF COMMUNITIES

Virtual communities are becoming more deeply embedded in all aspects of life. E-government initiatives are making online communities even more central to political life. (Japanese prime minister Junichiro Koizumi launched an e-zine, taking his message directly to the people, quickly attracting more than 2.1 million subscribers and surpassing any other online news site in Japan.[15]) Grassroots movements for environmental protection and global causes have been rapidly organized through online channels, posing a significant challenge for both government and corporate leaders. Virtual communities are also enhancing religious life. Sites such as Beliefnet.org have emerged to provide comprehensive information about different faiths, articles and commentary about spirituality, prayer rooms, church-finding search engines, and a host of other content and features. A survey of 1,300 U.S. religious congregations by the Pew Internet & American Life Project found that 83 percent of respondents said the use of the Internet has helped congregational life, 81 percent said the use of e-mail by ministers, staff, and congregation has helped the spiritual life of the congregation, and 91 percent said it helps the community stay more in touch with one another.[16] These communities are the new city centers, and companies that do not understand how to work with communities will be left outside of them.

Whatever the changes in technology and social organization, the reality of the centaur remains. The centaur interacts with both physical and virtual communities and often wants to look for intersections between the two, to derive the most value from both. The centaur at heart is still a "social animal" who desires community. This community needs to provide social value as well as economic value, and requires a tighter integration of the two. Companies have to find ways to combine economic and social interaction to build the value of each.

Action Memo

- Visit an online chatroom on iVillage.com or another community site, preferably one that is related to your business. What ideas are people sharing that could be valuable to your business? How are the interactions online different from those you see in focus groups and offline interactions with the company? **How can you use these insights in your business?**

- Ask your doctor how the Internet has changed interactions with patients in the office.

- Using several search engines, search for your company's name online. What are people saying about you? If nothing, is silence a good thing? **If not, how can you break the silence and increase the buzz?**

- Read what customers are saying about your business or others in your industry at one of the complaint sites noted in the chapter. **How can you address the potential for this type of broadcast feedback?**

- Ask your customers (either informally or formally through a survey) what communities, physical and virtual, they are a part of. Are there ways to build bridges between these communities and your business? Ask employees what communities they belong to. Are these the same as customers? **How can these connections with communities help expand or support your business?**

We invite you to share the results of these activities and suggest other action memos at the Convergence Marketing Forum (www.convergencemarketingforum.com).

NOTES

[1] This chapter draws upon: Balasubramanian, Sridhar and Vijay Mahajan, "The Economic Leverage of the Virtual Community" *International Journal of Electronic Commerce*, 5 (Spring 2001), pp. 103-138.

[2] Satya Prabhkar Interview, April 17, 2001.

[3] "Cult Brands," *Forbes*, April 21, 2001.

[4] Hagel, John III and Arthur G. Armstrong, *Net Gain: Expanding Markets Through Virtual Communities*, Boston: Harvard Business School Press, 1997.

[5] Lisa Kraynak, presented at the Wharton "Virtual Communities and the Internet," conference, April 7, 2000.

[6] Larner, Monica, "Infidelity Italian Style," *Business Week*, April 23, 2001, p. 16.

[7] "Big Music Fights Back," *The Economist*, June 16, 2001, pp.67-68.

[8] Bughin, Jacques and John Hagel, "Community Values," *The McKinsey Quarterly*, 2000 No. 1, pp. 34-35; Bughin and Hagel, "The operational performance of virtual communities-towards a successful business model?" *Electronic Markets*, December 2000.

[9] Kenny, David and John F. Marshall, "Contextual Marketing: The Real Business of the Internet," *Harvard Business Review*, November-December 2000, p. 122.

[10] Sparta, Christine, "It Takes A Village,"*Adweek*, Vol. 41, Issue 15, April 17, 2000, p. 66.

[11] Brad Handler, remarks to the Wharton Fellows in e-Business Program, July 11, 2001.

[12] Jerry Michalski, remarks to the Wharton Fellows in e-Business program, The Wharton School, Philadelphia, November 28, 2000.

[13] Appleman, Hillary, "What, You Don't have Skim Milk? This Means War," *The New York Times*, March 4, 2001. P. B-13.

[14] Appleman, Hillary, "I Scream, You Scream: Consumers Vent Over the Net," *The New York Times*, March 4, 2001, p. B-13.

[15] Cohn, Laura, "The Premier with Direct Appeal," *Business Week*, July 30, 2001.

[16] Larsen, Elena (principal author), "Wired churches, wired temples: Taking congregations and missions into cyberspace," *Pew Internet & American Life Project*, December 20, 2000.

5

CONVERGING ON
CHANNELS

I WANT TO CALL,
CLICK OR VISIT

"Give the lady what she wants."

Marshall Field

TRADITIONAL CONSUMER

"What I want is a well stocked store conveniently located with friendly salespeople who will give me what I want. Why should I go to all the trouble of hunting around online for what I need?"

CYBERCONSUMER

"No store can hold all the variety I want. With a click of a button, I can have access to an array of products that is an order of magnitude greater than any physical store. And I can search for what I want anytime, 24/7, without the interference of meddling sales people."

THE Centaur

"I want to find your company where I want you and when I want you. I will click on your site in the middle of the night, call you with problems, and drop in on you when I want to look you in the eye and pick up your products. I am everywhere, and I expect you to be everywhere I am. And you better recognize me when I come to you through multiple channels."

CONVERGENCE QUESTIONS

>>>*How can you create seamless interactions with customers across online and offline channels?*

>>>*How can you develop the right branding and internal structures to deliver this experience?*

CONVERGING ON CHANNELS:
I Want to Call, Click, or Visit

The power of the Internet is not in transactions that begin and end online, but in customer interactions that run across multiple channels, from online to offline and back. This chapter explores how companies can use convergence strategies to present a unified face to customers and develop coherent branding and internal structures.

Joseph Nelson goes online to look for tickets for a family vacation. With his extended family going along, he needs to purchase seven tickets. After painstakingly logging into a variety of sites, including Cheaptickets.com, Travelocity.com, and Expedia.com, he decides on a reasonable itinerary and puts a hold on the tickets. But because of the rules of the site, he finds that he can only reserve five tickets at a time. He breaks the order into two parts (five and two) and puts both sets of tickets on hold. He then calls his local travel agent to see what she has found out. Since her best tickets will cost several thousand dollars more, he decides to go with the online agent. And this is where his troubles begin.

First of all, he is reluctant to commit to buying the first set of tickets until he can put the second on hold. The web site is not cooperating. The online agent has a prominently featured customer service button that refers Joseph to its 800 number. He calls, and a very helpful customer service representative puts through the two ticket orders by phone. She asks him if he wants electronic or paper tickets, and gives him the confirmation numbers. He then receives a call that the airline carrier will not process electronic orders for more than five tickets, so he receives part of his tickets by mail and the rest electronically. He goes online to see if he can change his two remaining electronic tickets to paper tickets for consistency. He then finds that his order does not show up at all in his online account. This is troubling. So, he calls back to customer service, and is reassured that the order still exists on the telephone side of the business, even if it has dropped off the electronic one. And this is an online travel agent!

The service online and on the phone is very good, but the two sides appear to be separate worlds, which is particularly troubling when it comes to e-tickets where there is no hard paper to show you have a reservation. There is a disconnect between his first order and second, even though they are on the same flight, and a disconnect between the telephone and online experience. He finds that he is rapidly earning the money he has saved.

THE PERILS AND POTENTIAL OF CHANNEL CONVERGENCE

The need to have clicks and bricks is now fairly obvious, and the need to create a coherent customer experience across multiple channels is also becoming increasingly obvious. As Joseph Nelson's experience shows (based on an actual story), there is still a lot of room for progress.

People have always had a desire for speed, convenience, and relevant channel options. Integrated online and offline channels promise to offer more of all three. Consumers can locate information about products or services and purchase them much more quickly online. They have the convenience of dropping into physical stores or visiting a web site in the middle of the night. But a failure of integration or operation of the online and offline businesses can create slow and inconvenient interaction that undermines the reputations of both the online and the offline business. Putting the pieces together in the right way is critical.

The potential for companies in integrating their channels is tremendous. New online channels create opportunities not only to develop new businesses, but also to drive business across channels. Jupiter Media Metrix predicted that by 2005, U.S. consumers would be purchasing $199 billion directly online. But more than three times that amount, in excess of $632 billion, would be spent in offline channels as a result of research conducted online.[1] While the exact numbers of any future forecast may be disputed, the overall value of commerce driven across channels has been proven. As noted in the Preface, Staples customers who shop through the store, catalog, and website spend an average of about four times the amount spent by those who shop in the store alone. (Some of this effect may be the self selection of heavy buyers who tend to shop through multiple channels.) Many companies can derive more benefits from the online and offline spending by offering an integrated interface between the two. How can companies best design their businesses to create convergence across channels?

Although it is clear that a strategy that combines bricks and clicks can be more powerful than either one alone, the strategy for combining the two worlds has to be carefully developed. After initially replicating much of its store on its website, WalMart.com found it needed to develop ways to differentiate and integrate its value propositions online and offline. For example, Wal-Mart created a more limited selection of low-priced products on its website (dropping small products like the 25-cent plastic cup that costs $8 to ship). But Wal-Mart added more bulky items like patio furniture and appliances online, which take up valuable floor space in retail stores. It also created seamless pathways that allowed customers to start online with auto services, by ordering tires or scheduling installation carried out in the store. In this way, Wal-Mart integrated its online and offline experiences to take advantage of the strengths of each.[2]

There are two key concerns related to convergence of channels that we will examine in this chapter, as illustrated in Exhibit 5–1. The first, as highlighted in the example of Joseph Nelson, is integrating the customer experience online and offline. The second related issue is how to design the brand and

EXHIBIT 5–1 **CONVERGING ON CHANNELS**

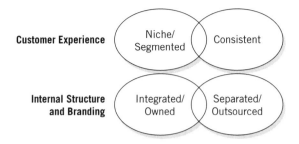

business architecture in a way that supports the customer experience *and* is profitable to the firm. The branding and structure of the business are highly correlated, so that businesses with separate brands are much more likely to be set up as independent operations.

It is important to note that while we are discussing online and offline convergence for simplicity, there is actually a complex and shifting set of technologies and channels that are converging. The rise of wireless communications and interactive television offer new

How can you combine clicks and bricks to improve the customer experience and increase the value of the business?

and distinctive ways to interact with companies. The insights on designing customer experiences online and offline apply as well to these new channels.

THE NEW, NEW RULES OF MARKETING

When Mark Goldstein took on the challenge of establishing Kmart's online presence (BlueLight.com) in 1998, he expected marketing to be transformed. And it was, but not in the way he expected. Three years later, as he stepped down as CEO of BlueLight to become Internet Advisor to Kmart, Goldstein found that the "new" rules of retailing he expected with the rise of the Internet had been replaced with "new, new" rules that reflected the emergence of the hybrid consumer.

In contrast to the strategy of Wal-Mart, Goldstein and Kmart made a deliberate decision to distance their web site from the Kmart brand. They established the Kmart e-tail site as "BlueLight.com," as an independent business with 60 percent ownership by the parent company. Kmart had twice tried to launch its own sites, without success. The BlueLight name played off the retro image of "BlueLight" specials in Kmart stores (where temporary sales were once marked with a flashing blue light).

BlueLight initially targeted customers who were not online. By offering a free ISP service and a site tailored to newbies, the company aimed to be the first face these Web neophytes saw when they went online. The company gave customers in the stores free CDs that encouraged them to go onto the Net. It didn't just build a site for its customers, but it built a bridge for its customers from the offline to the online world.

In contrast to Wal-Mart's more serious and conservative approach, Kmart intended to differentiate itself by being more fun. "We decided what was in our DNA to be more flippant and promotional," Goldstein said. "We don't want to compete with Wal-Mart against their core strengths. We had to approach it differently and simply go where they weren't." In the process the site would also begin to reinvent the Kmart brand across physical and online stores, and set the scene to bring back the BlueLight theme to all of the 2,100+ Kmart physical stores.

Goldstein explained that he didn't want to be "Kmart.com" because he didn't want to fight the losing battle General Motors waged when it tried to convince young drivers that its Oldsmobile line is "not your father's Oldsmobile." Instead, he wanted to differentiate the company from the Kmart brand to appeal to younger, higher-spending mothers. But while the BlueLight idea was successful as an independent brand, many of the hypotheses that Goldstein held about his business changed over the course of its first few years. "Our business changed," he said. "We thought we'd sell anything to anyone online, an Amazon-like company. What a difference a few years make. We realized we were all very wrong. All of the e-tailers were wrong. The analysts were wrong. The professors were wrong, in terms of the impact of the Internet on retail. We realized e-tail is not going to replace retail. Now we are not just selling online, but using the Internet to sell more in the store."

1998	2001
Revolution	Evolution
Destroy	Complement
Front end	Back end
Intelligent merchandising focusing on assortments from multiple dot.com merchants and own Kmart warehoused merchandise	Intelligent split shipping supply chain using multiple 'silent' warehouses and vendor partners
Best of breed software components	Integrated one-vendor supplied platform
Outsource to 'experienced partners'	Insource as much as possible to own staff
Portal partners	Leverage own store traffic
Unlimited free shipping service and coupons for all	Tiered membership services for active shoppers

Source: Mark Goldstein, BlueLight.com, presentation to the Wharton Fellows in e-Business Program, May 2001.

Goldstein summarized the shift in his view of retailing from 1998 to 2001 in the table shown in Exhibit 5–2.

Goldstein said they originally envisioned that e-tailing would be a revolution that would destroy traditional retailing, but discovered that it was an evolutionary process that would complement the offline businesses. Although they thought the battle would be won on flashy and effective front-end websites, in actuality the trench warfare was focused on management of back-end distribution. In contrast to the strategy of building their own warehouses and using intelligent merchandising, Goldstein and others found that split shipping, using the suppliers' warehouses was even more intelligent. In contrast to the strategy of assembling an unwieldy mix of best-of-breed software programs, they learned that a single, integrated platform was far easier to use and manage. Outsourced operations were augmented with insourcing.

Although Goldstein initially expected to get most of BlueLight's traffic through portal partners such as Yahoo!, these proved to be poor pathways to their online stores. A far better approach turned out to be to leverage their own store traffic to drive customers online and vice versa. In contrast to a scattershot, build-market-share-at-any-cost approach, they developed more carefully considered tiered membership programs focusing on active shoppers.

How have your own rules of marketing changed in the past three years, and what implications do these changes have for the development of online and offline channels?

STRATEGIES FOR INTEGRATING CUSTOMER EXPERIENCE

The first and foremost consideration in integrating online and offline experiences is the consumer. Many companies started with the technology and ended up with predictably disjointed customer experiences. Others started with business models, and again often came up short when it came to meeting customers needs. The most important place to start is with the experience of the customer. Then one must design channels that best meet customer needs. Among the strategies for creating consistent and coherent customer experiences are:

- *Give customers the best of both worlds:* Recognize the differences in how online and offline experiences create value and draw from the best of both worlds. As illustrated in Exhibit 5–3, online and offline channels have distinctive strengths and weaknesses. Depending on your goals, products and business strategy, you should combine the two in ways that emphasize strengths and minimize weaknesses. Build online interactions when information content and reliability are important, and when anytime, anyplace convenience is needed. Digital products, documents and some aspects of service can be delivered online. Build offline interactions when a personal touch is needed or creative insights and response are required. People looking for a

	Offline	**Online**
Access	Limited geography and often time	Anytime, anyplace
Search	Browsing is more holistic and experiential, but individual search is difficult	Simple to find specific information; information rich browsing
Selection	Limited to store size and design	Virtually unlimited
Pricing	Fixed	Dynamic
Experience	Tactile, directed to all senses	Intellectual, but becoming more tactile
Company cost of interaction	High for routine interactions, but sometimes lower for exceptions	Low for routine interactions, but high for exceptions
Customization	Difficult and time consuming	Simple
Delivery/Returns for non digital products	Simple and quick after the decision to purchase is made, but still requires a trip to a store	Complex, involving delivery channels
Delivery /return of digital products	More complex, requiring a trip to store	Easy
Time for first purchase	Very slow	Slow
Time for repeat purchasing	Slow	Very fast

hotel in a distant city might value the ability to actually see the rooms or fitness center or find out about dining options before arriving, but this has to be done online because of the geographic distance of the customer.

eBay offers an ideal channel for pooling demand for collectibles or offbeat used items that might not otherwise have enough interested buyers and sellers to create markets. But eBay also has discovered that its online auction platform is a particularly good channel for several types of new products from companies such as Disney or Sun Microsystems. These are typically products at the beginning or end of their lifecycles, when setting prices has traditionally been difficult. At the start of the product lifecycle, the online auction tends to be ideal for scarce newly released products such as Sony Playstations whose true value is difficult to determine independent of market demand. The online auction is also very effective for products at the end of their lifecycles, such as computers from Sun Microsystems that have eroding value as they become obsolete. Their price also is difficult to assess independently of demand. Finally, the eBay channel also works very well for closeouts, where pricing has traditionally been based on markdowns to move excess inventory. Companies such as eValue, which sells excess inventory of major department stores, have found the eBay auction an ideal platform for obtaining the best possible price for these products.

The right combination depends on customers and the company's product or service offering. In test markets, Home Depot allowed customers to place Internet orders that could be delivered or be picked up at the store in the morning. A contractor could log in at night and have the order waiting in the morning on his way to a job site. The Home Depot site also provides extensive how-to information for do-it-yourselfers. (Home Depot was initially resistant to online channels, but has since seen that the Internet is not as much a threat as an opportunity for established firms.)

Texas grocery store chain Randalls, owned by Safeway Corp., tracks the frequent purchases of shoppers who carry its shopping card into stores and then uses that information to create a "fast shop" list when customers log on to the website.[3]

To provide the best of both worlds you need to recognize the strengths and weaknesses of both approaches. An e-ticket, for example, has the advantage that it can be issued online or by phone and can never be lost, but if your flight is delayed and you want to take a flight on another carrier, your e-ticket may be much more difficult to transfer. Travelers have reported having to stand in line with an e-ticket at the first carrier to get a physical ticket to take to the second carrier. On the other hand, a physical ticket can be lost and if you show up at the gate without it, you will often have to pay a penalty.

It is also important to assess the strength of alternative channels and determine the share of customer spending that you are losing to competitors. Is there a way to integrate these other offerings and channels into your offering? For example, Charles Schwab set up a system of more than 5,000 independent advisors to create an advisory service to complement its financial services platform. It also created One Source to offer more than 800 mutual funds from a single source, significantly increasingly its presence in that business by integrating these

How can you offer customers the "best" of both the online and offline worlds? What needs are best met online versus offline?

offerings into its own channel. When it saw online trading companies begin to draw customers to their sites, Schwab expanded its online offerings. Finally, Schwab acquired U.S. Trust to offer services to higher net worth clients. By looking at the parts of its business that were flowing into other channels, online and offline, Schwab was able to reshape its set of channels to continue to offer greater value—and the best of all worlds—to customers.

- *Let customers decide how they want to interact:* Allow customers to choose how they want to interact. When Barnes & Noble places an electronic kiosk in its store, it allows customers to interact virtually with its entire warehouse of books using online search engines, but also allows customer to talk to a salesperson or find the book on the shelves of the store, with a map showing how to get there. Customers are not forced to choose between one or the other; they can fluidly move back and forth between the two modes of interacting at will, using the approach that adds the most value for them at the moment. This flexibility adds value by increasing the ease of doing business.

The importance of offering customers choice is shown in the rise and fall of Bank One's WingspanBank. Wingspan, an online-only bank was expected to turn financial services on its head when it rolled through the gates of the financial services industry in June 1999, like a Trojan Horse that threatened to destroy the industry. By mid June 2001, Wingspan's revolution ended not with a bang but a whimper. By the end of 2000, WingspanBank had signed up just 255,000 customer accounts compared with 700,000 at Bank One's online business (BankOne.com), and Gomez Inc. ranked Bankone.com's customer service higher than Wingspan's. The Bank One customers, in contrast to Wingspan customers, had access to ATMs and bank tellers, in addition to online banking. In June 2001, Bank One quietly announced plans to fold WingspanBank into its existing banking operations.[4] In retrospect, it may seem obvious that people would not want to conduct all their banking transactions online, but many intelligent managers and investors initially thought this model was the future of financial services.

How can you empower consumers to decide how they want to interact with the company?

What they failed to appreciate, once again, was the behavior of the consumer. It is also worth noting that this model may in fact be the future of financial services as electronic wallets replace physical wallets and consumers and companies resolve security and privacy issues online. But, even so, the pure online business is unlikely to meet the needs of the centaurs (except for small segments), and it will not be Wingspan that will capture these opportunities. It will be established financial institutions who can extend and integrate their business slowly from one model to the other as consumer preferences change.

- *Understand the context and timing for interaction:* While companies need to offer customers multiple channels, managers also should recognize that the channel often affects the type of activity and interaction that occurs. For example, 75 percent of electronic selling for Domino's Pizza in the UK is through interactive television versus 25 percent on the computer.[5] Why is this? Pizza and television go together, and the prime pizza ordering time in the evening coincides with prime-time television viewing time. On the other hand, retail products are rarely purchased on interactive television because they are not things that people want to buy at home. Online auction sites have found some of their peak times are Sunday evening (at home) and Monday morning (for users who log in through work computers). The context of the specific channel affects consumer behavior and by understanding this context companies can direct their offerings to the best channel. For example, Domino's would do better expanding its advertising on interactive television than increasing its presence in computer-based content.

- *Create seamless interfaces between online and offline experiences:* Increase the ease of moving from online to offline interactions and back. Companies are starting to allow online returns in their physical stores, but this is just the beginning of exploring the interface between online and offline experiences. For example, suppose a shopper for a minivan logged on to a car-buying site. After using a 360-degree camera to explore the vehicle and looking at all the product information, the customer could then press a button to send questions and other information to the dealer.

The customer also searches for loan rates and fills out an online loan application, which is preapproved before meeting with the dealer. This gives the customer peace of mind. The dealer could then meet with the customer at the dealership or bring the car out to the customer's home for a test drive. The dealer would be prepared to address the specific questions posed by the customer in real time or online. After the sale, the customer can chat online with other owners in the local region or send email to mechanics about a suspicious noise that may or may not be a problem. The online and offline experiences are seamlessly integrated. This integration adds tremendous value because it raises the level of service, saves the customer time, makes it easier to do business and gives the customer greater peace of mind.

Similarly, a physician could increase the peace of mind of patients by a call after surgery or a visit to the office. This could be enhanced by also providing an email address for the doctor and a web site that provides information on post-operation care, frequently asked questions, and links to a chatroom with others who have gone through the same procedure.

It is not enough to just give customers the option of finding you online, in physical space or on the phone. You also need to draw all these experiences together into a seamless fabric. This is often a tremendous logistical challenge for the company, but the customer is not looking at your legacy systems but the current overall experience.

Further development in computer-to-computer interfaces may allow car companies to remotely diagnose problems in the customer's car and allow physicians to monitor changes in a patient's condition.

How can you weave together online and offline experiences into a seamless fabric?

New technologies strengthen the interface between the customer and the company through online and offline approaches.

- *Treat consumers the same across channels:* Consumers want the company to treat them the same across all channels. A recent U.S. debut of a very popular Indian film "Lagaan" allowed filmgoers to purchase tickets online, in addition to purchasing by phone and through the box office. Phone reservations were not confirmed so customers had to arrive before the performance to pay for them at the box office or the tickets could be resold. For online sales, the theater directly charged the customer's credit card, and so the tickets were held at the box office. Imagine the anger of phone purchasers who arrived a few minutes late to find their tickets had already been resold, as they watched online buyers walk up and pick up their tickets. This is a recipe for disaster and led to angry exchanges in the theater lobby. From pricing to returns to service, consumers should be treated the same across all channels. They will be extremely disappointed if they are not.

- *Incorporate digital interfaces into the offline experiences:* While most of the attention of the digital revolution has focused on applying technology to online channels, there are powerful applications of technology in offline channels. Companies are establishing interactive kiosks in stores and dynamic store displays in their windows. For example, retailer Eddie Bauer has been testing plasma screen window displays in its stores to boost sales. The messages in these screens can be changed far more quickly than posters or window displays, tailoring the message to the changing mood of the passersby during the day—from the elderly "mall walkers" in the morning to the mothers with strollers in the afternoon to teens and "nine-to-fivers" in the evening. The retailer's studies found that early in the day shoppers tend to be more mission focused, more price sensitive and less brand conscious. In the evening, they tend to be more artistic, responding better to fashion and lifestyle messages. Managers reported that stores with dynamic displays achieved an improvement of as much as 50 to 60 percent over conventional print displays in attracting buyers into the store.[6]

STRATEGIES FOR INTEGRATING STRUCTURE AND BRANDING A CROSS CHANNEL

There are many critical issues to consider in designing online and offline businesses for convergence. These include brand, management skills, operations challenges, equity, culture, customer segment, pricing, channel conflicts, and capital requirements.[7] Among the key strategies for designing the right online/offline strategy are:

- *Develop the right brand or set of brands:* As in any branding decision, the decision whether to brand the online offering separately from the existing business depends on the target customer segment and the need for distancing experiments from the core business. If the web site needs to create a separate identity, a separate brand is in order. Procter & Gamble created a separate brand, Reflect.com, for its customized online site and this seems to have worked well for an offering that is distinctly different, and a bit upscale from, the standardized products offered by the parent company. Ford Direct, in contrast, used an extension of its existing brand for its customized car locator site, indicating continuity with the product line, but also differentiating it from the old business. At the other extreme, companies like Walmart.com or Barnes & Noble wanted their online businesses to be tightly integrated with the established business in image and offerings, so the uniform brand made sense. Kmart's BlueLight.com site, as discussed above, was initially envisioned as separate from the established brand, to break out of Oldsmobile syndrome, but ultimately was brought together into a more coherent branding strategy. The twist is that the online brand changed the offline branding strategy (through advertising emphasizing Blue Light). Another reason for setting up a separate brand may be to distance an offbeat online business from the original business, the way that Disney used the Touchstone brand to distance the more

What are the strengths and weaknesses of your current brand? Is it different online or offline, and how?

sophisticated and controversial movies of this business from its G-rated Disney image. If the online business has the capability to damage the reputation of the primary brand, it is important to create separation. Having a separate brand also may be important in targeting specific segments. For example, WingspanBank was initially targeted toward road warriors who were expected to have little connection to the parent bank, so the Bank One brand did not appear to have much value to the target segment. Similarly, BlueLight focused on a younger customer than the typical Kmart shopper. Finally, in developing online brands, companies need to realize that, given the global reach of the Internet, all online brands are global.

- *Leverage the assets of the existing business:* 1-800 CON-TACTS, discussed in Chapter 1, has a warehouse sitting in the middle of Utah jammed with 10 million contact lenses. From its telephone business, it is already skilled in taking orders, picking and packing, shipping and handling customer complaints, and return by mail. Adding on an online channel was a fairly simple addition that greatly increased its reach and made it easier for customers to place new or repeat orders while drawing upon the company's existing capabilities. Similarly, Tesco was able to leverage the marketing and real estate of its existing **How can you leverage your existing assets** network of stores **online?** to create an online business for a fraction of what it cost for a company like Webvan to develop a pure-play business from scratch.

- *Manage offline/online channel conflict:* Channel conflict is an important concern in pursuing these strategies. The optimal approach for the company or its customers may be different from the approach favored by powerful intermediaries. Iberia Airlines discovered this in Spain when it sought to move all its corporate business to e-ticketing and faced fierce opposition from travel agents. It compromised by requiring customers to do e-ticketing for travel close to the time of departure, but gave customers a choice of e-tickets or paper for trips with longer lead times. FordDirect manages this conflict by offering consumers the appearance of "direct" sales and customization while still directing sales through local dealers.

If the organization and its channel partners are focused on serving customers, then the channels need to be designed in a way that best serves the customer, not the tradional intermediaries. Any other course will ultimately drive customers away to other businesses that do a better job of responding to the customers' needs. At the same time, companies need to reassure their channels that they are not going to be disintermediated. While some suppliers initially saw the Internet as an opportunity to cut out the cost and expense of these intermediaries such as insurance agents or travel agents by going directly to consumers, many have since found that these intermediaries serve a very valuable function. They manage the customer relationship and help create trust. Companies should actively work with their existing partners to develop and implement new channels in ways that are mutually beneficial.

If companies want to conduct experiments in new channels without having to address conflicts with their existing partners, one approach is to set up an independent experiment that sells a different product. Procter & Gamble did this with Reflect.com, creating a customized product that does not directly compete with its standard products on supermarket shelves. This gives P&G experience with online sales, and customization without having to deal with the issue of channel conflict. The offering can be differentiated through the type of offering, the branding or the pricing. For example, Priceline.com differentiated its offerings from similar tickets of major airlines and agents by limiting the ability to choose exact departure times and cities until after the ticket was purchased.

Finally, it is important to distinguish between real and perceived channel conflict. Some managers will raise the specter of channel conflict as a way of blocking innovation. Managers should recognize the potential for conflict and then develop creative solutions to it, rather than use it as an excuse not to move forward with initiatives that add value for customers.

Sometimes channels need to be disintermediated. While joint optimization of the benefits for the customer, the firm and intermediaries is ideal, in many situations, this is not always possible. If the channel no longer adds value, it can be a liability. Whether the disintermediation is justified or not depends on the value created by the channel and consumer preferences.

- *Use partnerships and alliances to complement the weaknesses:* Toys 'R' Us had experience buying and selling through large retail stores. It knew how to get the right number of Barbie dolls or Playstations to stores at the right time and in the right mix to meet customer demands, and how to manage orders and staffing during the busy Christmas season. It knew nothing about dealing with online orders, remote customer service, picking, packing, shipping, and returns. Its initial foray online was a disaster, with such poor service levels on toysrus.com during the December 1999 holiday buying season that the company became one of seven online merchants that were fined a total of $1.5 million by the U.S. Federal Trade Commission. Similarly, Amazon knew little about the toy business. They joined forces in August 2000, with Toys 'R' Us continuing to identify, buy, and manage the inventory, while Amazon handled site development, order fulfillment, and customer service, using its existing infrastructure and distribution. The partnership led to sales that more than tripled in the 2000 holiday season,

  What are the weaknesses in your current offline business that can be strengthened online?

to $124 million from $39 million in the year before. This was at a time when rivals such as eToys and Sears suffered year-over-year declines. And the results, building upon the existing businesses and expertise of Amazon and Toys 'R' Us, was achieved without any radio or television advertising during the holiday period.[8] Similarly, Amazon partnered with Borders, which began selling books online in May 1998 (a year behind Barnes & Noble and three years after Amazon). By January 2001, Borders had written down more than half its Borders.com assets, which had lost $18.4 million during the prior year.[9] Like Toys 'R' Us, Borders teamed up with Amazon to take over the online operation of the Borders website and online fulfillment. To deliver and pay for online purchases conveniently in Japan, where there is low credit card penetration, Seven-Eleven Japan arranged for customers to pickup online purchases in its ubiquitous network of convenience stores. For many Japanese customers, this is more convenient than home delivery and allows them to make cash payments for online purchases.

- *Create the right degree of separation:* In addition to branding issues discussed above, companies also have to consider a range of other issues in deciding whether to create an online business as a stand-alone operation or an integrated business. Many established companies found that these entrepreneurial startups worked far better in Silicon Valley where venture capitalists and managers were used to operating on the frontiers of technology and business models. For example, both BlueLight.com and Reflect.com chose to set up shop far from corporate headquarters in Silicon Valley, to take advantage of the new economy culture and technological start-up expertise of the region. BlueLight and Reflect also involved venture capitalists to increase the depth of these insights. Companies that set up separate businesses also realized that existing organizational structures, incentives, and processes could kill these new initiatives. They realized that their homegrown executives had the wrong kind of experience to make these early businesses successful. But as these businesses moved from small experiments to operating businesses, like any startup, they ultimately may need traditional management. The degree of separation depends in part upon the culture and tolerance of the parent organization. If the organization can tolerate different cultures, different compensation systems and different strategies in its core organization without expelling these foreign bodies, there may be less cause to take the business outside.

- *Create integrated information systems:* The key to creating an integrated customer experience, where a customer who arrives by any channel is recognized as the same customer, is to integrate information systems. Whether the online business is a separate operation or an integrated part of the business, creating databases and systems across all channels is crucial to creating an integrated experience. In addition, information systems should allow companies to integrate

EXHIBIT 5–4 DESIGNING COMPLEX DISTRIBUTION WEBS

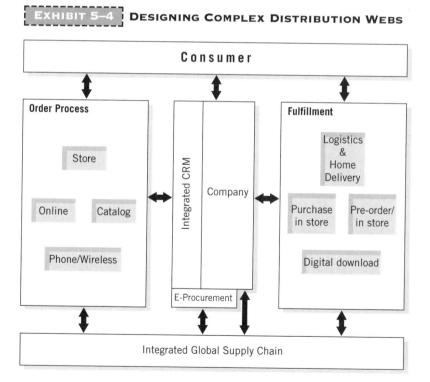

their customer interfaces with their supply chains. This way, the entire supply chain is linked and connected, so when orders are placed it ripples right throughout the chain.

- *Create integrated supply chains and logistics:* In addition to harmonizing information flows, companies have to rethink their product flows, service flows and financial flows in designing effective online/offline supply chains. There are a wide range of design paths that can lead from the customer order to delivery. Managers have to rethink these flows from the customer on back and design complex webs for distribution that allow customers to access the company from multiple channels and to receive their products in multiple ways, as illustrated in Exhibit 5–4. The design choices are much more complex, but for companies that can master them, they offer a much richer and more flexible experience for their customers. Information systems and networks allow companies to take advantage of electronic hubs such as Covisint and partners for e-procurement such as Ariba, CommerceOne or ClickCommerce. These and other outsourced partners can be tied into the company supply chain through information systems.

- *Manage the path of evolution:* As the Kmart and BlueLight example illustrates, the relationship between online and offline business evolves over time. A study of 58 companies by researchers Leslie Willcocks and Robert Plant found that leading companies migrated from a technology-focused strategy concerned with building platforms to a market focus on building market share and profitability. Along the way, the leading companies moved to either a brand strategy or service strategy during the transition to a market strategy that integrates both brand and service. For example United Parcel Service (UPS) began by creating a web site in the mid 1990s to compete with FedEx, then the leader in online customer service. By 1998, UPS had caught up on technology and built its strengths in customer service, permitting customers to see package signatures online, and offering an array of tools. With a market focus, it created an integrated customer experience, allowing customers to order, pay for, and track document and package delivery online. It also created capabilities for secure online document exchange. By 2001, USP was handling 55 percent of all e-commerce shipping compared with just 10 percent by FedEx. As UPS President Jim Kelly commented: "UPS does business where the virtual and physical worlds meet, where 'tires and wire' converge."[10]

THE NEED FOR TRANSFORMATION

Ultimately, the channel needs to be designed around the customer, not the customer forced into a rigid channel. People want convenience, choice, and responsiveness, and technology allows them to have it more than ever. Companies need to start by identifying the customer segments they are targeting, then they must come to understand how and where these customers want to interact with the company. Finally, they must use technology to build the appropriate channels. Customers will no longer be willing to adapt themselves to the supply chain of the organization. It must be the other way around.

We also cannot underestimate the organizational challenge of this process. What companies are increasingly realizing is that their e-businesses cannot simply be grafted onto their existing businesses. They cannot afford to create incoherent or inconsistent brands, service and pricing, nor can they afford the disconnect between culture and operations internally. Like Staples.com and Kmart's BlueLight.com, many companies are bringing their separate operations into the fold. In the process, they are beginning to transform their own organizations, as discussed in more detail in Part IV of this book. This broader transformation is necessary to move from a "bricks and clicks" approach—merely gluing together online and offline businesses—to an integrated business built around using new technologies to meet the changing needs of the consumer.

- Visit BlueLight.com and Walmart.com. How are decisions about branding and structure reflected in the design of these sites? What would you have done differently in creating online strategies for these businesses? **What are the implications for your own business?**

- Pick up a small order of commonly used office supplies at Staples or OfficeMax. Now place the same order at their online sites. How is the experience different? What made either the online or offline experience more convenient, pleasant, and efficient? **How can you use these insights in your own business?**

- Ask a young associate to shop on Drugstore.com and purchase a small set of items. Then ask them to go into RiteAid or other physical drug store and purchase the same items. Repeat the experiment yourself and compare notes. How are your experiences of the two channels similar or different from those of your associate? What are the strengths and weaknesses of the online and offline experience? How could they be better designed? How could they be better integrated? **What does this mean for your business?**

We invite you to share the results of these activities and suggest other action memos at the Convergence Marketing Forum (www.convergencemarketingforum.com).

NOTES

[1] "Online Retailers Missing Greatest Opportunity: Web-Influenced Spending to Exceed $630 billion in 2005," Jupiter Media Metrix, May 18, 2000.

[2] Zellner, Wendy, "Will WalMart.com Get It Right This Time?" *Business Week*, November 6, 2000, pp. 104–112.

[3] Keefe, Bob. "Online Shopping Isn't Extinct, It's Just Not All About Sales Anymore," *Austin American Statesman*, April 13, 2001, p. J-1.

[4] Coleman, Calmetta, "Bank One Clips WingspanBank, Folding Oline Unit into Parent," *The Wall Street Journal*, June 29, 2001, p. A-2.

[5] Reported by Jacques Bughin, McKinsey & Company, Wharton Fellows in E-Business Program.

6 "Eddie Bauer and Center Test Dynamic Displays," *Executive Technology*, June 2001, p. 14; Coleman, Calmetta, "Eddie Bauer's Windows Add Electronics," *The Wall Street Journal*, December 28, 2000, p. B10; Steele, Jeffrey, "The Ultimate in Flexible Manufacturing," *Point of Purchase Magazine*, May 2001, p. 32.

7 Gulati, Ranjay and Jason Garino, "Get the Right Mix of Bricks & Clicks," *Harvard Business Review*, May–June 2000, pp. 107–114.

8 Kemp, Ted. "Amazon Deal Helps Toysrus.com Shine," Internet Week, January 4, 2001, www.internetweek.com.

9 Wingfield, Nick and Erin White, "Amazon, Borders to Join Forces in Online Book-Selling Business," *The Wall Street Journal*, April 11, 2001.

10 Willcocks, Leslie P. and Robert Plan, "Pathways to e-Business Leadership: Getting from Bricks to Clicks," *MIT Sloan Management Review*, Spring 2001, pp. 50–59.

6

CONVERGING ON COMPETITIVE VALUE

GIVE ME MORE FOR MY MONEY

*"I found the greater the volume,
the cheaper I could buy and the better
value I could give to customers."*

Frank W. Woolworth, American Merchant

TRADITIONAL CONSUMER

"Frank is right. With the volume of a large retail store, I browse around and find a great selection of interesting products at reasonable prices. I get more for my money and see what I'm buying. The salespeople smile at me and answer my questions. And I can stop at the restaurant for lunch. I get a great price and leave the store with exactly what I want. Tell me again how an online retailer could improve on that?"

CYBERCONSUMER

"I don't need a Frank Woolworth buying for me in volume. I can search online across all sellers to get the best price. I'll create my own buying power. I'll propose a price to a seller on eBay or name my own price for a ticket on Priceline, and many times I'll get it for cheaper than retail. I don't need the seller to tell me the value of something. I can find that out for myself."

THE CENTAUR

"I'll decide for myself what I think value is, thank you very much. For me, at this moment, value may be going online or offline. It may be searching for your best price or giving you my best price. And I'm interested in a lot more than just price and product. I want peace of mind. I don't just want to buy; I want to have an experience, to learn to be entertained. Maybe a good product at a fair price was enough in Frank Woolworth's time, but I want more, much more. Now that you know what I want, let's see you deliver it."

CONVERGENCE QUESTIONS

>>>*How is the centaur reshaping the value equation?*

>>>*How can you use information, education, and entertainment to increase value?*

>>>*How can you creatively combine seller-initiated pricing with buyer-initiated pricing models?*

CONVERGING ON COMPETITIVE VALUE:
Give Me More for My Money

The value equation has become much more complex in a convergent world. In addition to traditional seller-initiated pricing, companies also have developed a wide range of buyer-initiated pricing mechanisms. New sources of value are being combined with traditional sources, and experience is becoming increasingly important in the overall value equation.

Filomena DiTomaso has a 15-minute wait for a train in Rome and she pulls out her cell phone on the platform. She recently joined 12Snap, a mobile entertainment and shopping channel, and on the platform she now checks out a 12Snap auction for a new MP3 player. She had been looking for a player, and now as she prepares for the train trip to Geneva, she realizes she's tired of listening to the same CDs and would welcome the opportunity to download new music. There are only a few minutes until the auction ends, so she places a bid and then increases it until she wins. She ends up spending a little more than she had hoped, but less than she had priced the players for in the store. Her credit card and address are already on file at 12Snap, so with a touch of the button, her purchase is speeding to her door even as she steps onto the train.

As Filomena takes her seat and the train begins to pull out of the station, she receives an offer on the phone to participate in a music contest sponsored by McDonald's. She had checked a box when she signed up for 12Snap allowing them to send certain contests and offers to her. In this contest, she will listen to clips of music on the phone and if she can name the artists, she will receive a free CD. With her knowledge of music, she aces the quiz and can now pick up the CD at a local McDonald's restaurant, along with a coupon for food. Every day, the fast-food company has millions of contacts with customers who walk into its restaurants and walk out with food, but it knows almost nothing about them. Now, when Filomena walks into the restaurant to claim her CD, they know where she lives, her taste in music, and other vital information. Before putting away her phone, Filomena checks a recording of jokes and then checks her audio horoscope delivered by one of the leading horoscope writers. Since 12Snaps has her birthday on file, she doesn't have to wade through all the signs of the zodiac, but hears only her own horoscope.

Services like 12Snap realize that the cell phone and cell service are not the only sources of value for users. (Successful wireless companies like iMode in Japan also recognize that entertaining content and ease of use are just as important as a clear connection or handset.) 12Snap offers auctions, gossip, shopping, sweepstakes, pre-releases of music, jokes, quizzes, news, and horoscopes at the touch of a button. The service is convenient. It can be accessed anytime and anywhere, and customers can go from impulse to order with a touch of the button. Perhaps because of the reduced entertainment value, 12Snap had less success with fixed price offerings than with auction formats. New pricing adds to the entertainment value of the experience, as well as new interactive models for delivery.

The centaur is reshaping the value equation and companies like 12Snap are accelerating this process. The centaur expects to be able to move between physical and virtual distribution easily, with the convenience of true integration of clicks and bricks (and, with wireless, everywhere in between). The centaur expects to be able to find information and purchase products anytime and anywhere. The centaur is not just interested in a product and service offering. The MP3 player that Filomena purchased is only part of the overall experience. It is the entertainment of the auction and the convenience of doing it during downtime on the railroad platform that also adds value. This is why a bidder on eBay or a ticket buyer on Priceline might sometimes pay more for some items than on other fixed-price sites. The centaur also expects to be able to move beyond standard pricing models to more flexible and dynamic pricing that puts the consumer in charge, rather than standard seller-initiated pricing.

All these are ways the value equation is being reshaped. The new value equation includes traditional sources of value offline. It includes sources of value online. And it includes "convergence value" that is created through the interaction of the two. As always, it is the "competitive value" offered by the company relative to rivals. In this chapter, we explore these sources of competitive value and strategies for using them.

THE NEW VALUE EQUATION

The value equation is changing as a result of e-business. While we often focus on price and product when we think of value (getting more and better product for your money), there has always been a lot more to value than just price and product. With the rise of the Internet, some of these other sources of value have been transformed or become more important. The components of the new value equation include:

- *Product/Service Offering:* It almost goes without saying that value is derived from the actual product or service itself, including its attributes, features, quality, and benefits. There is also value added through the variety and flexibility of options offered, which is much greater online.

- *Price:* Value also is derived through the price paid for the product or service and the consumer's perceived price/quality relationship. Pricing is changing in fundamental ways online, with new dynamic pricing strategies such as name-your-own-price and auction models, in addition to traditional fixed pricing. Much of the benefit of the Internet has been through the low-hanging fruit of improved efficiency and effectiveness, resulting in reduced cost of operations.

- *Service:* As the value equation has expanded beyond price and product, service before, during, and after the sale has become a key component of value. Typically, personal service has been very costly, but the Internet has the potential to offer online information and customer service at a much lower cost.

- *Brand:* The trusted value of the brand is another source of value. With increasing product proliferation online and offline, branding becomes more important. There are brands for the product, the seller, and the portal. As we are dealing with increasing product proliferation and more accessible information about price and product attributes, the brand becomes an increasingly important source of value.

- *Speed:* From one-hour photos to overnight express services, faster delivery is a source of value. The Internet has accelerated this speed for some products and services, moving from overnight delivery to instantaneous delivery for digital products (although physical products still need to find their way through on-the-ground logistics).

- *Convenience:* The ease of doing business with a company is also an important component of value. As discussed in Chapter 5, multiple channels do not only offer a new set of shopping options but can increase the convenience of the entire buying and consumption cycle: (1) pre-purchase search and decision; (2) purchase; (3) transportation; (4) storage; (5) retrieval and preparation for use; (6) use or consumption of the product; (7) discarding the waste; (8) post-usage evaluation and communication. The Internet transforms the "here and now" concept to "anytime, anywhere," with 24/7 convenience and virtual information and sales outlets that can be accessed from almost anywhere. This has become even more important with increasing mobile/wireless access.

- *Novelty:* The novelty of being a first mover or opinion leader also adds value for consumers, as witnessed by the premium paid by early adopters for the latest version of a personal computer or next generation Palm Pilot. The Internet can capitalize on its ability to be rapidly reconfigured and customized to generate value by creating something new.

- *Peace of Mind:* Security and trust adds value as well. Consumers are willing to pay more to purchase a product from a trusted company than from one that is unknown, in part because of peace of mind. In a virtual world, security and trust may be even more valuable, given the lack of a physical connection. This is becoming even more important as the complexity and uncertainty of buying a product increases. A reinforcing community can add to peace of mind.

- *Experience and Entertainment:* Consumers value entertainment and discovery. Fun adds value to the experience of interaction and purchase. Companies long have used giveaways, interactive contests, and other strategies to add to the entertainment value of their offerings. This is even more important in the interactive environment of online and offline business that offers richer opportunities for entertainment.

- *Information in Context:* Typically, the information gathering has been separated from the purchase decision, but now it can be presented in context. For example, book reviews at an online bookseller are presented with the books. With wireless devices, this information can be presented at a physical point of purchase. For example, Unilever has created a concept for a digital recipe book on cellular phones in Europe that will allow grocery shoppers in a store to call up recipes while shopping, complete with lists of ingredients (many chosen from Unilever brands). This "contextual marketing" places the message or information at the point where consumers need it.[1]

- *Education and Personal Growth:* Knowledge has value, not just in the degrees offered by universities, but in ongoing information, education, and personal development. People have been willing to pay for this training and ongoing advice on issues from computer software to personal finance, but this education is inexpensive and potentially more effective online because the learner can learn at his or her own pace.

- *Control:* There is a value to being in charge, to having control of the product or service development. Technology for customerization and personalization, discussed in Chapter 3, offers customers greater levels of control over the product and the experience, adding value.

- *Social/Psychological Rewards:* There are a lot of psychological benefits from using the technology effectively. Consumers gain a strong psychological benefit from a sense of perceived mastery of technology. Involvement in virtual communities and peer-to-peer communication also offers significant social benefits.

These are illustrative sources of value that indicate how the elements of the value equation are changing. Not every consumer will value all of these components, or value them all for every product or purchase occasion. These drivers of value are also interrelated, interacting with one another to increase or decrease overall value. Fundamentally, the new value equation leads to a rethinking of the traditional 4 Ps (product, price, promotion, and place) of marketing, as will be considered in Chapter 9.

We should also stress that we are discussing *perceived* value, typically in relation to other experiences, not only with peer companies, but also with companies in unrelated industries. For example, a company who receives overnight shipping from another company will expect a similar level of service from other companies delivering products. The customer expectation is not structured based on SIC (industry) codes, but rather in reference to their other experiences.

The changes in the value equation—new expectations for anytime, anywhere convenience, for example—are transforming consumer expectations online and offline. The value equation was changing before the Internet, but these changes have now deepened and accelerated, moving away from the traditional focus on price and product (although these issues continue to remain important). This spectrum shift has seen increasing attention to more intangible sources of value (in assessing value for both the customer and the company's investors). The first shift was reflected in an increasing interest in the impact of drivers such as customer satisfaction and brand equity on value in the 1990s. As the concept of value has expanded, it has moved increasingly from physical goods to experience. It has moved from seller-driven pricing to buyer-driven pricing, from fixed times and locations to "anytime, anywhere" convenience. Some of these shifts are summarized in Exhibit 6–1.

The Internet, with its capability for interactivity, flexibility, and real-time speed, is speeding up this spectrum shift. But even in online business, the initial focus of value creation was on more limited dimensions such as cost reductions through efficiency (which affects cost and time) or service enhancements. With a broader definition of value, the opportunities to create and transform value online clearly extend far beyond mere efficiency and effectiveness. In fact, for many businesses online, the efficiency of transactions was countered by the high cost of customer acquisition and logistics. It is only by looking at the value derived from interactivity, control, branding, speed, novelty, and other dimensions that we understand the true potential for value creation of online business.

How can you redefine the value equation in your business by using innovative pricing and distribution models and other components of the new value equation? How does your value equation differ online and offline?

Convergence Value

But even this expanded concept is only part of the value equation in an Internet age. There is also a "convergence value" in

Source of Value	Offline	Online
Product/Service Offering	Physical products and face-to-face services	Digital products and online services can be delivered more efficiently
Price	Fixed pricing models with discounting	Dynamic pricing models
Service	Traditional before-sale, during-sale and after-sale service that required real people	Automated service allows customers 24/7 access while reducing costs
Brand	Brand adds value by signaling status or product quality	Branding helps to increase trust in a virtual world and speed the ability to make decisions
Speed	Limited by physical value chain	Can deliver digital products in real-time but physical products face the same challenges
Convenience	Fixed locations, business hours	Anytime, anywhere
Novelty	Difficult to make new	Easy to make new
Peace of Mind	Physical relationship can contribute to peace of mind (eye contact, handshakes)	Virtual relationship may make trust more important and harder to achieve
Experience and Entertainment	Companies offer real experience, but have limited opportunities for entertainment	Virtual experiences offer tremendous opportunities for interactive entertainment and they are becoming increasingly realistic

EXHIBIT 6–1 CONTINUED

Source of Value	Offline	Online
Information in context	Off-site information is searched for and obtained, but often out of context	Information can be provided within the context of a purchase decision
Education and personal growth	Costly to provide	Inexpensive, accessible and more effective e-learning
Control	Customer has limited control or control is expensive (personal tailoring)	Through customization and personalization, customer has control over product and service offerings.
Social/Psychological	Personal interaction and other traditional rewards of offline activities	Enhanced by a whole new range of rewards through online interactions and empowerment through the technology

the way online and offline businesses work together. Virtual and physical businesses can work synergistically to create value or in opposition to destroy it. Well-coordinated online and offline strategies may give customers integrated solutions that create more value than the sum of the parts. On the other hand, mismatched efforts can erode value. To take a simple example, an integrated strategy that allows customers to buy a book online and return it in a physical store may increase overall value for most customers over a strategy that does not allow for returns across channels. This type of disjointed strategy, where the online and offline stores are totally disconnected, could decrease the overall value for customers.

Cost is also an important part of the equation. From the customer viewpoint, the higher the value the better, but companies have to be concerned about offering a higher value at a lower cost than rivals (or at least the same cost). The initial fear about e-business among traditional retailers was that competitors with much lower costs would come in and take over their markets. But the threat was not as great as it appeared, primarily because of these other dimensions of value. If the lower-price product comes from an unknown company without a strong brand, this reduces peace of mind. If the product is hard to return, this makes it less convenient. Online companies that focused primarily on product and price, as companies such as Buy.com and Mercata.com did, have missed important parts of the value equation and suffered as a result. For example, customers have shown their willingness to pay higher prices for books on Amazon,[2] because of non-price factors such as the rich content of user reviews that enhance the experience for customers who want to browse and the ease of one-click purchasing that enhances the efficiency for customers who want to save time.

Convergence value comes not only from combining online and offline strategies, but also in the way companies combine them. This value is increased through two types of convergence, as illustrated in Exhibit 6–2:

- *Buyer-initiated and seller-initiated pricing:* While pricing has traditionally been based on fixed pricing and discounts, the Internet has spread or created a wide variety of other pricing models from name-your-own-price frameworks such as Priceline to auctions such as eBay. How can you use and combine traditional pricing and new dynamic models in ways that increase value?

EXHIBIT 6–2 CONVERGING ON VALUE

- *Offering and experience:* The ambiance of retailers, like the piano player in Nordstrom, food samples in grocery stores, or the cappuccino bar at Barnes & Noble has always been a part of the value of the real-world shopping experience in addition to the product or service offering. But online channels offer greater opportunities to extend this experience through interactive entertainment and education as part of the shopping and consumption experience. The interactive, information-rich environment of the Internet offers greater opportunities for education and some types of entertainment. While the online experience was initially hobbled by primitive technology, it is now increasingly drawing upon sound and video, animation, special effects, interactive games and also bringing other senses into action. How can you draw upon all the senses in providing information, education, and entertainment to enhance the product/service offering?

CONVERGENCE OF PRODUCT/SERVICE OFFERING AND EXPERIENCE

The early assessment of the Internet was that it would add value primarily through more efficient searching and transactions. The advertising model was based on the ideas that customers would continue to receive passive ads for products and services through banner ads. The early Internet marketers were still looking at the world through the eyes of Frank Woolworth, who tried to increase volume and selection and offer lower prices. The ability to search for products and prices online is valuable, no doubt, but the real value turns out to be less a result of efficiency and more a result of interactivity. The Internet offers the potential for real engagement, entertainment, and education, increasing involvement of customers. As Jacques Bughin of McKinsey has noted, "curiosity is the killer app."[3]

Experience has always been a part of the purchase process. Certain experience goods, like cars and clothes, usually require a test drive or fitting before a purchase can be made. But due to the interactivity and other characteristics of the Internet, the consumer experience is enhanced and its importance increases. Companies that are selling products and services are not just offering products and services. Pharmaceutical firms are offering valuable information and education about the disease their drugs treat. Electronics makers are offering detailed information to help consumers understand the key dimensions for choosing a new stereo or DVD player. The experience is a key part of the value. The challenge for convergence is therefore to add experience (entertainment, education, information, and other experience) to the purchase and use of the product. In this way, companies join together the traditional value proposition of product/service offering and price, with other less tangible dimensions.

New technologies are increasing opportunities for adding experience. Streaming audio, video and animation have added to the sights and sounds. There are chips in development that add smell to the online experience. There are technologies such as the "talking heads" of LifeFX's Facemail that can transform a text message into a spoken message by a virtual agent, complete with smiles, frowns, and other expressions of emotion that are far more direct and engaging than traditional "emoticons" added to text e-mail messages. (Emoticons are the small smiley faces and other symbols designed to give context to email; for example :-) is used to convey a smile or humor.) Virtual reality can add three-dimensional vision along with touch and feel to the experience. The online experience is going to become richer and deeper as game designs, simulations and other technologies emerge.

Among the strategies for achieving this convergence of offering and experience are:

- *Increase novelty and entertainment value:* Companies can design their sites as games, to increase engagement and involvement with the site. To promote its Escape sport utility vehicle, Ford Motors' Canadian unit created a video game in which participants could drive the car through a race course on the moon. Of the roughly 29,000 unique users who participated in just over three months, an estimated 12 percent registered with the car company and 55 percent gave permission to Ford to send them marketing materials. Companies such as General Motors, PepsiCo, Honda and Burger King have designed online games as part of their marketing strategies.[4] Swatch used an original approach to take the experience of shopping for a watch to a whole new level on its Swatch.com website. Visitors are encouraged to hire or build a clerk from scratch. The "clerk generation" section offers visitors a chance to design their own clerk, adding eyes (or a single eye), hair, clothing, and accessories (such as angel wings or a space helmet) to a cartoon bust of a clerk. They can also give the clerk a name and choose an attitude for the clerk—New Yorker, Xtreme (Gen X), or Geek. While engaged in the process of designing the clerk, music is playing in the background of the site, and users have the opportunity to select from three music tracks using radio buttons. The choices during this process, along with age information taken when the visitor logs in, are enough for the "clerk" to offer a selection of four watches, with a text dialogue that reflects the attitude selected for the clerk. If the users don't like the clerk's choices, they can fire the clerk or modify it.

This playful approach adds a whole new layer of novelty and entertainment to the process of buying a product. In a certain sense, it has nothing to do with the actual product, but in another sense it has everything to do with a product that is designed for individual expression. For those who just want to buy a watch, the site also offers direct paths into a catalog or a set of questions that help identify potential selections.

The interactivity of the Web offers many opportunities to increase the entertainment value of the experience that go far beyond the experience of the product itself. The shopping experience and examination of the product offering is joined together with an entertaining experience of interacting with the virtual clerk.

Given the increasing richness of the online experience, offline businesses are also focusing on ways to increase the entertainment value of their offerings in ways that differentiate them from online firms. As buyers are offered more opportunities for grocery shopping online, physical grocery stores have created new offline experiences including restaurants, bars, and singles' nights. These are experiences that take them away from their core grocery business but also give them advantages that would be difficult to replicate online.

> **How can you increase the entertainment value of your product or service? How do you need to reshape your offline experience in light of the rich opportunities for expanded online channels?**

- *Create experiences that reinforce the brand:* Volkswagen AG created its own 24-hour online radio station to promote its automobiles. RadioVW features an eclectic selection of music designed to appeal to the carmaker's youthful buyers. Though a radio station may not seem like it has much to do with a car, the use of music is a core focus of Volkswagen's branding and of the experience of driving the car. Many of VW's television advertisements prominently feature music as part of the message. Steve Keyes, spokesman for VW's American unit that launched the Radio VW, explained that it reinforces the company's brand. "Music is a big part of the Volkswagen experience," he told *The Wall Street Journal.*[5] Similarly, BMW has produced short Internet films by professional directors, which feature its cars only peripherally.[6]

  > **How can you create experiences that reinforce the brand?**

- *Create pathways to entertainment that run from offline to online and back:* The motion picture industry, which has always blurred the line between fiction and reality, has come up with some of the most creative ways of using the Internet to zigzag across that line. Inspired by the word-of-mouth buzz generated around the low-budget film The *Blair Witch Project*, a number of promoters of movies and television shows have turned to the Internet to generate grassroots interest in their shows and motion pictures.

Some of these promotions have taken on a virtual life of their own. In pitching movies to the cynical youth audience, entertainment companies have taken the fictional identities of characters and given them life online. For example, an investigative reporter who shows up for a minute in an episode of HBO's hit series, *The Sopranos*, launched "his own" web site with inside information and updates on the characters as a way to increase interest and involvement by viewers. An even more obscure and elaborate online connection was established by promoters of Stephen Spielberg's movie *A.I.*, in which a scientist listed on the movie trailer led to her personal website that offered clues about the murder of her friend Evan Chan. Clues about the mystery were scattered in obscure corners of the Web and movie posters, creating a buzz before the show even aired. The storyline on the Web, created by a science fiction and fantasy writer, was only tangentially connected to the movie plot. These sites were not heavily promoted, which added to the intrigue and interest to insiders who could find them before they were ultimately made public through news stories.[7] Visitors to the advance online sites were invited to attend a preview screening of the film, using online interaction to ensure that the

How can you move experiences from online to offline and back?

film's greatest fans would see it before anyone else.[8] Similarly, computer games have enhanced their offline appeal and sales by allowing users around the world to play together for free online, for example through MSN's gaming site.

- *Integrate pre- and post-purchase experience:* Virtual communities can provide ongoing information and support before and after the purchase. Community members can answer questions about the intricacies of complicated products or offer candid feedback on their usefulness in different situations. After the purchase, these communities of customers can offer an integrated support system, working out bugs or other difficulties. For example, iVillage provides pre-purchase information and support as well as post-purchase information.

- *Invite spectators to play:* When chess masters match up in the real world, aspiring players can watch the board online and make their own moves to try to anticipate the strategies of the masters. These shadow games draw together offline and online experience in a way that transforms game spectators into participants. The more involvement and control you can give to people, the more they will value the experience.

- *Move more of the experience online:* New technologies such the manuals and virtual products developed by Livemanuals.com allow customers to "try out" a virtual product such as a radar detector by pushing its buttons, hearing its warning sounds, watching lights flash, and demonstrating its options. Some of the experience of experimenting with the product has been moved online because it has been digitized. Consumers also can download the entire product manual online (before or after purchase) for detailed information on product features. This online manual also provides a high level of customization. For example, an English-speaking foreigner who bought a phone in Turkey could discard the Turkish instructions and download the appropriate manual in English online. Online manuals also offer companies the potential for significant cost savings in printing and updating.

> How can you invite spectators to play and move offline experiences (such as reading manuals) online?

For some products and services, online experiences can offer a richer understanding of the offering than telephone or even direct sales. For example, most customers who purchase tickets to entertainment events select the seats based on sections or by a seating chart. By moving the experience online, however, customers could see an actual 360-degree video of the view from the seat, so customers would know exactly what they are getting before they purchase. In this case, moving the experience online could save costs on transactions and offer a richer pre-purchase experience for the customer.

- *Provide education:* Knowledge and expertise can sometimes be shared much more efficiently online and this education increases the value of the overall experience. From online investment advice to education and design tools for renovating a kitchen or building a patio, the Internet can offer the education of experts in the same space as it offers products and services. The Internet can provide just-in-time learning to students anywhere. Once this is developed, this can be used for the education of the consumer and training the company's own employees and partners. The potential in this area is enormous (for example, to customize the learning experience to address the learning style and preferences of the individual). Barnes & Noble has set up the Barnes & Noble University that offers free online courses for readers on dozens of topics, including literature, hobbies, business, history, science, and the arts, presumably based on books they purchase from the site.[9]

What opportunities are there to use education in your business online and offline?

CONVERGENCE OF SELLER-INITIATED AND BUYER-INITIATED PRICING

Pricing is becoming more fluid. Even before the advent of the online medium, industrial markets and bazaars have long followed a customized pricing mechanism based on bargaining and discount schedules. Now, in addition to standard pricing, there are a wide range of other pricing models to choose from, including dynamic pricing, auction pricing, and bundled pricing.

What are the opportunities to use new pricing models in your business online and offline?

Although pricing is increasingly interactive between buyer and seller, in general these pricing strategies can be characterized as starting in one of two directions:

- *Flexible seller-initiated pricing:* The online medium has made it feasible to apply dynamic pricing more broadly, offering prices that "change either over time, across consumers or across product/service bundles."[10] Online prices can be tailored to specific users and raised or lowered instantly for assessing and responding to consumers' price elasticity. The ability to create truly fluid pricing is only limited by customer acceptance. Technology is now available to vary pricing in ways that were not possible in the past. New in-store technology allows supermarkets to customize pricing based on specific times of the day through digital price labels or even to tailor discounts and coupons to individuals based on their past purchasing patterns. **How can you increase the flexibility of your pricing online and offline?** Further flexibility can be added to this pricing model through dynamic coupons, particularly e-coupons. These dynamic pricing strategies make it harder for customers to use shopping bots to make comparisons across different sellers.

- *Buyer-Initiated Pricing:* A more radical form of pricing is the rise of customer-set pricing. There are a number of models here:

    - *Name-your-own price:* Priceline.com and Deal-Time.com offer a reverse auction model of pricing, in which customers propose the prices (e.g., for such products as airlines, hotels, and mortgages) and producers determine whether they will accept them. This approach is more likely to work for non-customized products, such as airline seats, where the customer can easily shop around for the lowest price on the same product from a variety of sources.

    - *Auctions:* Companies such as eBay.com and Onsale.com have built successful businesses using online auction models that draw together large numbers of buyers and sellers in a virtual auction. Onsale founder, Jerry Kaplan, predicts that retail markets will operate more like stock exchanges in the future, with prices fluctuating based on demand. There is a trend to expand auctions in many markets and situations. Even in the exclusive domain of investment banking, companies such as W.R. Hambrecht and others have used Dutch auctions (declining prices) to set the price for IPOs.[11]

- *Aggregating Buying Power:* Another interesting transaction model was popularized by companies such as Mobshop.com and Mercata.com (which is no longer in business). The basic idea is to leverage the Internet to dynamically form a group of potential customers of a product (a "buying circle") to take advantage of quantity discounts. The time of sale is announced in advance. As more customers join the buying circle, the price of the product continues to fall for the entire group.

- *Fire sales:* This model, long employed for clearing out unwanted inventory in physical stores, is used by companies such as Basement.com. In the model, the company continually lowers the price of the products until they are sold. Buyers have to decide how long they are willing to wait before bidding, risking losing the product to another bidder, and the price keeps going down until one buyer accepts it.

- *Barter:* Barter is facilitated greatly by the Internet. It is common in the business-to-business realm, and has some interesting opportunities in the consumer realm as well.

- *Risk/Reward Sharing:* Some advertising and consulting companies are being paid for success instead of fixed fees, so they share more of the risk and reward for projects.

Convergent Pricing Strategies

Even as "dynamic pricing" becomes more popular, it does not necessarily mean that prices will decline, as shown by several research studies.[12] The convenience, time-saving aspects, and product matching features of online markets may increase the price a customer is willing to pay.

Centaurs are already finding creative ways to combine the different pricing models. For example, an executive was recently traveling from Austin to St. Louis on business. His company had paid full economy fare

How can you use buyer-initiated pricing strategies in your business online and offline?

to ensure he would arrive for his meeting in time. But he was now waiting at the St. Louis airport for 20 minutes for his wife and two children. His wife's family lived in St. Louis and she was anxious to accompany him on the trip, but he originally had decided it would be too expensive. Then on a whim, he offered a very low price on Priceline. He received a reply asking him to raise his price slightly and he had a deal. With a substantial savings, his wife and children were now accompanying him on the trip (but on a different airline). He had to buy his ticket through the company travel office and they valued a fixed and confirmed arrival and departure time, as well as the ability to make changes, over a lower cost. But his family valued cost savings over that flexibility.

This family acted like centaurs. The airline companies would not have gotten this revenue without this strategy because the family would have stayed home, so it added value for the consumer and the companies involved. Some tickets were purchased through seller-initiated pricing and others through buyer-initiated pricing. The buyer researched seller prices before making his own bid. The centaur can always find a lower-priced ticket, but he may not get the day, time, or airline on which he needs to fly. The question is, if centaurs are already combining the pricing strategies, is there a way for companies to do it for them?

How can companies effectively develop innovative pricing strategies that combine different pricing models while reflecting price elasticities of target customers, the competitive offerings, and the richness of the new value equations? Among the strategies for convergence of buyer-initiated and seller-initiated pricing are:

- *Offer multiple pricing options to the same customers:* eBay sellers have the option of creating a "Buy it Now" button with a fixed price for the product they are selling. If a buyer is willing to pay that price, the seller will stop the auction (provided there are no bids yet) and sell for a fixed price. In this way, the site combines both a fixed price system and an auction pricing mechanism, giving buyers more choices. Through its acquisition of Half.com, which offers used products at fixed prices, eBay also has offered fixed prices on used products for customers who like to pay fixed prices and auction pricing for buyers and sellers who prefer that approach (although not on exactly the same products and on separate sites).

- *Create consistent value propositions online and offline:* Whenever possible, it is important to create consistent value propositions or to consider the impact of differences in the value proposition online and offline. In April 2001, American Airlines instituted a $10 surcharge for customers who want paper tickets. The move was designed to encourage customers to use e-tickets, which are cheaper to issue, but travel agents often recommend paper tickets because they make it easier to rebook if the flight is canceled. American's pricing strategy creates inconsistent value propositions for online and offline, even though it may generate extra revenue. Will this policy ultimately be counterproductive?[13] Charles Schwab, which initially created different prices for its online and offline customers, recognized the importance of creating a consistent value proposition and significantly increased its business as result of moving to a single pricing structure.

- *Recognize that people look for more than price and product:* Insurance companies such as Geico advertise that you will receive the lowest rate, even if it means sending you to a rival company. Customers may be able to shop around and get better insurance rates online, but they still may buy their insurance from their local agent. They may look for information on a car online, but then want to go to the dealer. The reason may be convenience and peace of mind (knowing you have someplace physical and an agent you know to go to if you have a claim). These other elements of value help change the value equation and avoid comparison charts that focus on product features and price. How can you add value through service or brand? How can you increase value by reducing hassles or adding to peace of mind? Looking for other ways to create value helps differentiate the company's offering and add to its price. The control of customerization, the entertainment of interactivity, and the use of powerful decision tools and search engines are all non-price factors that lead to greater value.

- *Be aware of how dynamic pricing strategies affect other drivers of value:* Some powerful online pricing strategies may also be shortsighted by focusing too much on price. For example, one major cellular phone company showed different phone offers to web site visitors based on how they came to the site. Consumers who appeared to be less price-sensitive (because they went right to the high-end phone equipment and spent a lot of time exploring its features) were offered a monthly contract for $55 for 250 hours. On the other hand, consumers who first spent a lot of time shopping around through lower-priced phones ultimately were offered a contract of $39.99 for 700 hours.[14] This differential and dynamic pricing based on behavior is one of the powerful opportunities of e-business, and not so different from the salesperson who sizes up a customer before making an offer. **How can you combine different pricing strategies into a coherent portfolio of options?** But this online strategy has much more potential to erode the trust, brand loyalty, and peace of mind in the long term because it can be discovered more readily by customers.

- *Offer a limited version for free:* The idea of sampling can take on new forms online. Trial versions of software can be created that expire after limited test period. Similarly, a professor who was presenting to a faculty development symposium in an emerging nation asked the publisher of the book he was using to distribute complimentary copies to the attending faculty members. The cost of the books and shipping was more than the publisher wanted to contribute, but the publisher offered instead to send over an electronic version and gave the conference organizers permission to produce photocopies for a few days for participants of the conference. This allowed the participants to sample the book's content royalty free, and perhaps adopt it for their classes, but not receive an original book without paying. It was also a lot faster and more flexible because the organizers of the conference could print extra copies for late registrants. It was a win–win situation. To take this approach, however, companies need to recognize that books are more than their content. They are objects that people collect and keep in their libraries, so there is a value to a tangible book that goes beyond the "digital" content that can be distributed. Similarly, sampling of music does not necessarily lead to the erosion of CD sales. In fact, studies indicate that music sharing services such as Napster may actually have the opposite effect and that pirating of software may increase legitimate sales. One study has estimated that pirated software was responsible for attracting 80 percent of new legitimate buyers in the U.K., significantly increasing legal diffusion.[15] (On the other hand, the legal definition of a "book," particularly whether the electronic form is the same as the paper version, is being hotly contested by publishers and authors who want rights to electronic versions.[16]) The trick in offering a limited version is that there must be a way to differentiate the partial, free version from the upgraded version for which a fee is charged.

Could you increase your revenues in the long-term by giving away some version of your product for free?

- *Offer bundling of online and offline products:* The *Wall Street Journal* built a successful online Interactive Edition in part by cleverly bundling the subscription with its print version. It offered a lower price for the online subscription to

How can you bundle online and offline products and services?

paper subscribers (although it didn't give it away for free as many of its peers did), thus encouraging online and offline subscribers to take the other version.

THE DYNAMIC VALUE EQUATION

As new technologies, innovative strategies by direct and indirect competitors, new pricing models, and new customer behaviors emerge, the value equation will continue to shift. Better technologies for interaction should increase the value of online and offline convergence by boosting speed and efficiency, improving the overall experience, and providing more flexibility for value-based pricing reflecting the total cost of ownership. Customers will become savvier about the different types of pricing models and will be less likely to use them merely for novelty, as many early adopters of these new models have done. When this novelty value wears off, the underlying value will be seen. Smart agents who understand what aspects of value are important to customers will be more focused in making comparisons across products and services. This will further shift the dimensions that companies need to strengthen, just as the attention to product quality in the 1980s and 1990s increased the focus on this dimension of value.

Managers need to consider their online and offline value propositions in their totality. The heart of the marketing task is to define a coherent value proposition and articulate it to customers in a credible fashion. Too often, in the early days of the Internet, online and offline value propositions were not consistent and coherent. By understanding the distinctive strengths of online and offline approaches in creating value, managers can better harmonize their real and virtual value equations—and offer greater value than their competitors. This will create more value online and more value offline, as well as more convergence value between the two. This will provide greater overall value to customers and to companies that can develop revenue models to capture this value.

```
┌─────────────────────────────────────────────────────────────────┐
│                                                                   │
│  Action Memo                                                      │
│                                                                   │
│  • Sign up and buy a product on eBay. How did the auction         │
│    experience differ from a fixed price approach? Now, buy a      │
│    similar product on Half.com. What is the experience there?     │
│    How can you use these pricing models in your                   │
│    business?                                                      │
│                                                                   │
│  • Compare the price of a new computer or other big-ticket        │
│    item on eBay with prices through other sources. Is it higher   │
│    or lower? What are the advantages of an auction model for a    │
│    seller? What are the advantages for a buyer?                   │
│                                                                   │
│  • Price out an airline reservation online through               │
│    Travelocity.com, Expedia.com and Orbitz.com. Now, go to a      │
│    physical travel agent for a price. How is the experience and   │
│    the price different? Finally, if you have flexibility in departure│
│    time and place, go to Priceline.com and see if you can get a   │
│    lower price. How can you use these insights in your own pric-  │
│    ing decisions?                                                 │
│                                                                   │
│  • Visit the Volkswagen and BMW websites. What impact does        │
│    the experience of radio and video clips have on your per-      │
│    ception of their products, the companies, or the site? How can │
│    you integrate experiences into your own site?                  │
│                                                                   │
│  We invite you to share the results of these activities and       │
│  suggest other action memos at the Convergence Marketing          │
│  Forum (www.convergencemarketingforum.com).                       │
│                                                                   │
└─────────────────────────────────────────────────────────────────┘
```

NOTES

[1] Kenny, David and John F. Marshall, "Contextual Marketing," *Harvard Business Review*, November–December 2000, pp. 119–125.

[2] Brynjolfsson, Erik, and Michael Smith, "The Great Equalizer? Consumer Choice at Internet Shopbots," Working paper, *MIT Sloan School of Management* (July 2000).

3 Jacques Bughin, presented at Wharton Fellows in E-Business, Barcelona, February 2001.

[4] Vrancia, Suzanne, "GM is Joining Online Videogame Wave," *The Wall Street Journal*, July 26, 2001.

[5] Snel, Ross, "Volkswagen is Pushing Its Brand Name by Jazzing up Its Web Site with Music," *The Wall Street Journal*, April 30, 2001, p. B9A.

[6] Black, Jane, "Online Advertising: It's Just the Beginning" *Business Week*, July 12, 2001.

[7] Mathews, Anna Wilde, "Bizarre Web Game Pops Up To Promote Spielberg's 'AI'," *The Wall Street Journal*, April 30, 2001, p. B-1; Simons, Paula, "Edmonton Novelist Scripts A.I.," *The Edmonton Journal*, June 25, 2001, p. A-2.

[8] DiOrio, Carl, "Mecha Movie Moolah: Spielberg's sci-fi fantasy A.I. Bows on Top with $30 Million," *Daily Variety*, July 2, 2001, p. 1.

[9] www.bnuniversity.com

[10] Kannan, P.K. and Praveen K. Kopalle, "Dynamic Pricing on the Internet: Importance and Implications for Consumer Behavior," *International Journal of Electronic Commerce*, Vol. 5, No. 3, Spring 2000, pp. 63–83.

[11] John McCracken, WR Hambrecht & Co., presentation to the Wharton Fellows in e-Business, San Jose, July 13, 2001.

[12] Shankar, Venkatesh, Arvind Rangaswamy and Michael Pusteri, "The Impact of Internet Marketing on Price Sensitivity and Price Competition," *Marketing Science and the Internet*, Inform College on Marketing Mini-Conference, Cambridge, Mass., 1998.

[13] Engle, Jane, "American Adds Charge for Paper Tickets," *Austin American Statesman*, April 29, 2001, p. D-2.

[14] Ravi Aron, presented at Wharton Fellows in E-Business, May 2001.

[15] Givon, Moshe, Vijay Mahajan and Eitan Muller, "Software Piracy: Estimation of Lost Sales and the Impact on Software Diffusion," *Journal of Marketing* Vol. 59 (January 1998), pp. 29–37.

[16] Rose, Matthew, "Definitions are Key in Publishers' Dispute over Electronic-Book Rights," *The Wall Street Journal*, May 7, 2001, p. B-1.

7

CONVERGING ON CHOICE

GIVE ME TOOLS TO MAKE BETTER DECISIONS

"Many receive advice, few profit by it."

Publilius Syrus

TRADITIONAL CONSUMER

I give and receive advice from my friends and I like to shop where I can get a fair price and expert advice. I've bought my cars from the same dealer and stocks from the same broker for years. They know me and I think they look out for me. I don't trust the information I see online. How do I know where it came from or who paid to have it put there? Are those comparisons you see for real or are they designed to favor companies that paid for placement?

CYBERCONSUMER

Seriously, do you mean to tell me you really trust your car dealer or broker? Are they really looking out for your interests? The Internet puts me in touch with experts around the world. It allows me to search for products in ways that would have been impossible before. It gives me access to medical information that goes beyond what my doctor knows sometimes. It gives me the kind of financial advice you had to hire a financial planner for in the past. I am tired of being kept in the dark and manipulated by companies who want me to see their information through their eyes. I want to decide for myself. The Web is my path to liberation and power.

THE CENTAUR

Sometimes I like to get advice from live experts and other times I like to search information and decision-making support online. Other times, I like to do both. For minor health problems, I'll search on the Internet, but if I have a major problem, you can bet I'm going to make an appointment with my doctor. I'll use tools to search for a new house, but I'm not going to buy one until a real estate agent walks me through. And I even pay attention to advertising and might respond to direct mail, although I usually don't trust it.

CONVERGENCE QUESTIONS

>>>*Given that consumers have access to search engines and decision-making tools, how do managers need to reshape their approach to marketing?*

>>>*What mix between advertising spin and unbiased information should companies provide? When should companies push a message, and when should they give consumers the information to make up their own minds?*

>>>*How do companies profit from giving advice when rivals give it away for free?*

Converging on Choice:
Give Me Tools to Make Better Decisions

Information asymmetries have traditionally been a source of value for companies, and decision-making tools were jealously guarded. But now, better tools for search, decision making, and life management are in the hands of consumers. This chapter explores how companies need to combine human experts and decision models, third party and company information, and company push with customer pull in giving consumer tools to make better decisions.

Joseph Perry is up late thinking about his finances. With the strain of feeding both a growing family and a growing San Francisco business, he knows he's saved far too little for retirement. Now that his software firm is generating a healthy income and he's just turned 40, he's starting to worry about the future. At 1 a.m., he goes onto the site for Citibank (myc-iti.com), where he holds his credit card, and he instantly has access to over 100 financial calculators for automobile leases or loans, mortgages, credit cards, savings, budgeting, mutual funds, stocks, and bonds.

Joseph pulls up a retirement calculator that addresses the questions: "Am I saving enough? What can I change?" He enters in his age, income, expected age of retirement, planned savings, IRA contributions, and the income he thinks he'll need after retirement. As he moves through the series of questions, he is sometimes asked for a value he doesn't know how to estimate, but the program either suggests a default or offers him a pop-up help screen where he can find out more about the issue. After completing his own information, he enters the same information for his wife and clicks on the "results" button at the bottom of the screen. The program automatically computes his expected social security distribution and distributions from his savings. He finds out that his current savings rate, his retirement will be funded until he is 80 years old. He needs to save an additional $500 per month or decrease his expenses during retirement to stretch out his retirement income for 30 years. He checks another tool that helps him evaluate his investment portfolio and then makes the decision to increase his savings.

By 1:30 a.m., he has received the kind of advice that would normally have been provided by a professional financial planner, or tediously worked out by a mathematically-inclined individual with a good workbook. From the same computer, he can find out about mortgages, and apply for one, compare models of cars and see a 360-degree image of the interior, and find out what the monthly payments on his dream car would be. He can get several prices on a new laptop, compare several makes and models or review performance ratings, and then order one. He can research travel destinations and compare prices on tickets to travel from San Francisco to visit his family in New York across several airlines. He can set up a diet or exercise plan or obtain detailed information on a medical condition. From his computer, he can assemble a set of experts that a president or king might have trouble drawing together on such short notice at such an hour.

And yet, after filling out the retirement planner, Joseph doesn't click through to set up his IRA account on the Citibank site. Instead, he prints out the information and takes it to his accountant the next morning. Although he trusts the expert advice of Citibank, he doesn't really know them. His accountant knows him, knows his family, and knows his business. This knowledge and relationships is what is most important. So, when his accountant makes a suggestion that he could gain tax savings with a Roth IRA or put more away in an SEP account, Joseph listens attentively and accepts the advice. He might have found the same information on the Citibank site, but only if he looked for it. In such a complex decision, it is comforting to know that a knowledgeable human expert has actually looked at his case. But Joseph is more informed when he walks into the meeting and more apt to question his accountant's advice or ask pointed questions about levels of investment. Joseph leaves feeling that although his accountant may not be there at 1 a.m. or be the world's expert on retirement planning, the accountant provides a level of direct support and personal service that he would not trade for the most powerful decision-making tools in the world.

Joseph Perry and other centaurs want to make good decisions. To do so, they will draw upon the best advice from both personal experts and powerful emerging decision-making tools that offer round-the-clock access to information and decision-making support. The types of decision-making tools that were once in the proprietary systems of companies or advisors are now offered freely on the Internet. In forming their decisions, these centaurs will use search engines to find unbiased information, but will also be swayed by the marketing messages.

THE IMPACT OF DECISION TECHNOLOGY ON THE CHOICES OF CENTAURS

The Internet is a rich and active source of information that consumers use in making their decisions. Some 80 percent of Americans online use the Internet to search for information.[1]

And these tools have arrived none too soon. Consumers are overwhelmed with choices, with the rate of new product introduction and product line proliferation increasing rapidly. Of course, the centaurs are used to having what they want, so they wanted all these options, just not all at once. As Jack

Trout notes, in his book *Differentiate or Die,* from the early 1970s to the late 1990s, the number of vehicle models ballooned from 140 to 260, breakfast cereals expanded from 160 to 340, Colgate toothpastes from 2 to 17, running shoes have gone from 5 to 285 variations, over-the-counter pain relievers have grown from just 17 choices to a head-throbbing array of 141 analgesics, and even lowly dental flosses have expanded from 12 to 64 varieties.[2] An online proliferation of offerings and information has been even more prodigious, with websites appearing as quickly as people can register them.

What are the opportunities to put more decision-making tools and information in the hands of consumers online and offline? How can this benefit your business?

The overload of data, which has been accelerated by online technologies, has created the need for search engines to find information, decision-making tools to transform that information into knowledge, and life management tools (summarized in Exhibit 7–1).

EXHIBIT 7–1 ILLUSTRATIVE SEARCH ENGINES, DECISION-MAKING, AND LIFE MANAGEMENT TOOLS

Search Engines	www.altavista.com
	www.infoseek.com
	www.hotbot.com
	www.google.com
	www.ask.com
Decision Tools	www.mysimon.com
Comparison engines	www.dealtime.com
	www.edmunds.com
	www.expedia.com
	www.priceSCAN.com
Customer evaluations	www.bizrate.com
Expert evaluations	www.consumerreports.com
Life Management Tools	Microsoft Office
	My.Yahoo.com
	Ediets.com

- *Search engines:* At their simplest, search engines such as Google or AltaVista help users search for information on the Worldwide Web through keywords. While they have a common goal, the engines are organized based on different principles and so will have wide variations for any given search term. A study of these engines found that even the best one returns only 50 percent of relevant pages, although a combination of six engines gathers about 90 percent of the total.[3] With inboxes jammed with email and searches crowded with information, consumers also need ways to cut through the clutter. Structured and unstructured content management will allow consumers to automatically distill a long message to its core idea. These systems, using syntactic or semantic approaches, will sift through long-winded messages and crowded headers to give you the essence of the message.[4] Powerful new peer-to-peer technologies, such as the search engine InfraSearch (now owned by Sun Microsystems), allow users to search for information across networks of individual computers in the way people shared music files through Napster (although using a different technology).[5]

- *Decision-making tools:* Increasingly, companies are offering consumers tools to make better decisions about financial issues, purchases such as computers or electronics, health care, and other complex issues. Sites such as MySimon.com and Dealtime.com use comparison engines that provide price and product comparisons across multiple retailers. MySimon is also using conjoint analysis, a powerful marketing research methodology, to help customers think through their preferences for a particular product. These sites also draw together independent expert assessments (such as Consumer Reports) and customer feedback (on sites such as Bizrate.com). Bizrate, for example, gathers feedback from customers and provides customer-based ratings and comments on retailers. Tools such as the financial planners offered by Citibank and other financial services companies are changing the way consumers approach their decision making. There are also collaboration tools, such as eRoom, that facilitate group decision making, allowing users to share files, exchange ideas or information, and work on joint projects.

- *Life Management:* In addition to helping search for information or guide decisions, there are also tools that assist in life management. These tools help people manage diverse aspects of their lives, from health care to calendars to tracking financial portfolios. The Internet allows these tools to be interactive and updated continuously. Many of the personalized portals such as Yahoo! allow users to track their own stock portfolios, manage addresses and calendars, and follow news and information of interest to them. Most Microsoft products, for example, are designed as productivity tools to assist in life and professional management. Sites such as Switchboard.com allow users to search for people and then send them email, cards, or gifts. Other companies offer services to manage health care. Optiscan offers a blood glucose monitor to diabetic patients that is non-invasive for home use, with remote links to physician's offices. Customers of Photoworks can not only post their images, but also draw them together into online albums and invite their friends and relatives to see them. Automated shopping lists allow customers to rapidly repeat purchase items online. Consumers also have access to online job search sites and dating sites to help manage professional and personal relationships.

The power and richness of online search and decision-making tools can be seen in how personal ads and dating services have been siphoned off from newspapers to the Internet. Many newspapers have ceased to publish these personal ads altogether as online services have grown. Others have started publishing a sample from online sites. In contrast to traditional ads that offered several lines of acronym-laden classified ad type—advertising, for example, a DWF ISO SWM (divorced white female in search of single white male)—the online services offer a higher degree of anonymity, full photos, videos, and better search engines. MediaMetrix estimated that 5 million people visited personal ad web sites in December 2000, up 57 percent from the year before. Companies such as Match.com (owned by Ticketmaster), Americansingles, and Virtuallydating are growing rapidly. Other sites serve specific niches, such as Planetout.com, which touts itself as the largest U.S. gay personals site. Other sites target Catholics, Jews, African-Americans, and Latinos.

This area has seen the development of both search engines and some varieties of decision-making tools. Search engines save a lot of small talk. A single woman might search for all the men between 30 and 35, within a 30-mile radius of home with a certain education, income, and interests. Email exchanges help avoid the initial awkward first phone calls to test the waters before an actual meeting. The anonymity of the Internet makes it easier to meet people for those who are shy or not involved in social activities. But the anonymity of the Net is also a drawback, offering the potential for unsavory participants. This has given rise to a new set of decision-making tools, such as a service (whoishe.com) that provides a background report on the would-be cyber suitor. Another site, 24/7 Unite, offers handwriting analysis and psychological profiles. Of course, no matter how thorough the prescreening, the goal of online matchmaking is to end in a face-to-face meeting. Although the Internet can be used as a valuable search tool, there are some decisions that can only be made in physical space.[6] Whereas the cyberconsumer may meet, date, and even marry online, the centaur won't be giving up the candlelit dinners in a physical restaurant anytime soon.

THE CHALLENGE AND OPPORTUNITIES OF CHOICE TOOLS

Tools for searching for information, making decisions, and life management all change the relationship between the consumer and the company. In some cases, they shift the balance of power, erasing information asymmetries, and challenging current business models (as seen in the decline of newspaper personal ads). When investors can find analyst reports and other information online, what was the value of the expensive reports and advice from brokers provided offline? If shoppers could compare different prices for products through MySimon or Dealtime, wouldn't companies with higher-priced products need to slash prices to be competitive? Putting tools in the hands of consumers had many significant strategic implications for companies.

There are a couple of different ways companies reshape their strategy in response to the rise of these tools. First, companies can change their own offerings to meet the more informed consumers, providing more and different information, rethinking pricing or creating lock-in. Second, companies can offer the tools themselves. Instead of sending consumers out to a third-party site for product comparisons, companies offer comparisons right on their own sites. If you can't beat them, join them.

The tools that are developed for customers are often very useful for employees and partners, as well. For example, if an investment firm develops a platform for advice and trading for its customers, the same platform, augmented with selling tools and educational features, could be used by its employees and partners.

We have just begun to scratch the surface with the development of these tools. The spread of these tools will be facilitated by a variety of third-party companies such as Decidia.com that are developing consumer decision-making tools that companies can add to their sites. The sophistication of these tools will also increase.

Consumers will also drive the spread of these tools. To the extent that they are using these tools in their professional lives, either as organizational buyers in the B2B domain or as managers, they will be more likely to start experimenting with the use of these tools in their role as consumers. Most of the decision-making tools for improving management decisions—such as collaborative filtering, conjoint analysis, simulations, and rule-based expert systems (artificial intelligence)—are finding their way or may find their way to the consumer arena, provided companies can come up with a compelling business case.

Optimization tools can help identify the best set of solutions from a complex set of options. For example, an optimization program for air travel would be able to suggest the best flight, not merely on a search for connected cities and flights, but also by cleverly understanding hidden cities, schedules, and the consumer's own preferences and potential for flexibility. Marketing tools, such as conjoint analysis that use sets of tradeoffs to help companies understand consumer preferences, could be applied to helping individual consumers find or create their ideal product. The technology will become more active—moving from a responsive butler or concierge to a proactive skilled personal assistant.[7] Consumers will have more powerful agents that know their preferences and actively search for information and products to meet them, rather than passively responding to consumer requests.

What decision-making tools currently used by managers could you give to customers?

This means we are in the Stone Age of online decision-making tools at this point. These limitations are seen in current studies of decision support systems for consumers. A University of Minnesota study found that airline ticket buyers who used physical agents did better than those who bought their tickets on the Internet, despite the apparently much richer access to information and options online. The travel agents had figured out the system.[8] As electronic agents become increasingly sophisticated, this gap will be reduced, but it may not ever fully disappear. As we have seen in the slow progress of artificial intelligence, there are some surprisingly simple things that human beings can do that are hard for computers to replicate.

The Choices of Centaurs

The emergence of powerful decision-making tools is changing the face of marketing and the expectations of consumers. People like Joseph Perry are not willing to just accept what companies or even physical advisors such as doctors and brokers might tell them.

These centaurs expect to be able to find their own information and to call upon an experienced personal advisor when they have the need. The rise of decision-making tools and subsequent changes in the consumer present several convergence challenges for marketers, as illustrated in Exhibit 7–2.

EXHIBIT 7–2

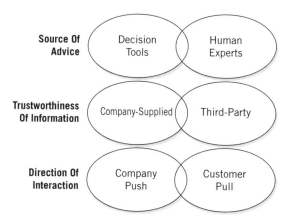

The first challenge is the *balance* between decision-making tools and experts. The proliferation of search and decision support tools has raised their expectations to receive support for their search for information and decision making. Most Internet users already have difficulty remembering the time a few years ago when a search for information meant spending hours in the library or hiring an experienced researcher or traveling to multiple retailers. Now it is often as simple as a few keystrokes in a search engine. Comparing prices once meant trips to multiple retailers, but now can be accomplished in seconds on a site like MySimon.com or Dealtime.com. Customers can compare trips across multiple airlines on sites such as Expedia.com or Travelocity.com without going to a traditional travel agent. They can look for and compare cars on a site such as Carsdirect.com. The centaurs now expect to be able to instantly find the information they need anywhere in the world and be given support in making decisions from purchasing computers and cars to setting up a diet and exercise program. And when they see an expert, whether it is their broker or their doctor, they are usually more prepared than in the past, so the bar for expert advice is raised. How can companies combine online decision-making tools with personal, expert advice?

The second convergence challenge is to manage the mix of company messages and third-party information. Centaurs are exposed to, and still respond to, advertising, PR, and direct marketing messages that are fired at them daily. But these messages are filtered out more rigorously by consumers that have access to third-party information and are increasingly skeptical about messages that are piped into their homes and heads. How can companies combine the advertising and spin of traditional marketing communications with third-party information sources? How can they balance the messages they want customers to hear with the information and insight consumers want?

The third challenge is related to the way the information flows. Traditionally, the communication has been piped down to passive consumer. Now the flow of information is two-way. The challenge is to effectively combine a mix of *company-pushed* messages and *customer-pulled* information.

There will always be different segments when it comes to advice and decision making. Some people want to do everything themselves. Others want to make the decision, but want some limited advice. A third segment wants nothing better than to turn the decision over to a trusted adviser and head for the golf links. Even a single individual will take these different approaches at different times, and across different types of purchases. A consumer may leave some investments to the discretion of a mutual fund manager while wanting personal control and detailed information for other investments.

In the following sections, we'll examine strategies for addressing each of these sets of convergence challenges.

CONVERGENCE STRATEGIES FOR COMBINING DECISION-MAKING TOOLS AND HUMAN EXPERTISE

Although more powerful tools will continue to erode the advantages of human experts, there will still be a need to cleverly combine human and machine-based decision support. A Wharton study by Stephen Hoch concluded that the strengths and weaknesses of humans and computer models in decision making are complementary. In comparisons of decisions made using models, experts, and a combination of the two, he found that the combination of humans and model leads to better decisions than either one alone. For example, humans are stronger in pattern matching, but weak in memory. The creative leaps of pattern matching are very challenging for machines, but they have much greater retention and access to memory.[9] Human experts also excel in knowing what questions to ask, providing subjective evaluation and adapting to changing conditions. Machines using models are less prone to biases of perception, emotion, or overconfidence. They are also better at weighing all the evidence to make optimal decisions. Finally, machines usually can provide more options than humans (a typical broker might offer customers only 4 or 5 of the hundreds of offerings available through the brokerage house because of limited knowledge) and employ broader criteria for choice.

The words of American writer Elbert Hubbard continue to ring true: "One machine can do the work of fifty ordinary men. No machine can do the work of one extraordinary man." But online decision-making tools will raise the ratio of the machine to the "ordinary" human far above 50 at the same time these developments will continue to raise the bar for what we consider "extraordinary."

When are computer-based models effective and when are human experts needed to provide advice to customers for making decisions?

How can companies combine online tools and personal experts, both online and offline? There are a variety of convergence strategies that can help you use these tools in ways that will be to the company's advantage:

- *Use virtual advisors and agents to increase trust online:* The design of support and advice systems online can increase trust by offering rich information and interactive virtual agents. An MIT study by Glen Urban, Fareena Sultan, and William Qualls found that a prototype site for selling pickup trucks was able to build trust through virtual advisors such as an independent mechanic (paid by the site, not truck manufacturers), a retired editor of an auto magazine or a contractor who has purchased many trucks.

Consumers in the study could also obtain research and information on the trucks and even listen in on conversations by peers in a virtual coffee shop. A combination of these virtual advisors, which used a dialogue-based computer graphical user interface, along with information-intensive sites actually gained more customer acceptance than the existing auto dealer system. More than 80 percent of participants in the study considered the Internet sites more trustworthy than the dealer and viewed the information quality and quantity as better.

How can you use virtual agents to increase trust online?

Some segments preferred straight information to the more lifelike virtual advisors. There was also some segmentation. In general, consumers who had the highest preferences for the virtual advisor were not knowledgeable about trucks, visited more dealers, were younger or were more frequent Internet users.[10]

- *Take the tools to the point of decision:* New portable and wireless technologies make it easier to take decision-making tools to the point where consumers are making decisions. Charlie Palmer's Aureole restaurant in Las Vegas offers diners a handheld wireless electronic book that displays its 3,600 bottle winelist. Customers can sort the list by categories such as red or white, grape type, winery, country, or region. They can also call up reviews and other information about the wines.[11] Portable technologies such as Personal Digital Assistants (PDAs), cellular phones, and electronic books provide opportunities to put decision-making tools right in the hands of consumers when they need them.

- *Charge for advice and decision support:* One of the limits in the development of more sophisticated decision-making models is that initially they have been given away for free. Companies should consider using value-based pricing, either directly or indirectly, for customers using valuable and powerful tools. The current environment, in which companies are giving away decision-making tools to draw traffic to their sites, has led to decision-making support systems that are far more limited than those offered at a premium to managers. These unprofitable business models have delayed the needed development of these systems. The more sophisticated systems used by managers are very expensive, but there is a tremendous opportunity in the middle ground, to offer powerful, easy-to-use decision-making systems directly to consumers and then charge them for this added value. While customers may receive some value from the personalized

Are there opportunities to charge for value-added decision-making tools offered to customers?

recommendations of Amazon, would they be willing to pay more for a much more sophisticated advisor who *really* knows their tastes, doesn't recommend a book related to one they bought as a gift and is right on the mark more often? There is no reason why corporations cannot develop and experiment with these tools.

- *Look for ways to put value-added tools into the hands of consumers:* The decision-making support systems of managers point the way to future developments of consumer tools. Although charging for such tools could make it easier for companies to offer data-mining, collaborative filtering (matching preferences with other customers) and other tools there may also be ways to offer more limited versions of management tools to consumers for little or no cost. There may also be ways to build interfaces to existing internal corporate tools to allow customers to access them directly.

- *Increase the expertise of human experts:* As more of the basic advice and information is available online, the questions that will come to human experts will be the tougher, more idiosyncratic ones—they will be posed by consumers who are much better informed. When patients come into their doctors, they may have more information about treatment options than the physicians (or more misinformation, in many cases). First the doctors need to have access to and facility in using the same information and tools as their patients, and then the physicians have to rethink the type of advice they give, usually increasing its sophistication. The same is true for brokers working with investors who have access to as much information as the brokers. These human experts may need access not only to the decision-making support systems offered to customers, but even deeper knowledge bases and more powerful tools. The interaction of consumers with these experts should also be seen as an opportunity for increasing the

How do you need to change the training and hiring of your human experts in the light of the information and support available to consumers online?

power of the online tools (adding frequently asked questions, for example, or presenting tools to automate solutions to common problems). This empowerment of the consumer offers opportunities for companies—the pharmaceutical firm or brokerage firm—to develop tools that are designed for both consumers and experts.

CONVERGENCE STRATEGIES FOR COMBINING THIRD-PARTY AND COMPANY INFORMATION

There are very different issues related to trust and credibility online and offline. On the one hand, because of the virtual relationship of online advice, it is often harder to establish trust with consumers. On the other hand, concerns about trust are certainly not limited to the online world. People are often suspicious of the motives of brokers and real estate agents (Are they looking after your interests or their own commissions?), lawyers and accountants (Are they just looking for ways to increase their billable hours?), and doctors (Are they trying to minimize costs in response to the HMO? Are they up-to-date? Did their junket to the pharmaceutical company's presentation in Las Vegas influence their decision to prescribe this drug?).

In addition to combining online tools and other expert advice, companies also have to combine the more credible third-party information sources with company information and marketing messages. There are several strategies for effectively combining third-party information with customer messages:

- *Be completely unbiased when you can:* Companies are often reluctant to offer unbiased decision-making tools on their sites because they are afraid of recommending a competitor's product. For example, a visitor might go to the Ford site, search for compact cars, and find out that the best deal for his money is a Toyota. This seems to violate a core principle of advertising, which is typically designed to encourage consumers to select your product over that of a rival. Recommending your competitor's product or service even seems to go against the instinct of organization for self-preservation. This doesn't appear to be something companies should willingly do. But the other way to look at this is that more powerful tools are going to become available, either on your site, on the sites of rivals or a third party, so it might as well be on your site.

Trust is a serious issue when it comes to offering tools on a company's own site. Many customers will assume that these tools will be tilted in favor of the company running the site. So visitors need to be reassured that this is not the case. One way to do this is through third-parties. For example, a recommendation from a site such as Bizrate or CNet might be expected to be more credible and less biased than the company's own site because it includes testing or customer feedback across a variety of sellers.

Another way to build this trust is to show more of the process of making the recommendation. If the process is more transparent, the consumer will have greater confidence that it is not tilted in some way toward the company making the recommendation. The limit of this greater transparency, however, is that the more the customer is exposed to the inner workings of these tools, the more complicated the process becomes. Companies need to balance the consumer's desire for a "black box" that spits out the right answer with the consumer's desire to be able to look under the hood and kick the tires.

There are different segments of consumers. Some "do-it-yourselfers" are very interested in plunging into the details while others are content to receive a straightforward answer that they can act on. Ideally, the company can offer a simple set of tools to the latter segments, but give users in the former segments the option of clicking down for more detail if they wish.

- *Provide both company and competitor information:* You can't afford not to play in this game. Although it may be very difficult to sell your sales organization on the idea of giving consumers these powerful decision-making tools, you will be worse off if consumers receive this information *and* they are already on another site. When American Airlines created its Sabre reservations system, it appeared to be aiding the comparisons of its offerings against those of rivals, but without such complete information on all the airlines, it would never have been accepted as the system of choice by all the travel agents. As a result, Sabre itself ultimately became more profitable for American than its low-margin airline operations. Leading the revolution in decision-making tools may take you in a completely different direction. Further, comparisons do not produce a clear "winner," but only a winner for a specific customer, given his or her unique set of preferences, so the same information that might hurt you in one case might be an advantage in another. (For example, one customer might turn your car down based on fuel efficiency, whereas another will buy the same car because of better performance.) The fact is that your own decision-making tools may lead your customers to purchase a rival product, but you don't have a choice. Either you do it, or someone else will. Either they find these tools on your site or they find them somewhere else. And once you have them on your site, you can influence their choice by the way you frame the decision, and have the option of using other ways to communicate information

How much information do you want to share with customers? Should the organization be completely transparent? What information should you share online or offline?

and messages to create a more meaningful experience. The battle is going to be on whose decision-making tools is the consumer going to use. How do I design the best possible decision-making tool so I can own the desktop (or laptop or Palm Pilot) of the consumer?

- *Offer third-party evaluations:* Companies can create a more compelling site by providing customer comments, such as Amazon's extensive customer reviews, consumer feedback on quality, and service feedback such as Bizrate's rating system. Independent reviews of technology by companies such as CNET can add credibility and information to help consumers make decisions. Although these types of independent information sources have been used as positive endorsements in company advertising in the past, to be credible online both positive and negative information must be included. This creates a challenge for companies who might be reluctant to help others say negative things about their products. This is less of an issue for retailers such as Amazon that offer a broad selection of diverse products, but is more of a challenge for companies. All in all, however, the credibility gained by offering unbiased advice often outweighs the negatives.

- *Differentiate:* In an environment of ubiquitous information, it is important to differentiate your company from the crowd along dimensions that are not easily lined up in a comparison chart. In addition to brand, personalization can also help differentiate your offerings from others. The more you can tailor your advice and your products and services to a specific individual, the less likely customers will be to look at your offering on a comparison chart with many others. If you can recommend the perfect laptop for a customer—and it really is the perfect laptop, not just one for which you have excess inventory—then you create an incentive for the customer not to look anywhere else. Insightful recommendations can add tremendous value to an information source. Consider a restaurant rating service, which pools customer evaluations of restaurants. These reviews are useful, but they might reflect the opinions of customers who have very different tastes and preferences. You may be a connoisseur of fine Italian food, but many of those surveyed may not even like Italian foods. It would be far better if you could sample the opinions of other Italian food aficionados.

How can you use brand and personalization to differentiate your company online and offline?

Recommendations based on a true understanding of the customer's tastes and how they match those of other customers will be much more targeted and valuable.

- *Make unbiased information a selling point:* The issue of trust is important in giving advice, and is becoming even more so. A RAND study reported in the *Journal of the American Medical Association* found that while Internet health sites influence the decisions of 70 percent of those who use them, the information about health found online is often incomplete, confusing, or contradictory.[12] When companies used comparative advertising and marketing pitches in the past, they tended to tilt the playing field in their favor. They looked at attributes on which they knew they could outperform the competition. Sometimes companies can gain greater trust by offering accurate and unbiased information. Sites such as Pricescan.com make a point of stating their neutrality. A FAQ on the site notes: "At Pricescan, we believe that consumers should have access to unbiased reporting on products and prices. It seems obvious to us that if a price guide restricts its listings to those vendors who have paid to be included, then its database more accurately reflects the source of its revenue, not necessarily the best products at the lowest price."

How can you make unbiased information a selling point online and offline?

- *If not, make your biases clear:* If you are tilting the field, you need to make a clear line between expert advice and promotion. This distinction is clear in the magazine world, but it less clear in online retail. For example, Amazon.com drew complaints from customers when it began charging publishers to increase their chances of receiving a top spot on the web site and to appear in customized email recommendations sent to customers. Amazon countered that these types of fees for placement are common practice in bricks-and-mortar bookstores, but the analogy to a physical retail store may be less applicable because the customer understands that product placement is part of marketing. The customer of Amazon treats recommendation much more as editorial. Amazon added buttons that allowed customers to click through to find the sponsored recommendations.[13] It is important to recognize that there are differences in the context of advice in an online and offline setting. There is a difference between product placement offline, where it is seen as promotion, and product "placement," online where it is seen as an expert recommendation.

CONVERGENCE STRATEGIES FOR COMBINING COMPANY PUSH AND CONSUMER PULL

The company once gave consumers the information it wanted them to hear. Now, this has changed. Consumers actively seek out the information they want and they know where to find it. Whereas the customer traditionally was passive, especially in respect to his or her relationship with experts, now the consumer is empowered. In the light of this new behavior, companies need to rethink their communications strategies in a variety of ways:

- *Recognize the limits of marketing messages:* The more information and decision-making tools consumers have at their fingertips, the less companies can control this information. Advertising and direct marketing are less appropriate vehicles for communicating information. For example, comparative ads could traditionally be crafted to favor your own product or service. These can still be used in some instances, particularly today when the decision-making tools are in an early stage of development. But, as consumers have greater access to their own tools that allow them to make unbiased comparisons on dimensions that are important *to them*, the strength of messages pushed through advertising, and other marketing channels may be diminished. If a consumer sees an ad for a new advanced camera, it is unlikely that they will rush out and buy it. They might read online product reviews or consumer feedback. This limits how much you can influence that decision.

- *Build credibility by creating a brand that consumers will recognize and value:* Some believed that the "perfect" information of the Internet would make branding less valuable. Why do consumers need a brand to convey information about product craftsmanship, innovation or quality when they can simply compare products on these attributes through search and comparison engines? The reality is that brands do matter in making products stand out and charging a premium over rivals. The challenge for companies is to create a convergence of online and offline branding that reinforces both.

- *Focus marketing messages on the intangibles and affect:* Although having a great product and excellent service is necessary, it will not always differentiate your offering from those of rivals. The tangible aspects of a product can be summarized in a table and compared with rival products and substitutes with a mouse click on any dimension. As the tangible aspects of a product become more easily compared (lining up products based on price or performance), it is the intangibles that become more important in differentiating your offering. The company's marketing messages can be more effective if they move from emphasizing *information* to increasing emphasis on *affect,* including the type of people and occasions associated with the brand. The aesthetics of design of the product and the promotion are more

As tangible benefits have become more searchable and commoditized, what are the ways to focus your marketing message on intangibles online and offline?

important. Victoria's Secret doesn't emphasize the construction and performance of its products in its online or offline advertising, but rather the romance that they represent.

TWO TYPES OF KNOWLEDGE

Samuel Johnson once said, "There are two types of knowledge. One is knowing a thing. The other is knowing where to find it." The Internet offers powerful tools for both kinds of knowledge. Powerful search engines help consumers find the information they need.

New tools for choice have empowered consumers. But while these tools are providing clear value to consumers, they do not always benefit companies. Given the reality of these empowered consumers, the challenge for companies is to raise the bar for their own offerings to find new ways of creating value for their shareholders and their customers. Companies can create value by offering more powerful tools or providing better integration through combining online tools with human experts and unbiased information with traditional marketing messages.

NOTES

[1] Pew Internet & American Life Project Survey, November-December 2000; May-June 2000; July-August 2000.

[2] Trout, Jack. *Differentiate or Die*, New York: John Wiley & Sons, 2000.

[3] Bradlow, Eric T. and David C. Schmittlein, "The Little Engines That Could: Modeling the Performance of World Wide Web Search Engines," *Marketing Science*, Vol. 19 No. 1 (Winter 2000), pp. 43-62.

[4] Discussed by Steve Andriole at the Wharton Fellows in e-Business program, Philadelphia, May 11, 2001.

[5] Roderick, Daffyd, "File it Under Sharing," *Time*, June 4, 2001, p. 58.

[6] Lotozo, Eils, "Love at First Byte: Personal-Ad Web Sites Booming," *The Philadelphia Inquirer*, April 20, 2001, p. A-1.

[7] More powerful preference models are being developed that make more accurate recommendations than collaborative filtering. See, for example, Ansari, Asim, Skander Essegaier and Rajeev Kohli, " Internet Recommendation Systems," *Journal of Marketing Research*, Vol. 37 (August 2000), pp. 363-375.

[8] Chircu, Alina M. and Robert J. Kauffman, "Show Me The Money: Comparing the Business Value of Traditional and Electronic B2B Procurement Systems," working paper, Carlson School of Management, University of Minnesota, 2000.

[9] Hoch, Stephen J., "Combining Models with Intuition," *Wharton on Making Decisions*, Stephen J. Hoch and Howard C. Kunreuther, eds., New York: John Wiley & Sons, 2001, pp. 81-101.

[10] Urban, Glen L., Fareena Sultan, and William Qualls, "Design and
Evaluation of a Trust Based Advisor on the Internet," Working Paper, July
19, 1999, MIT, http://ebusiness.mit.edu.

[11] Shriver, Jerry, "Las Vegas Diners Mull Wine Selection Digitally," *USA
Today*, June 29, 2001.

[12] Pugh, Tony, "Online Medical Advice is Incomplete, Study Says," *Austin
American-Statesman*, May 23, 2001.

[13] Wingfield, Nick and Matthew Rose, "Amazon Plans to Charge Publishers
Fee for Online Recommendations," *The Wall Street Journal*, February 7,
2001, p. B-1.

PART
3

MASTERING
CONVERGENCE
MARKETING

The rise of the centaur means that organizations that had rethought their approaches to marketing with the emergence of the Internet now need to rethink them again. We examined, in Part 2, some of the ways the interaction of the consumer and technology leads to new solutions in the critical 5 Cs of customerization and personalization, community, channels, competitive value, and choice tools. What do these changes mean for marketing and business strategies?

Marketing has traditionally played a boundary role between the organization and its environment, yet the shape of this boundary is changing. The boundary between the consumer, technology, and company is the area in which both marketing strategy and business strategies are converging. And these changes are calling for a new set of convergence marketing strategies.

Marketing, in the context of the changing interactions of the company, consumer, and technology, requires a new role, as shown in this figure. In addition to just assuring marketing excellence as it relates to marketing decisions, marketing offers a perspective and guiding principles for all business and corporate decisions. Marketing must play a key role in identifying growth opportunities and using creative approaches to capture these opportunities by offering solutions that create value for the consumer, the firm, and other stakeholders. Marketing can also be applied to internal constituents to help guide organizational change and connect different parts of the organization with consumers and other parts of the environment.

This section explores these implications of the hybrid consumer at the intersection of the consumer, technology, and the company. In Chapter 8, we focus on the growth opportunities created by the convergence of traditional marketing and cyber-marketing and the convergence of marketing and business strategies. In Chapter 9, we explore some of the new "convergence marketing" strategies in more detail, including how the centaur is transforming marketing's traditional 4 Ps.

8

TRANSFORMING MARKETING

*"There are two fools in every market;
one who asks too little, one who asks too much."*

Russian Proverb

TRADITIONAL CONSUMER

"The marketers on the Internet thought they could ignore traditional value equations, giving things away that had value. They asked too little, and lost their businesses as a result. We need to bring back traditional marketing approaches."

CYBERCONSUMER

"The traditional marketers undermined their reach and development by focusing too much on short-term profitability. They don't understand that the dynamics of the Internet are fundamentally different. When you have critical mass and interaction, that is priceless. In a winner-takes-all network economy, the only thing that counts is capturing market share as soon as possible."

THE CENTAUR

"Instead of arguing over price, we need to redefine how we see value, positioning, and other marketing fundamentals. How does the new hybrid environment allow the company to rethink its value equation? What new opportunities are created by redefining markets? The value is not in what you charge, but how you rethink the business."

CONVERGENCE QUESTIONS

>>> *What does the new hybrid consumer mean for the practice of marketing?*

>>> *What new opportunities are created by the global reach and interactive nature of the Internet?*

Transforming Marketing

As the consumer connects much more directly to the company, marketing may appear to be "disintermediated." But actually it has a deeper role to play in spanning the complex organizational boundary to create a combined marketing and business strategy. In this chapter, we examine how the centaur is reshaping the role of marketing and creating new opportunities.

Harry Shaw is Chief Marketing Officer of a major retailer. He watches the rise of Amazon.com at the end of the 1990s with horror, as each department in his store is slowly added to the menu tabs at the top of Amazon's home page. Books, music, videos, tools and hardware, electronics, cameras, toys, gardening, health and beauty, kitchen, and housewares. Would this juggernaut never be stopped? How could he respond? He hastily throws up a web site, creating a separate organization to run it, and then sits back and waits.

Not only are customers not pleased by the move, but they are upset—with him. They want to be able to return the products they buy online in the retail stores, but his systems can't handle it. They want a broader selection and integrated customer service by phone and e-mail, but he is just not prepared for the volume. Then they begin posting complaints about his online operations in chatrooms. And then, worse still, they just ignore him. He pumps up his banner advertising, but the millions of dollars he invests flashed by without result. He just can't figure out how to market online, so he turns his attention back to his tried-and-true newspaper circulars and television ads, hoping to make the best of it. As Amazon's stock price rises into the stratosphere, surpassing $100 per share, Harry Shaw's spirits drop into the basement.

At the beginning of 2000, a little joy comes back into Harry Shaw's life. The dot-coms plummet and investors start to nip at the heels of Amazon. Harry Shaw breaths a sigh of relief as he watches Amazon's share price continue its free fall, bottoming out at just north of $8 per share by April 2001. It is all a bad dream after all! But, just as he begins to relax, Harry Shaw receives another shock. He notices major retailers such as Wal-Mart and Kmart creating coherent Internet strategies that capitalize on both bricks and clicks. These players are already his competitors. He watches as Amazon begins to forge powerful relationships with offline retailers such as Toys 'R' Us and Borders. This virus of the Internet is not gone; it has mutated into a more deadly strain. The dot-coms were just the warm-up act. The real players are arriving. These companies and their customers are reshaping the value equation and their business models. How can he transform his marketing strategy for this new hybrid world? But more fundamentally, how is his business changing and what are the opportunities for growth in this new environment?

THE IMPACT OF THE CENTAUR

The changes in the consumer described in the preceding chapters have significant implications for the practice of marketing. The demand for customerization means that the process of building products and targeting segments has been transformed. The establishment of physical and virtual communities means that the nature of the interaction of companies with customers has been changed. The creation of new channels means that companies need to manage across complex webs of marketing and distribution. The rise of new pricing models and value equations means that traditional approaches to pricing and revenue models need to be reconsidered. Technology creates greater interactivity and transparency, and has transformed product development and the supply chain. Finally, placing powerful decision-making tools in the hands of consumers means that the balance of power between companies and customers have been radically altered. The new hybrid consumers expect to be able to balance standardized products with customerization—from the products and services they buy, to the information they seek, to the price they are willing to pay. They expect to get what they want, when they want it, 24 hours a day seven days a week.

Most important, many consumers are no longer content to be passive recipients of marketing messages. They want an active role. They want to be able to engage the producer in the kind of tussle that used to characterize the bazaar. Only now this ad hoc and localized activity has become universal, free-flowing, and non-stop on a global scale.

THE DISINTERMEDIATION OF MARKETING

Marketing has traditionally served as the interface between the company and the external environment. It was, in effect, an intermediary. But like most intermediaries in a networked world, its role is now fundamentally changing in an environment in which customers and the organization can connect much more directly. Like airline travel agents, booksellers, and other intermediaries, marketing has to reinvent itself. Instead of being the intermediary between the organization and the external world, marketing is now a dynamic facilitator of direct connection between the company and consumer.

To meet the reality of the hybrid consumer, companies have to meet two convergence challenges as illustrated in Exhibit 8–1. First, they need to join together their traditional marketing and cybermarketing strategies. Second, as the interaction with customers becomes more integral to the business, companies also need to more closely align their marketing strategies with business and coporate strategies.

Is marketing being "disintermediated" in your organization? What new roles can marketing play as an intermediary between the company and its environment? How can you combine traditional marketing strategies with cybermarketing strategies?

EXHIBIT 8-1

SEEING NEW OPPORTUNITIES FOR GROWTH

Marketing, at its core, is focused on identifying new opportunities for growth. Where are the new customers? What do they want? How can existing product and service lines be extended or new ones be created to reach them? And how can we build and deepen our relationships with current customers?

The emergence of the Internet—which has made industry and geographic boundaries more fluid—significantly changed the shape of these opportunities and the tools and strategies available to marketers to understand them. Now, the emergence of the new hybrid consumer is creating a new set of growth opportunities. In an environment of rapid change, the role of marketing is changing and its importance is deepening. If you expect more of your future growth to come from businesses or markets that are not your traditional ones, then the process of identifying these new opportunities is vital to your success, and perhaps survival.

The identification and development of opportunities comes from focusing on ways customers, competitors, or the business environment might be changing. Some companies have developed sophisticated systems for tracking current competitors and others have focused on the emerging needs of customers. But managers need to look beyond their current rivals to new industries that might present threats and opportunities if the industry boundaries are reconfigured. Current competition is often defined too narrowly. A bank may define its competitors too narrowly as other banks, but competition may come from brokers, life insurance companies or even a company such as Microsoft. Managers also have to go beyond talking to their existing customers to identify the potential new markets that might emerge. You need to consider: What are the opportunities created by the new technology? What is it now possible for you to do that you couldn't do before? What current opportunities will continue?

Consider several examples of opportunities for convergence marketing opened up by this new hybrid consumer: redefining markets, reaching forgotten segments, and focusing on maximizing the lifetime value of the customer.

Redefining Markets:
Selling Beverages and Competing for Time

The convergence of online and offline markets can present opportunities for reshaping the competitive space. A classic example is the breakthrough cross-industry merger of offline Time Warner and online AOL, that redefined both their industries.

AOL Time Warner sees its competitors not only as other media companies or online portals, but any activities that compete for the time and attention of the consumer. "AOL is competing for time," Joseph Ripp, Executive Vice President and CFO of America Online, told a session of the Wharton Fellows in e-Business program in New York. "The consumer today is very busy and the things we offer take their time. Ours is a product you must consume with your eyes, minds, and heart. Anything that takes that time is a competitor. We take the amount of time spent online as a measure of success at AOL."

This view changes how the company defines its markets and approaches these markets. It also explains why AOL did not see itself as an Internet Service Provider or portal, but rather an entertainment and information company, a view that already has significantly expanded its marketing opportunities.

But managers in any single industry can also think creatively about redefining their markets based on a consumer perspective. For example, The Coca-Cola Company, which had long seen itself locked in fierce but narrowly defined cola wars with rival Pepsi, redefined the playing field in its 1999 annual report. In the report, the company reported that it sold 1 billion servings of its products daily, but rather than gloating about its market share, it pointed out the sobering fact that it had "47 billion to go." The report notes, "This year, even as we sell 1 billion servings of our products daily, the world will still consume 47 billion servings of other beverages *every day*. We're just getting started." Instead of competing against other sodas, the company redefined its market as all beverages, putting it head-to-head with tea, coffee, and water.[1]

General Electric found that forcing all its business units to be number one or number two in their industries led managers to create narrow and rigid definitions of their industries. So GE leadership asked managers to take a very different approach: to define their markets in such a way that they would have a mere 10 percent share or less. As the executive team wrote in the 2000 annual report, "Rather than the increasingly limited market opportunity that had come from this number-one or number–two definition that had once served us so well, we now had our eyes widened to the vast opportunity that lay ahead for our product and service offerings."[2]

Online interactions with consumers create new opportunities for understanding potential market shifts. eBay's creation of product categories, based on customer postings on its auction site, allows it to reinforce and identify patterns of the market that are appearing among its membership base. In addition to monitoring these micromarkets of individual sellers, the auctions conducted by companies such as Sun Microsystems and Disney on its site offer eBay a unique window on customer interactions in other industries and markets. The company sees where the parade is going and then gets out in front to "lead" it by establishing internal sales groups that develop these categories such as autos, computers, and consumer electronics. This approach of redefining markets focuses on the customer's view of the world and optimization of benefits rather than **How can you use the Internet to redefine your market to create new opportunities? How can you redefine your current market so that you have less than a 10 percent share?** traditional industry SIC codes. It also looks to future market definitions rather than being limited by the current reality.

Rethinking Global Markets and the Digital Divide

The Internet creates a convergence of global markets. There are no passports, visas, airline tickets, and reservations required. The Web gives companies in the developed world access to markets they would traditionally not find attractive to approach. These "invisible" markets could represent important markets today and they will be even more important markets in the future as these nations rapidly develop and incomes rise. The new technology is also spreading rapidly in these regions. A study by Telecompetition predicts that the use of wireless devices for data will grow twice as quickly in underdeveloped parts of the world between now and 2010 than in the so-called First World.[3]

As an example of how quickly new ideas can penetrate global markets, when Wharton recently launched an online research newsletter—Knowledge@Wharton—it attracted more than 1,000 subscribers from 33 countries within the first 48 hours, without advertising.

But having a passport to the world is not enough. When you arrive, you have to understand local languages and customs. And even more important, you have to understand how different the dynamics of marketing to emerging economies are from marketing to developed ones. As we have seen with hybrid consumers in developed countries, new "online" markets in developing nations will require an understanding of the virtual connections and the human quirks and needs of the potential consumer.

Most of our marketing strategies are targeted toward the developed world, with GDP per capita above $10,000, or to high-income segments of developing nations. This has left more than 80 percent of the world's population completely out of the sights of most marketers.[4] Although these poorer parts of the world do not have high disposable income individually, they collectively represent a huge market. Companies, such as Colgate in India, have carried their marketing for toothpaste and toothbrushes into remote villages. The microbusinesses supported by Grameen Bank also show the potential of creative strategies for reaching these markets.[5] For example, instead of selling wireless phone service to individuals, entrepreneurs in small villages buy the service and then sell calls to individuals in the village. If you continue to tailor your messages and strategies to the elite (either focusing on developed nations or high-end segments within developing countries), you will miss the opportunities of these markets. What physical local presence do you need to build the trust and the expertise to establish online markets? How do you use powerful tools for customizing language and other aspects of the product to quickly offer it to a variety of diverse markets? How can you tap into local communities to build online communities? How do you have to change your logistics to deliver your products and services to these regions? How do your existing products and services need to be changed to meet the specific challenges of these markets?

Tools for language customization open opportunities for reaching these markets. Where products once had to be shipped with instructions in a specific language, virtual product manuals now allow consumers to pull up product information in their own languages. These systems also allow companies to offer information in far more languages without the time and cost constraints of printing and distribution. Although English remains the dominant language on the Internet, with 230 million English speakers expected online in 2003, Chinese speakers are projected to rise to 160 million in that period, Japanese speakers to 58 million, and Spanish speakers to 60 million. Multiple languages and automatic language translation will be increasingly critical for websites, telephone, and other interaction with consumers from diverse locations.

The size of these invisible market segments may be underestimated by looking at the number of computers with Internet access. Customers may enter through a community center, school, office, library, or a shared connection that can support a far larger number of customers than may be apparent by tracking online connections. Like the multiple readers that swell magazine circulation, Internet access is far wider than can be seen by counting machines and online accounts. This is particularly true in developing nations, where constrained resources make sharing equipment more likely. Also, growth of the Internet in areas such as Korea and China has exploded rapidly, so today's numbers may have little to do with the future potential. Customers in these countries may not have credit cards, but they can be reached with pre-paid debit cards that can be used for online shopping.

Similarly within developed countries, forgotten segments are coming online. The worthy public policy concern over the "digital divide" may blind managers to how quickly this divide is closing on its own. With the growth of the Internet, the digital divide appears to be narrowing and there has been rapid growth across the whole spectrum of socioeconomic segments.[7] Companies need to understand these segments and tailor their strategies to them. There is only so much potential for Internet penetration in the U.S. and developed nations, and this field is quite crowded. The future may be found across the digital divide to the untapped segments that have been traditionally overlooked. These present tremendous opportunities for companies with the vision and understanding to reach them.

How can you use the Internet to reach "forgotten" markets at home and abroad? How do you need to transform your marketing strategies to reach these emerging markets?

Maximizing Lifetime Value of the Customer

As companies have become more sophisticated in building and maintaining relationships—the kind of relationships that the Internet and new technologies help stimulate, monitor, and support—the focus on the value of long-term relationships with customers has intensified.

There are a variety of strategies for maximizing the lifetime value of the customer. First, in the short-term, the company needs to develop migration strategies to move customers to higher-value services. Companies have analyzed their own customers to discover ways to increase their overall lifetime value. If banking customers have a mortgage and checking account, their overall value might be much higher if they also had a credit card. It might be well worthwhile for the bank to take actions to encourage them to accept the credit card.

The second stage is to move to lifetime management. For example, online discount brokerages have allowed more people to invest in the market, and as these families grow, the companies can provide more service and advice on issues like planning for college or retirement. This focus has always been a general principle in some industries—such as automobile makers who created full lines of cars to try to develop loyal buyers for life (for example, moving customers from the BMW 3 series to 5 to 7). But now, across virtually every product category, there is greater attention to understanding and maximizing the lifetime value of the customer, and there are far more sophisticated tools for analyzing and improving the lifetime value.

The third level is to focus on "life event" management. SEI Investments, for example, is developing services that focus on the overall financial wellness of the customer. They take care of any issue the customer has—from providing information online to referring the customer to specific experts for solutions to life events and offering solutions to the associated financial challenges or opportunities. For example, if a client has a serious medical crisis, advisors would help find medical assistance while addressing the financial challenges of paying for health care.

Some companies, such as credit card firms, have used sophisticated analytics and strategies to "cherry pick" just the most valuable customers from rivals (for example, by offering balance transfers). The combination of online and offline channels affects this value in two ways. First, it offers additional ways for companies to develop new, long-term revenue streams from customers. These online revenue streams can be added to the offline streams for a single customer, *if* companies have integrated databases to make such assessments. But the second, and more, important way the Web creates opportunities to maximize the lifetime value of customers is its power for establishing and strengthening ongoing relationships. Although a traditional music company might be able to count on one or two purchases from a customer, online music communities such as the model pioneered by

What is the lifetime value of your customers? What can you do to increase and capitalize on the value through online and offline relationships?

CD-Now (now part of Bertelsmann Music Group) might be able to count on multiple sales from customers who share information and passion for different musical groups. Loyal customers interacting in a community with similar musical tastes, and subscription models, such as the one under consideration by Napster/Bertelsmann, could also lead to recurring revenue streams from these customers.

NEW BUSINESS PARADIGMS

The opportunities illustrated above, and the changes in marketing as a result of the new hybrid consumer, create the potential for new business paradigms and associated new value propositions. These paradigms are not merely new approaches to marketing, but new approaches to the business. The rise of the centaur offers a chance to shift the value proposition, reshape the concept of positioning, and develop new business and revenue models.

As discussed previously, the value equation is being rewritten by new consumer capabilities and business applications, including new pricing and distribution models. The value equation is also transformed by customerization, community, and decision-making tools. These and other changes can undermine existing business models and create opportunities for the development of new ones. As Xerox CEO Paul Allaire stated candidly in explaining Xerox's free-fall during a conference call with analysts, "We have an unsustainable business model."[8] Many other companies have found their business models challenged by the changing realities of the market.

Moving to Integrated Solutions and Pricing Models

One substantial shift in the business paradigm is the move from selling products to offering complete solutions—integrating online and offline, product and service and information. Consider the example of a pharmaceutical firm that has traditionally focused on developing and selling pills as shown in the lower left of Exhibit 8–2. The customer doesn't just want a pill, however. The customer desires wellness. A pill might help achieve wellness, but the customer might also use exercise, diet, nutraceuticals, acupuncture, prayer, and other approaches.

Instead of selling a pill, the company might connect the consumer to other resources in achieving wellness. For example, the consumer could be linked to a web site with exercise programs on streaming video, tools for planning exercise and diet regimens, recipes and diet plans tailored to patients with the particular disease, and online support groups that create a community. The company could even link the consumer to others who might provide therapies such as acupuncture or spiritual counseling. By providing these additional online offerings, the pharmaceutical firm moves closer to the concept of offering "wellness" instead of merely selling a pill.

Pfizer, for example, announced an innovative public/private partnership in June 2001 with Florida to provide health care to Medicaid patients. The program combines innovative technologies with face-to-face care by trained nurses to encourage patients to take a more active role in managing their own health while reducing expensive trips to the emergency room. The program uses technology-based disease management to educate and track patients. It also includes health literacy and

EXHIBIT 8–2 MOVE TOWARD INTERGRATED SOLUTIONS

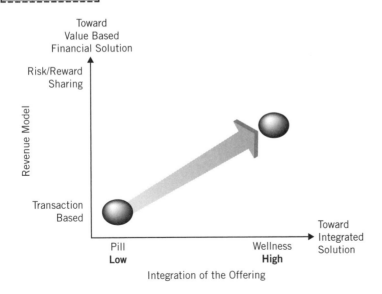

training, as well as expanded drug donations. The improvement of health care management is expected to save the Florida Agency for Health Care Administration $30 million, primarily in emergency care costs.[9]

There are opportunities for similar shifts from focusing on products to integrated solutions in other diverse industries, including telecommunications and financial services. Some of the more progressive financial services companies, such as Charles Schwab and Fidelity Investments, offer a wide range of information, connections, and solutions to consumers, addressing financial questions that go far beyond their own specific products and services.

New Revenue Models

The challenge is that if companies change the nature of their offerings and their business models, they also need to rethink their revenue models, as presented in the vertical dimension of Exhibit 8–2. If a pharmaceutical company begins to deliver total wellness solutions, but is still charging by the pill, it will incur huge additional costs to support these new activities without a return on these investments. As they create total solutions, companies have to simultaneously move to more innovative, relationship-based revenue models—sharing the risks and rewards and ideally establishing recurrent streams of revenues—as shown by the pathway in Exhibit 8–3. Integrated product and service solutions allow companies to price by total cost of ownership (the cost of the product, usage, maintenance, and disposal across its entire life cycle) and to bundle together products and services, rather than pricing the product alone.

More integrated views of the product/service offering can lead to revenue models in which the "product" may be given away with a commitment to a set of services. Kevin Kelly calls this strategy "follow the free" in his book *New Rules for the New Economy*, and notes that "plain old phone service will soon be essentially free, but consumers will pay for mobile phones, call waiting, fax lines, modem lines and caller ID blocking."[10] This strategy also has been used increasingly with personal computers and Internet access and one can even

EXHIBIT 8–3 COHERENT REVENUE MODELS FOR INTERGRATED SOLUTIONS

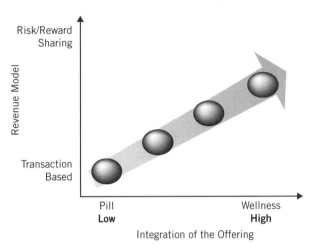

imagine that it might be applied to automobiles within a few years. Automakers may give away their low-end models if customers sign up for insurance, wireless service, maintenance plans, and other ongoing services.

This leads to a shift that author Jeremy Rifkin describes as moving from selling products to providing "access." He notes the example of a company that sold lawn sprinkler systems that moved from selling the hardware to selling access to "sprinkling." It integrated its sprinklers into a sophisticated weather tracking system so the watering of the lawns could be automatically tailored to local weather conditions.[11] The sprinklers are physical, but the information about weather conditions and regulation of the sprinkling are virtual, information-based services that are easily distributed online. As the company moved to this new business model, its revenue model shifted from a one-time transaction of the purchase of a sprinkler to an on-going relationship in the form of a subscription to its service. The delivery of these integrated solutions also has significant implications for the design of the entire supply chain.

One of the initial challenges of moving to new pricing models with recurring charges for value-added services was that in the early development of the Internet, new companies believed that it was a "winner takes all" game, so they focused on building traffic at any cost. This led to revenue models that were absurd in any other context. (As the joke goes, the concept was to "sell at a loss, and make it up on volume.") Since companies were giving away valuable services, it made it harder to implement revenue models that extracted the value created from providing integrated solutions.

How can you offer more integrated solutions to your customers? How do you need to rethink your corresponding revenue models?

The renewed focus on profitability has made it easier for companies to introduce new revenue models that capture the true value created for customers.

New Sources of Value

In addition to reshaping the value proposition and revenue models, companies need to recognize new sources of value from online activities. Wharton Professor Raffi Amit and Christoph Zott of INSEAD, examining e-business firms, found four key sources of value that account for a significant portion of the value created by the companies:[12]

- *Novelty:* The novelty of the offering can add to the value it creates.

- *Lock-in:* Value is created by switching costs or other ways that customers are locked into the site. For example, customers who create a customized "My Yahoo" page are less likely to invest the time to go through the process at another site.

- *Complementarities:* The Internet offers the ability to bring together diverse resources. For example, the small business site Everdream has brought together a bundle of computers, Internet access, and support for small businesses that increase the value of its overall offering.

- *Efficiency:* Efficiency is the most obvious source of value from e-business models. The Amazon one-click makes the purchase of books much faster, and Peapod's standardized lists speed repurchasing (although as we have stressed throughout the book, customers are not always interested primarily in efficiency).

Other studies indicate other drivers that may contribute to the performance and survival of companies, including the extent of verticalization, enthusiasm of its customer base, consistency in product execution, and metrics-centered culture.[13]

CONVERGENCE OF MARKETING AND BUSINESS STRATEGIES

Although marketing, technology, and business decisions have typically been considered in separate spheres, they need to come together in convergence marketing. All key business decisions should start with a consideration of the consumer in his competitive environment, including:

- What business to be in (note the implications of the customer-driven business paradigm shown in Exhibit 8–2)?

- What type of business models?

- What type of revenue models?

- What portfolio of countries?

- What portfolio of segments?

- What merger and acquisition strategy?

- What strategic alliance strategy?

- What location, etc.?

Since the centaur is found in the intersection of the consumer, technology, and company, these issues need to be considered together. Fundamentally, there is no business decision one can make without reflection on its implications for customers. Even IT strategy should reflect not only the technology needs of company users, but also how the technology could be used to help solve the problems of customers.

Too often, managers determine strategy by looking internally, but we also have to take into account how the systems we develop can help meet customer needs. Since marketing has the concepts and methods to better understand the changing consumers, and their likely actions and reactions, marketing can play a critical role in all business strategy.

Make the Voice of the Customer Heard in Every Decision

One of the roles of marketing today is to ensure that we inject the presence of the voice of the hybrid consumer in to everything we do. We need to make sure the voice of the customer is heard in every decision.

In R&D decisions, we need to make sure the voice of the customer is heard. Even though we can't always expect the consumer to be the innovator and develop new products for the company, we have to understand how a new product or technology fits into the changing lifestyle of the consumer. Working collaboratively with consumers leads to products that more closely meet their needs. The closer consumers from the various target segments work with the company on the development of new products and services, the faster the new product development process and the higher the likelihood of success.

In designing customer-relationship management systems, we need to focus on more than minimizing costs but rather to make them most effective from the customer point of view. Many corporate decisions are driven by concerns about internal efficiency rather than the joint optimization of benefits to the company and the consumer.

In human resources, we need to treat recruiting, nurturing, and retaining employees from a marketing perspective. How can we position the company to these external "customers" and how can we keep them loyal so we retain them after they are hired? These are not human resource questions, but rather marketing questions.

The consumer is rapidly changing and the only way to understand these changes is to keep your eye on the customer. While companies often start with their own organizations or technologies, this becomes dangerous in an environment in which the customer is changing. Today, more than ever, you need to start with the customer and work your way back to the business. Every question, every deliberation should start with an identification of the customers and their changing needs.

This ultimately leads to a need for market-driven strategy supported by a market-driven organization.[14] Marketing perspectives are deeply integrated into the strategy process. And a marketing perspective is woven into the fabric of the organization so that managers across the company can focus on the value creation process.

How do you need to change your business strategy to support convergence marketing and reach the new hybrid consumer?

Implications for Marketing Strategies

How can these broader opportunities for growth and new paradigms be translated into specific marketing strategies? How do we need to reexamine the 4 Ps and other marketing fundamentals in the light of the emerging hybrid consumer? Building on this overview of the shifts in marketing, Chapter 9 examines specific "convergence marketing" strategies for meeting the hybrid consumer.

- Create a set of websites for your business based on radically different pricing, promotion and distribution models. Appoint individual champions to create these sites and then invite a small test market of consumers to come onto these sites. What approaches are effective? What strategies should you roll out across the organization? **How can you use these insights to design a second generation of experiments?**

- Identify new opportunities for business and marketing strategies. In what ways are your business, technology and marketing strategies separate? **How can you bring them together?**

- Reexamine the role of marketing. To what extent can marketing considerations and likely customer reactions be integrated into your corporate decisions?

- Using the GE model, how can you redefine your markets so that you control less than 10 percent of your market? What are the opportunities in this view?

- Pick a single developing country to study. What businesses have been successful there? What strategies are they using? How could you change your strategies to reach these "hidden" markets profitably? **Where else can you look for similar opportunities?**

- Take Exhibit 8–2 and develop it fully for your business. How can you move toward an integrated solution? How would you need to change your pricing to realize that solution? Can you identify several combined strategies along the diagonal of Exhibit 8–3?

We invite you to share the results of these activities and suggest other action memos at the Convergence Marketing Forum (www.convergencemarketingforum.com)

NOTES

[1] Coca-Cola, 1999 Annual Report.

[2] General Electric, 2000 Annual Report.

[3] Study by Telecompetition Inc., July 2001, http://www.internetnews.com/prod-news/article/0,,9_794381,00.html.

[4] Mahajan, Vijay, Marcos V. Pratini De Moraes and Jerry Wind, "The Invisible Global Market," *Marketing Management* (Winter 2000) , pp.31-35.

[5] Yunus, Muhammad and Alan Jolis, *Banker to the Poor: Micro-Lending and the Battle Against World Poverty*, New York: Public Affairs, 1999.

[6] Andruss, Paula Lyon, "Speak the Language and Be Heard," *Marketing News*, June 4, 2001, p. 3.

[7] Pew Internet & American Life Project, November-December 2000, and Wharton Virtual Test Market, 2001.

[8] Colvin, Geoffrey. "It's the Business Model, Stupid!" *Fortune*, January 8, 2001, p. 54.

[9] "Pfizer and Florida to Work Together on Innovative Program To Improve Health Care for Approximately 50,000 Florida Medicaid Patients," Pfizer company press release, June 26, 2001.

[10] Kelly, Kevin, *New Rules for the New Economy: 10 Radical Strategies for a Connected World*, New York: Viking Press, 1998.

[11] Rifkin, Jeremy. *The Age of Access*, New York: J. P. Tarcher, 2001.

[12] Amit, Raffi and Christoph Zott, "Value Creation in e-Business," *Strategic Management Journal* Vol. 22, pp. 493-520, 2001.

[13] Columbus, Louis, AMR Research, personal communication.

[14] Day, George S. *The Market Driven Organization*, New York: The Free Press, 2000.

9

CONVERGENCE MARKETING STRATEGIES

"I know that half the money I spend on advertising is wasted; but I can never find out which half."

John Wanamaker

TRADITIONAL CONSUMER

"Advertising is tried and true. It gets results, even if some of them are not directly measurable. I'm sticking to traditional ads. If half my ad budget is wasted offline, as John Wanamaker says, I'm pretty sure the entire ad budget is wasted online. We shouldn't get swept away. We should keep using the same approaches to marketing we always have."

CYBERCONSUMER

"The Internet allows us to approach marketing in a way that is more customized, more interactive, more targeted, and more precise. Unlike John Wanamaker, we know who is clicking through on our ads online. And this is just one of the many ways the Web has changed the practice of marketing forever."

THE CENTAUR

"The power of the Internet is in reshaping the value equation for the consumer and the company. The centaur can be brought directly into the organization and work in collaboration in building communities, designing customized products, and setting prices. It is not an us-against-them battle in which ad dollars are the ammunition."

CONVERGENCE QUESTIONS

>>>*How do the traditional 4 Ps of marketing need to be rethought in the new environment?*

>>>*What market-driven business strategies are needed to meet the emerging needs of the hybrid consumer and take advantage of the combination of online and offline channels?*

Convergence Marketing Strategies

What do the changes in marketing discussed in the previous chapter mean for marketing strategy? In this chapter, we consider how managers need to rethink the traditional 4 Ps of marketing, along with strategies for segmentation, positioning, customer relationships, branding, and marketing research.

Paul Mansey, the CEO of a major music company, arrives in his office early in the morning and is preparing for a meeting with his brand managers later that day. He is deeply concerned about his marketing strategy. The entire strategy is built around selling CDs through recording company brands, each with a clear identity and market niche. But the night before at home, he was talking to a classmate of his teenage daughter who spent every evening downloading music through Gnutella. He stifled his immediate reaction to express outrage over the theft of intellectual property rights, and listened to the somewhat eclectic and rapidly shifting musical tastes of this young music fan. Her interests cut across artists and genres and were driven more by recommendations by friends and communities online than by anything he was firing out at her through his marketing organization. While he was spending tons of money promoting the label, it made no difference to her. She was only interested in the content.

He realizes that this 16-year-old girl is fundamentally changing his business. His product, which he saw as the atoms of CDs, is rapidly dissolving into downloadable bits. His pricing, which was based on selling customers a full album for a single high price, is being challenged by people who would download a single song and expect to get it for free or very little. His promotion, which was based on advertising on MTV and other networks, concert tours and radio play, is now being swept away by more powerful word-of-mouth communities. And the location of his business, once clearly centered in the record stores, is being blown to the winds. His brands were the focus of his efforts, but it is obvious that his customers only cared about the artists. The brand plays no role in their purchase decisions.

When he had earned his MBA, he learned about the 4 Ps of marketing (product, price, promotion, and place), but now all of these 4 Ps are being challenged by this one teenage centaur. He had, of course, known that all these changes were taking place in his industry, but it is the combination of his discussion with his daughter's friend and his forthcoming planning meeting with his brand managers that causes him to step back and take a look at the big picture. And now he is surprised by what he sees. He pulls down his old college marketing textbook. As he thumbs through the pages, it seems to him in many ways that some of the concepts are quaint anachronisms.

On the other hand, as he thinks more about it, he takes comfort in the fact that the revolution is not absolute. He is still selling a substantial number of CDs, according to his traditional models, and even quite a few through new channels such as Amazon. His company has formed a joint venture to create an online music service, with subscription revenues. Through this strategy, in combination with legal attacks against the music swapping services, he expects to be able to lure many of the renegade Napster and Gnutella users back into the fold.

But still, his strategies for marketing—and perhaps his marketing organization—cannot remain the same. He needs to be able to address new consumer demands that he has never had to address before. He needs to allow for greater customization of the product. He has to find a way to tap into communities of customers. He needs to integrate the new channels into his existing organization. He has to rethink his value proposition. And he has to look for ways to offer new tools to help customers find music they like.

As he prepares for his meeting with his brand managers, it seems that his entire marketing strategy and organization are out of sync with the emerging world his daughter and her friends inhabit. How does he need to rethink the 4 Ps of marketing in the age of the centaurs? How does he need to rethink his strategies for segmentation, positioning, customer relationships, branding, and marketing research? What should he say to these brand managers when they walk through the door of his office?

TURNING MARKETING ON ITS HEAD

Modern marketing and its tools came of age during the heyday of television and mass markets. Convergence marketing comes of age during an age of customer empowerment, interconnectivity, a time of increasing customization, customer-driven processes, and interactive communications.

The Internet turned marketing on its head, as illustrated in Exhibit 9–1. Traditionally, the company dictated the flow of communications and used back-office technology as a tool in this process. The rise of the Internet changed the balance of power, putting technology and tools in the hands of customers. These empowered customers began finding their own information, creating communities and making demands for changes in company pricing, service, and other strategies. The flow was reversed. At the same time, companies armed themselves for this new challenge with sophisticated technologies for datamining and personalization.

The flow of convergence marketing is no longer one way but rather two way. Technology is not the arsenal used by customers and companies, but rather it is the glue that connects the company and consumers. It is a collaborative, co-production

EXHIBIT 9–1 REVERSING, THEN CONVERGING

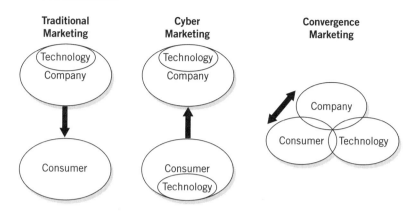

Traditional Marketing · Cyber Marketing · Convergence Marketing

process. The reality for marketing, as for the consumer, is a hybrid of the old and the new. The arrows flow in both directions. To meet the challenge of the centaur, companies need to understand the intersections between traditional and cyber marketing, keeping some traditional approaches to marketing, adding new approaches, and modifying others. Companies need to manage a new set of relationships with consumers.

Even our traditional marketing metaphors fail in describing these new relationships. We use hunting metaphors such as "targeting" customers, or military metaphors such as "guerrilla marketing," as if marketing were a form of a hunt or a battle, when in fact we are now much more concerned with "interaction" with customers and the creation of value networks.[1]

THE FOUR Ps REDEFINED

Although they are by no means comprehensive, the "4 Ps" (product, price, promotion, and place) have been a convenient shorthand that is a cornerstone of traditional marketing strategy. The changes in these 4 Ps offer insights into the impact of the hybrid consumer on marketing. Each of these Ps continues to be important today, but each has been transformed by the Internet. This transformation raises new challenges, new wrinkles in how these are applied, and new opportunities. Consider each of these in turn.

Convergence of Product

The whole definition of the product is changing. There is a convergence of physical and digital products, and bundling of products and services into a total customer experience. The ability of the customer to configure the product means a greater interaction before purchase. The product may be linked to community. For example, in marketing the movie *The Perfect Storm*, AOL Time Warner offered downloads of movie clips and other interactions related to the film on its AOL site. The experience extends beyond the product itself.

Digital products can be downloaded instantly, and their knowledge content is separated from a physical product. This has sparked major battles between Napster and the music industry over the definition of a piece of music and between book publishers and authors over the definition of a "book" in electronic format.

Given the rapid pace of technological change and obsolescence, companies can benefit by building platforms that can be easily updated.[2] Nokia, for example, designs its line of cellular phones with this option and so does Bernina, the premier sewing machine producer. Companies are involving customers in this design process and creating platforms and modular components from which consumers can create their own customized products. This collaboration with customers can also help to speed the product development cycle. As product life cycles shrink, an increasing number of firms focus on innovative, concurrent new product development processes. Companies are also engaging in concurrent development of product, production processes, and supply chain.[3]

How has the digital revolution changed your products? How can you use online and offline capabilities to initiate or take advantage of these changes?

Convergence of Price

Pricing has been a key focus of traditional marketing strategy, but as pointed out in Chapter 6, the centaur has introduced a new value equation and the Internet has enabled the development of innovative pricing models. For example, pricing has been very challenging in the computer industry, with intense competition and rapid product cycles leading to obsolescence that makes setting fixed prices a moving target. As Sun Microsystems CEO Scott McNeally commented, computers are like bananas, that have no value once they exceed their shelf life. Sun was very successful in selling its computers on eBay, allowing market demand to set prices through dynamic auctions in addition to its traditional pricing models. Similarly, Walker Digital created an offline system for fast food franchises that prompted restaurant workers to offer a complementary product or discounts on products that were reaching the end of their shelf life. A customer who ordered a hamburger and fries might be offered a free upgrade to a cheeseburger based on inventory.

Companies have an opportunity to experiment with new pricing strategies and create a portfolio of pricing models *online and offline*. The Internet increases transparency so companies need to make sure pricing is consistent online and offline. For example, a major corporation noticed a jump in sales from a customer in Thailand, where its prices were lower than in the United States. It turned out the customer there was taking orders online from U.S. customers, buying the products at Thai prices and shipping them out to the United States at a discount on U.S. prices. Even with shipping, the Thai company was turning a profit. These problems can be avoided if the company distinguishes its online and offline offerings. For example, Sun's use of the eBay auction model allows some comparisons with standard prices, but only after the auction has ended.

Ongoing and experiential models lead to pricing models based on subscriptions rather than transactions. As customers interact with the company over a period of time, firms can use new pricing models for access rather than ownership. Experience-based pricing creates recurring revenue streams in contrast to the one-shot transactions. While free services online have faded in popularity since the early dot-com focus on building market share, there may still be opportunities to offer free services and free trials, especially to encourage consumers to experiment with new technology. AOL and other ISPs have been very successful in attracting new online users by flooding mailboxes with CDs offering free hours of service. RealNetworks offers a limited version of its RealPlayer through a free download and attempts to sell an upgraded version. Similarly, Adobe offers free versions of its Acrobat Reader, to create a critical mass of users to sell its premium software for creating and editing Acrobat files.

Similarly, in a business-to-business context, Hewlett-Packard used value-based pricing in a $500 million contract to supply computer equipment to Qwest Communications International. Under the plan, Qwest would pay only based on generating revenues and achieving objectives. HP expected to receive $1 billion in 3 years. In addition, as part of this arrangement, Qwest would buy 95% of its Windows computers and 75% of its UNIX servers from HP.[4] Increasingly, companies are looking for value-based and revenue sharing-based pricing as an integral part of their business strategies. Nissan, for example, is using a new contract with its advertising agency, TBWA/Chiat/Day, by paying based on performance—the sales generated—and thus linking the objectives of the two companies.[5]

Similar risk/reward sharing is possible in the business-to-consumer market. For example, most consumers feel that broker pricing in financial services is unfair because the broker makes money whether the customer does or not. The alternative would be to come up with creative pricing where the broker shares in the risk and reward of the investor.

Yet we should also note that not all consumers are price sensitive. Visitors to online travel sites can often find much better fares if they search carefully (one vacation that cost $2,400 on the home page of one site could be had for just $1,399 deeper in the same site with more research). But many visitors either don't know this or can't be bothered. One major travel site reported informally that 29 of 30 visitors take the higher fare without comparing prices.[6] And while it is extremely easy for a book buyer to compare prices on Amazon and Barnes & Noble online, it is fairly uncommon for customers to do so. Even the site "10percentoffamazon.com"—which seemed like a shoe-in for success in the efficiency-focused early days of the dot-com bubble—was not successful in moving any meaningful traffic away from its obviously higher-priced rival.

The real challenge in the pricing area is not just to look at this as making a pricing decision, but framing it as part of the revenue model of the business. As discussed in Chapter 8, the change in the revenue model has to be aligned with the product/service offering.

> **What pricing strategies are used in your industry? What new pricing models can you introduce online that might increase your revenue growth and profit?**

Convergence of Promotion

Traditionally, the interaction of advertising and promotion has been fairly limited, as readers or viewers of ads and promotions could respond by calling or writing for more information, engaging in word-of-mouth communication, or making a purchase. Now, promotion can be integrated into an immediate and ongoing dialogue between the company and the consumer. For example, Opel developed an interactive television advertisement for French digital satellite television subscribers that begins like an ordinary ad showing beautiful women driving cars through magnificent scenery. But the interactive advertisement allows viewers with a click of their remotes to find out more detailed information about the car (including choice of colors, interior, costs, and financing). Then, they can design their own dream car online and email it to Opel, who matches the dream car with inventory on the lots of local dealers.[7] The traditional time gap between the marketing message and the customer response has been reduced to zero, with a much richer interaction than dialing an 800 number.

This is just the beginning. Future technologies might allow viewers to click on items in a television program—a chair on a set or a skirt on an actress or even a recording of a theme song, increasing interaction and further blurring the line between programming and advertising. Further, sophisticated set-top boxes will be able to filter advertising to better match the viewer's interest.

In an interactive medium, the standard approaches of static advertising, such as banner ads, have proven to be ineffective. Targeted and interactive promotions are usually far more effective. For example, a company called Ezula (www.ezula.com) developed a technology that automatically highlights words in online documents allowing readers to click on the words and be transferred to related company marketing messages. This is just one of many innovations in this area.

The next generation of online advertising has been far more successful than the more static "billboard" banner ads. For example, advertising created by Ad4ever uses animation and translucent advertising that floats across the screen to attract attention and then leads the user to a reminder ad and an interactive message such as a game or interactive "movie." In a series of experiments by a leading automaker, the approach generated an average clickthrough rate of 25 percent, compared to clickthrough rates for the average banner ads of less than 0.5 percent. What's more, the viewers did not just clickthrough, but most of those who clicked proceeded to interact with the movie or game, and an amazing 80 percent of those took some action (printing a coupon, going to the advertiser's site, or requesting information). The exact response rate obviously depends on the quality of the creative work, and the technology also benefits from the fact that it is novel. (The results might be diluted if the Web were crawling with these ads.) But this does show the power of creative new technologies and strategies for promotion that have the potential to bring advertising on the web to life.

This is one of a number of on-going experiments with new online advertising approaches that could transform the nature and effectiveness of online advertising. The spread of interactive television and mobile phones creates many opportunities for other creative approaches to advertising.

Promotions can be made across channels, using in-store promotions to drive customers to the web site and web site promotions to drive people into the stores. Online promotions also can be very effective if they are targeted (rather than undirected spam). For example, advertising agency T3's interactive division created an HTML email for Dell's Small Business division that generated more than $1 million in revenue within three days from a single message. The campaign averaged a 10 percent response rate and a 3.4 percent conversion rate. Customers who were interested in one of the products could purchase it with as few as four clicks. Unlike traditional promotions, Dell and T3 could determine what was working very quickly, to build on successful campaigns and scrap unsuccessful ones. Part of the reason the campaign was successful was that the messages were part of an integrated campaign for small business customers, which included a monthly catalog, a quarterly newsletter, web site content, and advertising. Promotions can be much more effective as part of such an integrated set of relationships with consumers.

The content of the communications is changing, and there are greater opportunities for the effective convergence of interactive promotion, education, and entertainment. Customers are no longer the passive recipients of ads and commercials, but are active participants in an interactive "edutainment" process, seeking opportunities to learn about the products and services (education) while being entertained and inspired.

Another critical convergence challenge is the need to integrate all the communication vehicles, messages, and strategies across channels. Companies such as Vignette, nCompass, Documentum, and Interwoven offer content management software and services, which allow companies to manage their content across different points of online and offline contact and offer an integrated interface to customers. For example, a banking customer can keep track of online and offline balances and transactions on a single page or click to connect to an online teller.

Companies also have to be able to coordinate media advertising, Internet communication, public relations, packaging, customer service, and any other point of contact between the firm and its customers and prospects, regardless of the device. New software and services such as BlueMartini's campaign management can help develop, manage, and track results of campaigns across email, web site, direct mail, and other channels. At the extreme, technological advances allow the firm and its customers to have continuous dialogue and interaction at any point of contact.

What is your current approach to promotion? How can you use new technologies to engage in more interactive promotions with customers?

Convergence of Place

"Place" has traditionally referred to distribution, getting the product out in front of the customer. In a digital age, however, consumers expect increased speed and convenience, to be able to find products 24/7, anywhere in the world. This is reflected in Fidelity Investment's "call, click or visit" call to action. The challenge for companies is to manage a global, integrated supply chain that leads to both online and offline outlets, and in which the customer is an integral part. The supply chain is concerned with getting components to the manufacturer, but the new "marketing network" belongs to the customer. The challenge is to create an unbroken chain between the customer and the many suppliers in the network who are providing the product or service so when the customer clicks the "buy" button, the information ripples down the entire line. When information can flow up and down the line, the company and its suppliers can design their production around actual orders and the customer can know where the product is at any give time. Historically, the supply chain has been left to the "production people," but now it is equally the concern of marketing.

Companies also have to retool their logistics strategies to deliver products directly to customers' doors rather than retail shelves. For digital products and services, this is a fairly straightforward proposition because the product (a magazine article, a software package, a recorded concert, a movie, for example) can be downloaded and billed entirely online (although protecting intellectual property in this case is more complicated but new technology makes it feasible). An e-book, for example, can be downloaded anytime and anyplace. For physical products such as wine or flowers, the problem is more complex because the digital component is only part of the equation. (Of course, creative entrepreneurs are finding ways to digitize even these items. A site called www.virtualflorist.com allows visitors to send free digital flowers while offering them the opportunity to pay for shipping real flowers to the same person.) For physical products, the marketing network must be joined to a logistic network that is either owned by the company or outsourced to a specialist such as Fed Ex or UPS. But, even here, there are many possibilities. For example, Spanish grocery retailer Caprabo offers customers the option of having groceries delivered in a two-hour window or picking them up in the store. As noted in chapter 5, in Japan, where customers are wary about using credit cards over the Internet, Seven-Eleven allows customers to pay cash and pick up the online purchases in its network of convenience stores. Seven-Eleven reports that some 75 percent of Japanese Internet shoppers pick up their purchases in bricks-and-mortar stores.[8] Other companies offer delivery of products to hotel rooms or to workplaces at the end of the day.

Companies need to focus on the entire "marketing network," from the customer on back to the initial product inputs. Digital technology has reshaped the supply chain in a variety of ways.[9] Increasing numbers of companies offer their suppliers real-time access to their customers' orders, thus achieving just-in-time inventory and a truly customer-driven global integrated supply chain. Specialist trading companies, such as Li & Fung, tailor a virtual, integrated supply chain for each order. The use of technology on the business-to-business side can help integrate the supply networks, reduce product inventory, streamline processes, and as a result cut cost and speed up the development, manufacturing, and delivery of products and services.

The greatest opportunity is not just from combining channels, but using the new combinations to rethink the overall shopping experience online and offline. The combination of channels can allow companies to increase the "stickiness" of the shopping experience in the store. For example, outdoor outfitter REI has incorporated kiosks in the store that allow new outdoor enthusiasts to ask questions they might be reluctant to raise with experienced store employees. Increasingly, high-end stores are creating events (fashion shows, music, meet-the-designer events) and creating cappuccino bars to augment the offline customer experience.

How can you use multiple channels to deliver products to customers and how can you best learn which channels are preferred by different customer segments? How can you reshape your supply chain and shopping experience?

OTHER MARKETING STRATEGIES

The changes to the traditional 4 Ps and their interaction indicate the new marketing challenges and opportunities created by the rise of the hybrid consumer. But these are just the tip of the iceberg. There are a variety of other changes in marketing strategy that result from the rise of the centaur. These include rethinking of segmentation, positioning, customer relationship management, branding, marketing research, and other aspects of marketing.

Use Reverse Segmentation

Segmentation is changing with the rise of personalization and customization. With sophisticated data-mining, companies have been able to move from mass markets to segments to segments of one. With databases and tools such as collaborative filtering (where a company such as Amazon recommends products based on purchases of consumers with similar profiles), companies have taken a finer and finer cut on the market, but their basic idea of "targeting customers," either as broad segments or as individuals, has not changed. Companies are using this customer information and tools to *personalize* the customer experience, actively tailoring their offerings to the perceived needs of individual customers. But given the complexity and quirkiness of individuals, it is challenging for companies to completely understand the needs of these micro "segments."

The adoption of new communications technologies also creates segments of experienced, inexperienced, and non-users that further segment the market. As Geoffrey Moore points out in *Crossing the Chasm*, it is a challenge for companies to move from the smaller segment of initial adopters to the larger mass-market segment of later followers.

There are many different ways to segment. Every company has to develop its own segmentation scheme. In developing this segmentation, it is important to move away from general demographic segmentation and include idosyncratic segmentation based on benefits, the way customers use the product, and perceptions and preference for online and offline options. Managers need to manage a portfolio of segments, which might include 1-to-1 segments, reverse segments (customizers), and other traditional segments. The key is to manage this diverse portfolio of segments and use the segmentation strategy that works best for particular situation.

In addition, the information-rich environment of online interaction offers greater opportunities to use data mining to target specific segments. Overlooked segments can be extremely valuable. For example, Providian Financial grew its credit card business from $100 million to a $12 billion through careful data mining and analysis, and targeting credit products toward the low end of the market, which had traditionally been overlooked.[10]

To the extent that the buyer differs from the end users, companies also need to be sure that the segmentation captures the critical characteristics of the buyer, the user, the decision maker, and others who influence the decision.

How should you segment your market to reflect the changing consumers' perceptions and preferences for online and offline offerings?

Design for Customer-Led Positioning

The new business paradigm and value equation also affects the way companies communicate this shift to the world through the positioning of their product and service offering. In traditional marketing, the company "positioned" its product for the consumer, emphasizing the most important benefits sought by the consumer, and trying to make sure the consumer would perceive the product or service as being superior, or at least comparable, to rivals along these dimensions.

In the malleable digital environment, the consumer can now choose the important dimensions directly. Whereas it would be impossible for customers to redesign a physical retail store based on the product attributes they seek, this is quite easy online. With a few mouse clicks on a service such as Peapod's online grocery shopping, the entire store could be reconfigured based on fat content, or calories, or price. This is not remotely possible in the physical world. Although the company will still position the product through its own advertising, it also needs to think about ways to allow customers to do their own positioning. How do companies position their products in an environment in which customers, using search engines, decide what factors are important and can sort based on these factors? How do companies position a product when consumer chat rooms and other interactions allow for real-time global flow of "word of mouth" communication?

Companies need to offer consumers the frameworks to do their own positioning on the attributes that are most important to them in the broader context used by the consumer. By carefully observing these positioning strategies, companies can then reshape their offerings to come up favorably on these attributes. For example, if Peapod finds most customers are organizing the store based on fat content, this would be a clear signal to stress low-fat positioning and add more low-fat offerings to its product mix, or if it found an increasing number of customers looking for organic foods, it would expand its positioning efforts in this area. The *Field of Dreams* idea that "if you build it, they will come," is replaced with the concept that "if you build it *with* them, they will stay."[11]

Focus on Emotion

In today's environment, company-initiated positioning should focus not only on traditional benefits that appeal to logic, but also on feelings or affect associated with the product or brand. We discussed in Chapter 6 how Volkswagen has created an online radio station, BMW has added movies, and Swatch created a site that allows customers to build their own salesclerks. These had little to do with cognitive arguments about the benefits of their products and much more to do with an emotional attachment to the product or brand. Similarly, NextCard has been very successful in marketing its credit cards online, but not by stressing cognitive benefits such as rates, but rather emphasizing the ability of customers to put their children's artwork on their cards. "Leah's first masterpiece, age 7. (We're so proud.)" reads the caption on one ad depicting a child's crayon drawing on the front of a credit card. In a world in which benefits, features, and prices are easily searched for and compared, the customer's feelings toward a product are increasingly important.

This emotional appeal, that was once used primarily in marketing fashion, perfumes, and other image-based products and services, is being applied increasingly to hard goods such as computers (for example, the "think different" positioning of Apple's iMac and iBook) and automobiles (for example, Mercedes-Benz's new positioning as an American treasure). As the facts of products and services become more widely known, they are less powerful drivers of the brand's purchases. Instead, companies position on more psychological or social dimensions. This is also reflected in the increased attention to design. (Is an Apple iMac a computer or a fashion statement?)

Although initial text-heavy online offerings focused on logical arguments, the more entertaining and interactive approaches today provide the opportunity for more emotional relationships. Also, the ability for customers to interact with virtual products and customize them (including emerging drag-and-drop design systems) create more opportunities to develop these connections. The positioning is based on the ability to establish a strong emotional link between the company and consumer.[12]

Companies are developing what Marc Gobé, President and CEO of d/g*worldwide, calls "emotional branding." This is branding that engages the senses and emotions of consumers—the head, heart and gut—through relationship, sensorial experiences, imagination and vision.[13] The interactive and dynamic nature of the Internet offers opportunities to add new dimensions to the emotion and experience associated with brands. For example, eBay has created a brand focused on community, empowerment, and a sense of quirkiness and fun in addition to providing the more rational benefits of an efficient global marketplace. This leads to a definition of their brand essence as something they call "way enlightened trading."

It is important to note that the emotions associated with the brand are not merely an element of marketing communications, but rather integrated into a total experience. Every contact or interaction with the customer reinforces or undermines these emotional associations. They must be integrated and orchestrated **How can you augment your feature/benefit-driven positioning with emotional appeals to the customer?**

to reinforce the overall image. eBay's positioning as a safe and protected community, as well as a fun, global flea market, is reinforced by its communications with members and its stringent privacy policies. It is important to recognize that these emotional brands do not belong to the company, but are co-created with the consumer.

Build Strong Customer Relationship Management

It is clear to most companies today that the organization must be centered on the customer. As Thomas Siebel and Pat House note in *Cyber Rules*, "Whatever the role of software agents, and indeed of technology in general, in the networked future as in the pen-and-ink past, *only the customer-oriented organizations will survive*.... On the Web, as in any other venue, you've got to follow your customers, and only the vendors who accept that fact have a chance of succeeding."[14]

But because our organizations were designed around internal systems and processes, this goal of a customer-centered firm is often very difficult to achieve. The customer experience is tremendously hampered by fragmented internal systems. At one point, a major bank had 45 different systems for interacting with customers and many of them were not directly connected. Customer service reps had to log in and out of systems to respond to customers. This fragmented design means that many companies don't even know who their customers are across divisions. A major investment house has systems that are designed to track *accounts* set up by customers, not the customers. So when customers set up multiple accounts or joint accounts with their spouses, they are treated as different accounts.

This fragmentation also means that companies provide different answers across different channels. A Gartner study found that when people looked for information by phone and online, 78 percent of the time they got a different answer.[15] Companies also have different policies for responding. For example, in many organizations, a telephone response is immediate, but email languishes because it is handled by customer service only after all the calls are taken.

Companies have to provide excellent customer service no matter how the customer reaches them. Given the limitations of legacy information systems, this integrated customer service is a serious challenge for many organizations. But customers expect to be able to "call, click or visit" in the call to action of Fidelity Investments, and have an integrated and positive customer experience across all these channels. They expect the results of phone calls will instantly show up on their account online and they expect customer service representatives on the phone or in the office to have access to all their online information. There is tremendous work to be done, not only in the infrastructure of customer service, but also in its basic design. In an age when many products are moving toward commodities, the management of this customer relationship has become a crucial competitive advantage. Companies that achieve high levels of customer service across multiple channels will be differentiated from those who don't.

Customer Relationship Management is the deliberate process of building the systems and processes for focusing the organization on the customer. It builds bridges between the internal systems and the external operations, as illustrated in Exhibit 9–2. The customers and prospects, no matter what channel they use to come into the company, meet a coherent interface in Customer Relationship Management. This is linked to customer service, sales, and marketing. It is also attached to a unified database where customer information from all parts of the organization is gathered. Finally, systems for partner relationship management and employee relationship management help to ensure the staff and partners are also focused on the needs of the customers.

Siebel Systems and other companies have created integrated platforms to bridge the gap between the customer and the organization. Siebel reports that companies using CRM have seen improvements of more than 12 percent in revenue growth, 20 percent in customer satisfaction and 20 percent in employee productivity.

In contrast to information systems that were focused on internal transaction efficiency, these systems are focused on improving the customer relationship and experience. Beyond

EXHIBIT 9-2 **FOCUSING THE ORGANIZATION ON THE CUSTOMER**

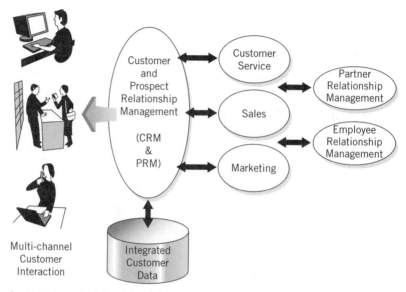

Source: Based on a Siebel Presentation by Kevin Nix to the Wharton Fellows in e-Business program.

the software, Siebel Systems also has designed its culture and incentive systems to focus on the customer. For example, the payment of sales commissions is tied to independently audited customer satisfaction levels. A focus on the customer is fully integrated into the culture and the technology of the organization.

Jerry Shereshewsky, Group Director of Direct Marketing at Yahoo!, points out that *prospect* relationship management is focused on establishing and sustaining a dialogue. This process in the offline world has often required a series of interactions moving from "no" to "maybe" to "yes." Most car buyers do not say "yes" immediately. The same is true online. As long as the customers are talking to the company, there is an opportunity to draw them in. "Most of us are dealing with prospects and not customers," Shereshewsky said at a conference sponsored by the Wharton e-Business Initiative and the Marketing Science Institute.[16] "We need to focus on prospect relationship management. It is the management of that process at a distance that characterizes the difference between online marketing and everything else." Siebel looks at a whole system of interactive selling, beginning with an eCatalog where customers can browse through products, to an eConfigurator where customers can create customized products, to an eAdvisor where customers can receive expert advice, and finally to an ePricer that dynamically establishes pricing.[17]

This coherent focus on the customer allows organizations to build and strengthen long-term relationships. Customers not only become repeat purchasers, but also evangelists for the firm.

Focus on the Total Customer Experience

This emphasis on customer relationship management should go beyond merely focusing on the customer to thinking about creating an outstanding total customer experience. How do the pieces of the customer interaction fit together? What kind of relationship do customers want with the company? How can you enhance the total customer experience rather than just provide a smooth and pleasant transaction? Companies need to appreciate the context of interaction and provide information that relates to the customer and the context.

One financial service company, for example, is creating a large interactive database and decision support system (DSS) that includes, in addition to a real-time depository of all the customers activities with the company, the capability to allow continuous dialogue with each customer. Customers who apply for a loan may get a note about the status of the loan application when they use an ATM, look at their statement, or have any other point of contact with the company. The database, which is augmented with external data including Internet usage, offers the potential for targeting individual customers and developing and offering each customer the products and services that will maximize his or her lifetime value to the firm. As noted above, the experience also needs to be integrated across cultures and languages, tailored to **How can you use an integrated approach across different channels to improve the overall customer experience?** local markets. The customer experiences this as an on-going dialogue with the company rather than a series of disjointed interactions.

Preemptive Communications Strategy

With the speed of online communications, companies cannot wait to hear complaints to fix relationships after they go sour. They have to engage in a proactive process of customer relationship management—across all physical and virtual interactions—focused on "pre-crisis management" instead of traditional "post-crisis management."

Because of the rapid spread of buzz in a connected world, managers need to ensure that their communication strategies are well integrated and anticipate potential problems. With one button, customers can find information in any part of the world or transmit complaints and problems like wildfire around the globe. Where companies might have been able to engage in crisis management after a problem emerged, they do not have a second chance in the digital economy. Intel discovered this when minor problems with its Pentium chip ultimately led to a recall. A story about a Nike customer who was turned down when he wanted to customize his shoes with the words "sweat shop" traveled the planet (and ultimately sparked interest in Nike's customized shoes, proving that any publicity is good publicity as long as the reporters spell your name right.) [18] Managers need to be much more proactive, to engage in "pre-crisis" management, managing problems and anticipating potential negative messages before they occur.

How can you build strong communications channels online and offline that can increase interaction and loyalty?

Create Coherent and Trusted Global Brands

In the early days of the Internet, digital technology was expected to undermine the power of brands by putting more perfect information in the hands of consumers. Actually, evidence suggests that branding has become more important. With many options to choose from and less personal relationships online, customers may turn to trusted and trustworthy brands as an indication of more intangible qualities. As the issue of trust becomes a central concern online, branding may become more important. Nike's brand still has power in this environment because it conveys an image about the purchaser. But an airline brand that relies on low prices and on-time performance may be eroded because the information it conveys about budget prices and on-time service can be determined empirically through easily conducted information searches.

One of the central challenges of branding in a hybrid world is to create a coherent brand across different channels and across different geographical, cultural, and linguistic domains. Given the transparency of the Internet, companies need to create consistent brands across different countries, language, cultures, competitive environments, market institutions, supporting institutions, online and offline. This means that the branding needs to focus more on common human experiences that cut across cultures rather than those that are focused on the idiosyncratic characteristics of a single culture. An online business can be an opportunity to create new brands, as in the case of Amazon, to extend existing brands, as in the case of Wal-Mart and many other established companies, or to rejuvenate a tired old brand as Kmart has done with "BlueLight."

As companies move to the more integrated solutions discussed above, cobranding among diverse companies becomes more important. For example, Amazon joined with Toy 'R' Us and Sotheby's, where the cobranding offers the consumer better confidence and therefore provides value for both companies. And customerization creates the opportunity to "cobrand" with the consumer by creating "my brand" along with the corporate branding. There are companies whose brand emphasizes this customerization, such as myCFO, inviting customers to co-brand.

The convergence of different industry and market spaces also makes branding more challenging online. Several years ago, Lexus successfully defended its automobile brand against a suit by research service Lexus-Nexus, noting that the two businesses were in completely different industries. But in 2001, Internet price comparison site MySimon.com lost a suit filed by real

How are you using branding online and offline? Do you have a coherent global brand? If not, how can you enhance your global branding or use the Internet to help transform your existing brands?

estate investment trust Simon Property Group and was ordered to stop using the "Simon" name. A federal court judge issued an injunction ordering MySimon to cease the use of its name, its "Simon" character and the mySimon.com website.[19]

Augment Marketing Research with Modeling

Advances in technology and the explosive growth in Internet access challenge all aspects of traditional marketing research. Traditional data collection—mall intercept, telephone interviews, self-administered mail surveys, and hybrid approaches such as Telephon Mail-Telephone (TMT)—are augmented with Internet surveys and most important, with automatic capturing of Internet-behavioral data. The results are tremendous amounts of data, reduced costs of obtaining some of the data and much greater speed in getting the required information.

But this information can be overwhelming for marketers, presenting the age-old challenge of moving from data through information to understanding and insight. Companies need to use the extensive multichannel data for data-mining, modeling and reporting to develop insights into the market and make better management decisions. The database and modeling can also be used to support rapid experimentation. The online environment offers many opportunities for real-time marketing research and experimentation. Instead of large-scale test marketing, the company can create many different options and quickly determine which approaches work by interacting with customers online. Companies can give customers "experience" with potential new products through "information accelerators" (exposing them to television ads, newspaper articles and product information, and word-of-mouth recommendations in video interviews).

What are the opportunities to transform your current approach to marketing research using the tools and modeling based on the Internet and other new technology?

Companies also can conduct global conjoint surveys online within a day or less that offer meaningful insights into customer preferences. Although these studies are rapid, they are often very accurate. One study of a web-based virtual product and conjoint analysis system found a 90 percent correlation between its measures and consumer's actual preferences.[20]

Develop New Competencies for Marketing Excellence

What are the competencies that organizations need for marketing excellence in this environment? In addition to traditional marketing competencies and leadership traits, organizations also need to develop new sets of competencies to meet the convergence challenge. Among these competencies are:

- Understanding the customer and other stakeholders, and their changing needs in light of their interaction with technology.

- Mastering sophisticated analytics to turn an avalanche of online data into actionable insights on consumer behavior and market opportunities.

- Developing the creativity to develop innovative options and solutions. Many managers focus on low-hanging fruit, the easy solutions that may lead to improved efficiency in the short term, but do not fundamentally change the business.

- Taking risks and designing and implementing bold experiments.

- Mobilizing and leading cross-disciplinary and cross-cultural teams under conditions of rapid change and ambiguous authority.

- Developing a balanced perspective that allows them to manage the convergence, to mix the old and the new and to avoid the extremes of thinking about either/or.

- Passion, commitment, and ability to execute.

MARKETING IS NOT AN ISLAND

We need to develop broader capabilities for marketing across the organization. This will help the company move from viewing marketing as a function in the organization to seeing it as a philosophy. The marketing perspective is pervasive rather than limited to a certain part of the organization, the consumer bringing into every decision.

Ultimately, the transformation of convergence marketing requires a shift that goes beyond the marketing department. Organizational silos and separations, by their nature, tend to work against the process of "convergence." Breaking the organization into online and offline structures, functional areas, brands or other separations work against providing an integrated experience and interaction with customers. The tectonic shifts of the rise of the Internet and hybrid consumer are moving these separate islands together and creating a need for a more "convergent" view of the organization.

The organizational architecture as a whole needs to be reshaped, rewired to meet the reality of the new hybrid consumer. In this transformation, a "c-change," the 5Cs that have helped drive the emergence of the centaur outside the organization can also be applied to reshaping the internal organization, as discussed in Part 4.

Action Memo

- Examine your marketing strategy under three assumptions: 1. The whole world is the traditional consumer, 2. The whole world is the cyberconsumer, 3. The whole world is made up of centaurs. How well are you prepared for each of these worlds? What do you need to do to be prepared?

- Look at your own interactions with the companies you purchase from. How are you, as a centaur, transforming their marketing strategies? What would you like them to do? How can you apply these insights to your own business?

- Look at your marketing organization. What are its weaknesses? If you were designing it today, what would it look like?

We invite you to share the results of these activities and suggest other action memos at the Convergence Marketing Forum (www.convergencemarketingforum.com).

NOTES

1 Sawhney, Mohan and Philip Kotler, "Marketing in the Age of Information Democracy," *Kellogg on Marketing*, Dawn Iacobucci , ed., New York: John Wiley & Sons, 2000.

2 For a discussion of the implications of the digital world on new product development see Sridhar Balasubramania, Vish Krishnan, and Mohanbir Sawhney, "New Offering Realization in the Networked Digital Environment," in Wind and Mahajan, *Digital Marketing*.

3 For a discussion of 3-dimensional concurrent engineering, see Charles H. Fine, *Clock Speed*, (Reading, MA: Perseus Books), 1998.

4 *Business Week* (May 31, 1999), p. 126.

5 *Advertising Age*, "Nissan Ties TBWA's Pay to Car Sales" (June 7, 1999).

6 Ravi Aron, presented at the Wharton Fellows in e-Business program in Philadelphia, May 7, 2001.

7 Schenker, Jennifer, "Death of a Salesman," *Time*, June 4, 2001, p. 64.

8 "Over the Counter e-Commerce," *The Economist*, May 26, 2001, p. 78.

9 For further discussion of the integrated global supply chain, see Marshall Fisher and David Reibstein, "The Digital Era: Implications for the Supply Chain," in Wind and Mahajan, *Digital Marketing*.

10 Hill, Sam and Glenn Rifkin. *Radical Marketing: From Harvard to Harley, Lessons from Ten that Broke the Rules and Made it Big*, New York: HarperBusiness, 1999.

11 Although popularized by the movie *Field of Dreams*, this idea actually can be traced back to Ralph Waldo Emerson, if not earlier.

12 Vijay Mahajan and Jerry Wind, "Got Affect? Moving Positioning Beyond Features and Benefits," *Marketing Management*, forthcoming 2002.

13 Gobé, Marc. *Emotional Brands*, New York: Allworth Press, 2001.

14 Siebel, Thomas M. and Pat House. *Cyber Rules: Strategies for Excelling at e-Business*, New York: Currency Doubleday, 1999, pp. 222–223.

15 Kevin Nix, Siebel, presented to Wharton Fellows in E-Business, June 12, 2001.

16 From a presentation at the Wharton conference; "From Browsers to Buyers: Online Conversion Workshop," May 30, 2001, The Wharton School.

17 See note #15.

18 "Nike Gets Traction from Sweatshop Spat," *The Wall Street Journal*, February 28, 2001.

19 "Judge Grants Permanent Injunction Against MySimon," *PR Newswire*, January 25, 2001.

20 Paustian, Chuck. "Better Products Through Virtual Consumers," *Sloan Management Review*, Spring 2001, pp. 14–15.

PART 4

C-TRANSFORMING THE ORGANIZATION

The challenge of the centaur goes beyond marketing and business strategies to the heart of organizational architecture. Many firms, believing the Internet was merely a new channel for reaching consumers, did not fully appreciate the depth of the impact of the new hybrid consumer. The expectations of consumers have been raised.

Technology has moved out of the back office into the customer interface, giving customers much more direct access to the company. In the old world, a sales rep or retailer could create a friendly façade for the company. These intermediaries knew how to navigate the complex channels for interacting with the company so they could present a fairly coherent face to the consumer (even then, the system was often slow, frustrating, and inefficient). But

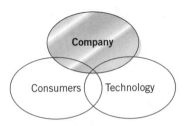

today, when the centaur is much more directly wired into the company, managers need to be able to organize to interact with customers and truly have a coherent architecture for meeting the ever-increasing demands of the centaur. Most organizations are not designed for this.

As illustrated in the figure above, this section of the book focuses on the organizational architecture the company needs to create to run with the centaurs. How can companies meet these rising expectations? The very technologies that create these new challenges often offer the potential for solutions, if they can be applied correctly. The technologies for customerization and personalization, building community, designing and managing channels, reshaping the competitive value equation, and providing decision-making tools can all be applied within the organization. In Chapter 10, we explore how managers can apply the 5Cs of convergence within their organizations to create a "convergent organization." But just as the emergence of the hybrid consumer has been a challenging and circuitous process, so the process of implementing organizational convergence presents substantial challenges. In Chapter 11, we examine the pathways to convergence and strategies for implementation. How do WalMart and Amazon make their way to the hybrid model? What are the organizational issues involved in implementation? Finally, in the conclusion, we explore lessons learned and offer a few strategies to help you initiate your own process of transformation to meet the challenge of the new hybrid consumer.

10

DESIGNING THE CONVERGENT ORGANIZATION

*"There is only one valid definition
of business purpose: To create a customer."*

Peter Drucker[1]

TRADITIONAL CONSUMER

"Drucker is right. We need to create a customer. We need to find potential customers for our products and services, and then make them our own by focusing our entire organization—from R&D to marketing to operations—on the customer."

CYBERCONSUMER

"Drucker has it backward. It is the customer who creates the company. The empowered online customers will pull together the knowledge and products they need. There will be no loyalty to a particular company. Companies need to reshape themselves to the reality of this empowered customer."

THE CENTAUR

"The purpose of the business is to create <u>with</u> the customer. It is not to create the customer. It is not to create for the customer, but instead to collaboratively work with the customer in developing and delivering products and services. To do this, we need to rethink how we are structured and how we connect with customers, online and offline."

CONVERGENCE QUESTIONS

>>>What does the new hybrid consumer mean for the design of the organizational architecture?

>>>What kind of organizational convergence is needed to make the company more flexible and connected to the consumer, and to support the implementation of the convergence strategies?

>>>How can companies apply the 5Cs of convergence marketing to the design of their own organizational architecture?

DESIGNING THE
CONVERGENT ORGANIZATION

How can organizations address the gaps between their architectures and the needs of the hybrid consumer? This chapter explores how the same technologies and approaches that led to the emergence of the hybrid consumer can be applied within the firm to create a convergent organization. This organization can use the 5Cs to redesign culture and values, processes, structure, customer interface, boundaries, performance measures, and human resources.

John Sanderson, the CEO of a major packaged goods manufacturer, has been up all night wrestling with a problem he was thinking about on a trip back from California to Chicago. As he returned home from a meeting with leaders of the company's online startup, based in Silicon Valley, he was thinking about how his organization has already begun to transform its approach to marketing to meet the new hybrid consumer. It established this separate company to create a customized line of food products online. It began to build online communities around recipes and cooking, linked to sites with similar interests. The company has experimented with auctions and other pricing models for higher-end products and bulk orders. And it has offered customers engines for comparing products, sorting based on many attributes, creating and analyzing diets, and searching for difficult-to-find ingredients.

But the more the organization tries to "run with the centaurs," the more he feels it keeps tripping up. The company is not flexible enough. It is weighed down by traditional information systems, organizational structure, and processes. Perhaps most significantly, it is hampered by legacy mindsets. The technology is there to do much more, but the organization is not designed to take advantage of it. A traditional airplane cannot be expected to travel at supersonic speeds merely by adding an engine. It needs an entirely new design.

As he stretches out in first class on the red eye home, he realizes that he needs to do more than transform his approach to marketing. To deliver on the promise of the 5Cs —customerization, community, channels, competitive value, and choice tools—he needs to challenge his current view of the business and transform his entire organization. This is what keeps him awake on the flight home.

Could he transform his successful organization without destroying it? If he undertakes a radical overhaul, can the organization still meet its earnings targets? Will the current employees be able to operate in this new environment? What will it do to the organizational culture? And after all is said and done, how can he be sure that this organizational change will actually better meet the needs of the hybrid consumer? Sanderson is not alone in this challenge. Companies such as WalMart, Kmart, and Staples are wrestling with similar questions as they draw together their online and offline businesses.

Then it hits him: the same approaches that have created the challenge of the hybrid consumer can be applied within the organization to create solutions. Sanderson pulls out a legal pad and sketches out a chart, illustrated in Exhibit 10–1. For each of the 5Cs, he examines implications for organizational architecture. As he has done in exploring consumer markets, he now examines what has changed as a result of the new technology, what are the opportunities to do things differently, and what aspects of the organization remain the same. He is excited to see the possibilities for transforming the organization.

EXHIBIT 10–1 **APPLYING THE 5CS TO THE ORGANIZATIONAL ARCHITECTURE**

5Cs	Implications for Organizational Architecture
Customerization	Using customerization technologies, the organization can be dynamically "reconfigured" for employees, suppliers and customers so they see different views of the same organization.
Community	Developing real and virtual communities inside and outside the firm can help bridge traditional organizational "silos" to develop more modular, networked and flexible organizations.
Channels	By integrating physical and virtual interactions with customers, companies can conserve resources while delivering higher value to customers.
Competitive Value	As the value equation is redefined, companies need to develop new metrics to track lifetime value of customers and provide new ways to provide value to employees through more fluid work relationships. Companies can also outsource smaller segments of their processes, as with the move toward web services.
Choice Tools	Powerful tools for employee information, decision making, and managing the business can offer employees the real-time information and support to keep pace with the fast-changing and savvy centaurs.

Sanderson realizes that while the new hybrid consumers want to interact with the company in diverse ways, they also expect to have a coherent experience across all these channels. It is difficult to deliver this type of coherence with a piecemeal organization. In the past, when the customer was distant from the organization, the complexity was not apparent, but now that the customer is more directly connected to the organization, the inconsistencies, the complexity, and divisions within the organization have become much more transparent. Sanderson realizes that to achieve coherence, he needs to find ways to bring the separate parts of the organization together. He needs to achieve an organizational "c-change," redesigning his organizational architecture to meet the challenge of the centaur.

In this chapter, we'll examine how the 5Cs can be applied within the organization to create innovative organizational designs that are better suited to meet the external

How do you need to change your organization to support convergence marketing?

challenges of delivering the 5Cs to consumers. We'll explore how companies are engaged in transforming their organizations to meet the challenge of the centaur and to take advantage of the new technologies and approaches offered by the 5Cs.

THE NEED FOR ORGANIZATIONAL CONVERGENCE

Changing the organization appears to be essential in making technology investments pay off. Erik Brynjolfsson and Lorin Hitt, studying both econometric data and individual company cases, found that the returns from investments in IT are far greater in firms that make complementary changes in their organizations—such as new business processes, new skills, and new structures. The impact of these changes may be as much as an order of magnitude larger than the investments in the technology itself.[2]

The communications and information technologies that drive convergence work against the grain of the traditional organization. The traditional organization is built upon separation and specialization. Because of the need for specialization, poor communication mechanisms, and high coordination costs, the large organization could not operate as a total organism. Instead, it was broken down into component parts, divisions and strategic business units (SBUs), brands and product lines. The supply chain was broken into suppliers, manufacturers, and buyers. Industries were broken into fairly neat sets of competitors. The car companies in Detroit could look out their corporate windows and see their competitors. The customer was outside the organization, and there was a clear boundary between the inside and outside.

This led to the creation of a variety of ways to slice up the traditional organization into "silos" by function (finance, operations, marketing, etc.) brand, customer, and geography, as shown in Exhibit 10–2. Each of these silos creates pieces of the organization that are separated from the whole. While this creation of silos may facilitate management and control, breaking a complex organization into small pieces reduces interaction among the pieces and increases complexity for customers. For example, one customer may be forced to interact with several separate divisions of a single company. Is customer relations a marketing, information technology, or operations issue? Is a telephone customer with a cell phone and several landlines a "business" or "residential" customer? Should a road warrior who buys a laptop be viewed simply as a customer in his home country? What geographic division should serve a customer in Singapore who orders online from a U.S. business unit? Should an upscale customer in Manhattan be considered part of the same "U.S." market as the poor Hispanic worker in Los Angeles?

The implementation of e-business initiatives has, in many cases, added to the silos in the organization. The rise of e-business has often led to the creation of independent e-business units within organizations. For example, Procter & Gamble created Reflect.com as a separate unit or Kmart set up the independent BlueLight.com website. Without careful management, the separation of online and offline businesses can lead to a rift between these organizational units and reduce the likelihood of seamless convergence.

While pharmaceutical firms usually market brands, their customers, who often suffer from multiple ailments, are seeking integrated wellness solutions. Separate marketing campaigns target doctors and consumers, yet physicians are a part of both

EXHIBIT 10–2 SO LONG TO SILOS

Over the years, the company has been sliced and diced in many different ways. While these divisions facilitate managing large organizations, they create silos that can create barriers to convergence. There is a critical need to bridge and break these silos. Among these silos are:

- **Function:** Companies have traditionally been managed by functional areas such as finance, operations, marketing but many business challenge such as new product development span these functional areas. There are further silos within each of the functions. For example, the marketing function is further divided into silos such as sales, advertising, public relations and other components of marketing strategy.

- **Brand:** Companies manage their businesses by brands, such as P&G's brand structure and its associated category or group product management that groups together a number of related brands. Yet even these efforts have not encouraged coordination across company /industry-defined brand categories, which may not be relevant to the consumer.

- **Industry:** SIC codes are often quite common. AT&T, for example, has proposed reorganizing into business lines of business (residential, wireless and broadband services), but the lines between these offerings and markets are increasingly overlapping.

- **Geography:** Companies typically break their organizations into geographic units by region and countries, and within countries by Census-type regions, but the Internet is erasing many of these geographic distinctions.

- **Team:** Even organizations that create cross-functional teams often find that the teams create their own silos and start competing with one another.

- **e-Silos:** The rise of e-business has led to the creation of independent e-business units within organizations, but these can become silos that are separate from and competing with the traditional business.

- **Across companies:** Historically, we have treated the company as a silo, separate from its partners, but companies are increasingly moving to become part of integrated supply chains and value networks that bridge these boundaries.

audiences. The organizational separations do not make sense. But how can companies remove the brick walls of these silos without losing the benefits of specialization and their ability to manage the business?

To counteract the weaknesses of these silos, companies have moved to matrix structures, in which one silo is overlaid upon another silo. But these matrix organizations often become complex to manage, eroded functional expertise, made accountability more difficult to assign, and presented the customer with an even more complex organization.

The Web and the centaur are all about openness and connection, but organizational "silos" create barriers to openness and connection. With the change in the balance of power, the walls of this "fortress" corporation need to be reconfigured. From the customer's perspective,

How does your current organizational structure facilitate or create obstacles to convergence? What are the major silos of your organization and what are you doing to facilitate their convergence?

the ideal would be to organize the company around the customer, but such a customer-centric model makes the organization difficult to manage. Is it possible to do both?

Bridging Silos

Now, these silos are converging. Advances in information technology are shattering walls between industries and between companies and customers. Microsoft's research agenda, for example, is focused on using technology to leap across a variety of barriers including: reality barrier (virtual reality), barriers between people, barriers between people and computers (language, speech), barriers between people and information (data mining), barriers among computers (high speed networking), and barriers between work, car and home.[3]

These information and communications technologies are creating what information technology expert Colin Crook has called the emergence of a "global grid." This grid is a network of users and portals, offering free communications, scalability for even the smallest corporations, globalization, total connectivity, and universal digitalization. In this new environment, simple rules often produce complex outcomes, as can be seen with fractals or traffic patterns on the Internet. The boundaries between organizations and customers and suppliers are breaking down. The boundaries between once-separate industries are blurring. And, finally, as we have explored in this book, customers are running zigzag over the dividing line between online and offline businesses.

5C STRATEGIES FOR CREATING CONVERGENT ORGANIZATIONS

The same technologies and approaches that have led to the rise of the hybrid consumer can help deliver on the vision of the convergent organization. *Customization* technology and approaches can help to tailor the organization differently for customers and employees in different parts of the organization, offering different filters on information. *Community*-building technologies and approaches can be used to bridge silos, drawing together virtual teams to address specific challenges in real-time in the organization or to create communities between the outside customers and inside employees. The technologies that provide customers with seamless, *multi-channel* solutions and timely responsiveness and value can be applied internally as guiding design principles. New *competitive value* equations and metrics can be developed, focusing on lifetime value of the customer and other measures in addition to short-term financial returns. Finally, automated *choice tools* for gathering information, decision making, and management give employees more information and support in responding to customers. These tools also offer customers increased access to the resources of the organization without using the precious resource of physical experts.

The following strategies illustrate ways that managers can apply the 5Cs internally to transform their organizations to meet the challenge of the centaur. Some of

How can the 5Cs help address the organizational challenges of convergence?

the examples are drawn from business-to-business organizations, but they illustrate principles of organizational design that can be applied to business-to-consumer organizations.

Create a Customizable, Modular Organization (First C)

Like mass customization of products, a "plug and play" organization developed from modular processes can be easily reconfigured to meet the shifting opportunities of new technology and changing demands of the hybrid consumer. A "digital fabric" can tailor the view of the organization to the individual while maintaining its existing structure.

In an environment in which the core technologies and organizational capabilities need to shift, the organization has to have the agility to be quickly reconfigured. Nokia is implementing an approach that Senior Vice-President of Strategy and Business Structure Mikko Kosonen calls the "plug and play" organization.[4] Core processes across the organization are being systematized and modularized so that they can be rapidly reconfigured. The organization identifies "best of breed" solutions from outside partners and makes sure they are designed to fit together well with company systems through modular processes and web-based interfaces. "The fact that we can reuse modules provides us with tremendous cost, speed, and flexibility advantages," said Kosonen.

"Every time we create a new module, it is in the library and can be used by everybody." In contrast, most processes that are built from the ground up, like integrated hardware and software systems, are not easily upgraded or transferred to other parts of the organization.

Leaders of business units still decide how these standard modules are put together, so they retain control over the strategic direction of their units without the time and expense of developing custom solutions from scratch. By assembling the organization from these building blocks, the Nokia group lowers its costs of implementing and supporting new technologies without significantly eroding functionality.

In the past, companies have always had to trade off agility with economies of scale in their organization in the same way they have had to choose between efficiency and customization in their manufacturing. The larger the organizations became, the harder they were to restructure.

Nokia's new technologies and processes offer ways to reduce these tradeoffs. The combination of modular design and technology that can bring these components together into a system creates an organization that can be customized on the fly. This type of flexibility is crucial in very uncertain and fast-changing businesses such as wireless communications. "We want to be the first company in the world to combine economies of scale with agility," Kosonen said.

This approach creates a very different role for IT. It is neither a passive tool for leaders of businesses nor an overarching architecture that imposes a uniform model across the organization. Instead IT works with the business leaders in developing technology and processes to support their business strategies. It extracts common elements of these processes and creates corporate-wide best practice components. IT ensures that these processes are modular and have a common interface that allows them to be joined with other processes. When it faces its next organizational design challenge, it can then pull these standard modules out and use them as a basis for

> **How can you use web-based applications to systematize your processes to create a modular design for your organization that will increase its flexibility?**

developing a solution to the strategic challenge. In this way, the business strategy remains squarely with the business, but the organizational design to execute that strategy is shaped by IT and senior business leaders.

Digital Fabric: Bridging Silos without Breaking Them

Sometimes it is not necessary to actually reconfigure the physical organization, but rather to create a customized interface so the organization *looks* different to different employees, customers, and partners. Trintech—a company that provides software and support to financial services organizations for handling credit card transactions in physical, online, and wireless transactions—has pioneered an approach CEO John McGuire calls the "digital fabric." Trintech has begun to create an organization that is neither a functional organization nor a matrix organization. Instead, like a customizable web browser, the organization looks different to different viewers. It is the same organization underneath, but different people see it differently.

Just as Windows was able to overlay a graphical user interface on DOS, and Web browsers were able to create a user-friendly interface for the Internet, the organization can create a customizable interface for users in different parts of the organization. The organization can be "configured" to be viewed by product line, by function, or by customer, without changing the underlying organization. Finally, the organization can be opened up to customers in ways that were never possible in the past. For example, customers can directly access their accounts, design new products or check on orders, so they are invited inside the organization. The matrix can be sorted in different ways to take whatever cut of the organization is needed.

Trintech is organizing interactions with each customer around an online "eRoom," as illustrated in Exhibit 10–3, a collaboration technology that allows sharing of documents and interaction, drawing relevant experts from different parts of the organization together in a single virtual location. This means, in essence, that every customer has a virtual micro company within the larger organization. Functional managers retain depth in specific areas, such as finance, marketing, or engineering, and retain their identification with these areas. They do not become generalists, but see the organization as a collection of specialists working together to create customer solutions. The leaders of product divisions see the organization as a set of product divisions that are managed for P&L by segment. The CEO and top managers see the organization as a set of key metrics on the revenue and order pipeline that can be dynamically sorted using data lenses, where they can click down for greater detail. The management team also manages by exception through operational red flags.

The organization can still be structured by traditional functions such as finance and marketing, or by brands, but the customer or employee doesn't have to see the messy infrastructure. This allows the organization to *bridge* functional silos and product divisions without *breaking* them. "We need the

EXHIBIT 10–3 TRINTECH'S CONVERGENT ORGANIZATION

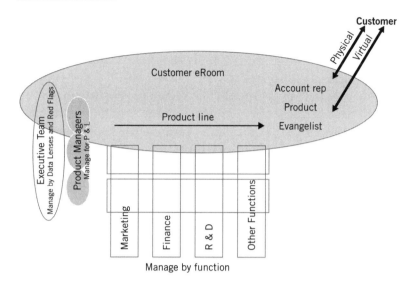

traditional value of brands, and the P&L focus has to be honored," McGuire said. "You also can have functional depth and efficiency so you have best practices across all the brands. It is through the digital fabric that we are able to break down those silos yet maintain the discipline of functional depth."

Mohanbir Sawhney describes such a customizable interface using the metaphor of a Palm Pilot, which has a HotSync button to automatically synchronize information with a computer. Instead of breaking down the walls to "homogenize" the organization, the company uses technology to "synchronize." The product lines and functions of the organization can be kept separate, but the information layer is drawn together to create integration.[5]

> **How can you create a seamless "digital fabric" in your organization?**

Organize Around Community (Second C)

In addition to customization, the second "C", communities, both physical and virtual, can reshape the boundaries of the firm to draw together customers and suppliers into value networks. These communities are built upon entrepreneurial values and flexible architectures.

The community-building power of the Internet that has transformed interactions with customers can also be used to change interactions within the company. New business paradigms, such as those based on delivering a total solution instead of stand-alone products, lead to a redefinition of the boundaries of the firm. Companies can build communities around knowledge, value-creating processes (such as new product development, demand creation, etc.) or around areas of interest that might cut across functional or business lines. Companies also can find value in linking the vibrant and valuable private communities of their intranets and extranets with the open communities of the Internet. Joining together the public and private communities can help to harness the social energy inside the firm and link it to social energy outside the firm, in ways that create value for the firm.

For example, AOL Time Warner realized its decentralized commercial printing was diffused across 500 vendors. Rather than moving to centralizing printing, which would have increased coordination costs and hampered the freedom of divisions, the company instead used printing software (Printcafe) and the Web to create what AOL's CFO Joseph Ripp called a "virtual community of printing."[6] This strategy drew together members of the company's private community of employees and connected them to a more limited set of 50 printing suppliers outside the community. Employees still had a choice of different vendors to meet their specific needs, but the virtual consolidation extracted $150 million from the company's costs. "The Web gives you the opportunity to create communities across the company, to give people access to the cookie jar," Ripp said.

Similarly, Trintech's connections with customers and ideas within the organization have transformed its approach to developing new products and businesses. Customers and employees are wired together by something Trintech CEO John McGuire calls an "idea vault." Trintech has created a systematic process for capturing new ideas from customers, employees, and competitors and channeling them into new business initiatives. The system takes suggestions gleaned from customers, and ideas created independently by employees, and channels them to an "idea council." The idea council screens and filters the ideas and moves promising ideas forward. The ideas are also tracked in an idea pipeline that is similar to a sales pipeline. The company then has a systematic method for screening and developing new ideas. It also can recognize and reward the employees who create them.

Use Lighthouse Customers to Point the Way

In a world that is rapidly changing, companies can use their interactions with customer communities to keep ahead of change. In the 1990s, at a time when online business was just taking off, McGuire found his way from Dublin into the office of a tiny start-up named Netscape in California. He met with Marc Andreessen, who was just starting the revolution that would transform the computing industry and business world forever. How did McGuire find his way from Europe into a small company on other side of the world? Trintech had identified a set of "lighthouse customers" who were at the forefront of adopting new technologies. It worked closely with these customers to understand and monitor these emerging technologies.

One of these lighthouse customers, a bank called Swedish Post in Sweden, was carefully monitoring IP (Internet protocol) technology. Swedish Post mentioned they had bought a few servers from a company called Netscape. McGuire immediately called the head of Netscape Europe and got him on the phone at 8 p.m. that evening. The European executive patched McGuire into Netscape's San Mateo headquarters. Within a few days, McGuire was in California hammering out a deal for collaborating with Netscape. Within a week, he and a representative from Netscape were making a joint presentation to the Swedish bank. "If you are close to your customers and listen to your customers and see what they want, you will find what you need to do," McGuire said.

"We saw the emergence of the Internet as a means of global connectivity," McGuire said. "What we were trying to do was to use the Internet as a means of connectivity so all consumers could access their accounts anywhere in the world. We looked at projections of transactions over the Internet. Global airline reservations systems were doing electronic commerce to sell airline tickets, beds in hotels and travel packages. All of their networks were proprietary networks. The Internet represented a huge growth opportunity and Trintech was going to capitalize on it."

How can you link your internal and external communities? Can your pacesetting customers lead you to the next Netscape who will define core technologies for the future?

Create a Convergent Culture: Put the Organization on Wheels

Like customer communities, internal communities are held together by a set of social interactions and shared values. To meet the challenge of the hybrid consumer, companies need organizational cultures that can combine the executional excellence of the best traditional organization with the entrepreneurial energy and creativity of technology startups. These organizations are not one or the other, but rather "ambidextrous."[7] These organizations keep a stable set of organizational values and culture, but conduct ongoing experiments with new approaches to the business. As these experiments are proven successful, they are then absorbed into the culture of the broader organization. This is a delicate balance, but is what is required to create a convergent organization.

The physical organization of the community can reinforce its virtual interactions and values. For example, at the headquarters of SEI Investments, all of the desks and file cabinets in the organization are on wheels and all the telephone and computer connections come down from huge cables suspended from the ceiling (the next generation will be wireless). Employees can literally create self-organizing teams and reconfigure their groups in new patterns by moving their desks. This is a physical metaphor for an organization designed for change in response to new opportunities and changes in its markets. It is a clear sign to new and existing employees that the organization wants to attract people who are comfortable with change and entrepreneurship. Prospective employees who are not comfortable with this type of creative environment, also signaled by the modern art throughout the offices, quickly self-select out. Everyone also has the same desk and no one has a secretary, including Founding Chairman and CEO Al West, who answers his own phone and sits on the open floor with everyone else. This creates an environment of flat and open communication. The company has been very successful, achieving 30 to 40 percent annual growth. SEI was named one of the top companies on *Business Week's* 2001 ranking of Standard & Poor's MidCap 400 index and earned a spot on *Wall Street Journal's* "honor roll" for the highest shareholder returns, with five-year average annual returns of 73.6%.

In addition to workplace design and culture, company actions also set the tone for the values of the community. For example, General Electric stresses values such as annihilating bureaucracy, digitization, relishing change, and creating a "boundaryless" organization. These are values that encourage people to work creatively and break down organizational barriers across the organization. GE has made a commitment to weed out what it calls "Type IV" managers,[8] those who deliver results, but at the expense of the company's values. This is a demonstration of its willingness to sacrificing short-term earnings to protect the long-term culture.[9]

How can you create a convergent culture?

Build Convergent Channels (Third C)

Combine physical and virtual interactions with customers strategically in ways that meet the relational and information needs of customers, reduce internal costs and offer insights into the future of markets.

Just as hybrid consumers are combining different channels in their searching and purchasing processes, companies also need to explore ways to combine physical and virtual channels. For example, Trintech has created a customer interface that combines physical and virtual interaction in a way that creates value for the customer and reduces cost for the company. In the old days, Trintech would send out a technical sales rep and a sales engineer. These two—inseparable like "Laurel and

Hardy"—would fly into town and meet with clients together. This meant two salespeople had to be transported around the world, put up in hotels and flown back home to create a proposal based on the meeting. This was a process that generally took two weeks, after the proposal was drafted and run through engineering, legal, and other reviews.

The new model combines the physical and virtual, sending the sales rep out to shake the hand of the client and patching in the engineering rep virtually, either on the videoconferencing screen at one of Trintech's local offices or even on the laptop of the sales rep (through NetMeeting). The engineering rep, known as a "product evangelist," can handle calls in this way with sales reps in Europe, North America, and Asia, all from his home base in California. The same rep can handle more calls, and clients have access to the product evangelists with the deepest knowledge. After discussing the technical concerns with the client, the product evangelist logs off and the sales rep takes the client out to the pub.

To further leverage the strengths of the engineering reps, they are very well supported. In the background, assistants listen in on the call and sketch out a solution that they turn into a formal proposal. Meanwhile, a fresh team of assistants come into the room to provide support for the product evangelist's next call. Where Trintech would have needed 30 engineering reps to support 30 sales reps, it now has just three key evangelists, one in each of its product areas. Even with the added support staff positions, the arrangement saves Trintech an estimated 60 percent over the old Laurel and Hardy model. At the same time, it means that every customer has a much more experienced engineering rep at the meeting. "There is one expensive person who is really deep in knowledge," McGuire said.

The process is also much faster. The proposal itself goes into the client eRoom, where legal, engineering, and product managers come into the room and populate the document, working off predefined templates. The salesperson comes in with a pricing matrix and the proposal is kicked back to the product evangelist for a final review. Then it is sent electronically to the sales rep, who can print it out and deliver it to the client, very often the next morning.

There are some new positions that are needed to make this process work smoothly. Trintech has created the position of "program manager," who is responsible for managing the eRooms and making sure that proposals and other projects are acted on in a timely manner. This program manager, dubbed "captain clipboard," is responsible for pinging people to make sure they are delivering on time. Since the process is diffused and needs to be completed rapidly, this coordinating function is crucial to make sure all these virtually connected parties are brought together.

How can you combine physical and virtual interactions with customers to maximize value for customers and reduce costs for the firm?

Separation vs. Integration

As discussed in Chapter 5, another key channel decision for organizations is the degree of separation or integration of its online and offline businesses.[10] Greater separation can facilitate entrepreneurship while greater integration can improve control, synergies, and efficiencies. In developing their online businesses, companies can create separate units, engage in joint ventures, develop internal ventures or establish fully integrated online operations. Often companies will initially set up their online businesses as independent units to give them room for their entrepreneurial energies to run and then integrate the businesses into the organization when their potential has been demonstrated and they have worked through their early stages of growth.

The level of integration also creates tradeoffs for consumers. They may benefit from the innovation and fresh approaches of a separate online business but be disappointed when they are treated like different customers across different channels. Companies also lose the opportunity to market across channels if they have poor integration. As discussed above, however, integrated interfaces and databases can help to draw together the online and offline, even if the actual organizations remain separate.

Redefine Competitive Value through People and Technology (Fourth C)

As the value equation changes for customers, companies correspondingly need to redesign their internal value equation. More flexible environments mean companies need to rethink the value proposition they offer to their employees. Technological offerings such as web services can redefine the way value is carved up and delivered through new technologies.

Convergent Careers:
Forge New Relationships with Employees

With the erosion of corporate loyalty and long-term employment, companies also need to rethink the value proposition they offer to employees. The relationship with employees in the organization is far more fluid today. Employees are finding jobs and companies are finding employees electronically through job sites.

The new technology creates opportunities to change relationships with employees along the entire spectrum, from recruiting to employment to post-employment. Many companies are using their own corporate web sites more effectively in recruiting. For example, Cisco reportedly tracks the questions of visitors and when they start asking highly technical questions about products, showing a high level of knowledge, the company shows them employment advertising. Cisco also holds contests on issues such as optical network engineering, providing the company with another source of contacts for potential employees with expertise in these areas. Other companies are creating alumni lists, where they connect former employees with other current and former employees, but also gather current employment information at the same time. Companies are also keeping in touch with applicants who are not hired, sending them e-mail every six months asking them to "update their resumes."[11]

Just as it has empowered consumers, the Internet is also placing more power in the hands of workers. Sites such as salarysource.com give employees access to salary surveys. Other sites such as vault.com offer profiles of the company and candid chatrooms with current employees of companies, who give inside reports on everything from dress code to job interview questions to working environment. The employer no longer controls this flow of information. Companies such as reference.com and refer.com allow people to post references in their personal networks and receive a reward if the person they refer is hired.

The new environment is changing the way companies find and relate to employees. Employee referrals and the Internet account for 70 percent of hiring at Motorola's broadband division.[12] As workers are finding greater opportunities and perhaps even loyalty to external job markets such as Monster.com, companies are forging their own internal job markets to keep employees within their companies. All of this is changing the relationship of the company with its employees and creating far more interactive relationships using both physical and virtual channels.

Candice Carpenter, founder of iVillage, said that given the more fluid nature of employment, companies need to focus on helping employees understand and build their baseline work personality. There are tests that can provide useful insights on current capabilities and companies can also help employees chart their own career paths. One approach Carpenter used is "aspiration-centered mentoring." Employees were asked to identify the job they would like to hold in five or six years and then identify someone already in that job and interview them. The employees then developed a list of skills they had to develop to achieve this goal and could then focus their work at the company on acquiring those skills.[13]

Companies also have to recognize that the core values of today's workers, who are also today's hybrid consumers, are changing. Companies need to address a shift from the traditional Protestant work ethic to the new "hacker ethic."[14] The old work ethic was focused on discipline, building a career and earning money as a reward, while the new ethic is based on passion and freedom, peer recognition and money as an enabler of freedom.

Finally, many of these employees will not be formal employees per se. Nokia's Kosonen expects that the future growth of the company will come without expanding the size of its

How can you use technology to develop new value propositions for employees and potential employees to attract and retain the best people? organization. Instead, he envisions an organization with about the same number of core employees but a much larger network of independent "employees" who are outside the formal organization, through alliances and outsourcing.

Retool Technology

The value equation for technology traditionally required large initial investments in internal systems with long and uncertain payoffs. This is changing as smaller technological components can be outsourced into "web services." These web services are the next step in the diffusion of technology from large legacy systems to client servers to web-based systems. Web services create greater flexibility in serving customers across channels.

Obviously, technology is a critical enabler or facilitator of convergence. It is the heart of the changes that have created the centaur. From the company perspective, however, the difficulty is that traditional legacy systems often have trouble talking with one another and have even more problems communicating with new consumer interfaces. As managers try to untie this Gordian knot, web services offer a creative solution to cut through it.[15] They offer a common, Internet-based, technological platform for information technology services. There are an increasing number of companies that are adopting this approach, such as PeopleSoft or Microsoft with its ".Net" strategy. There also are new companies such as 12 Entrepreneuring that are building their strategies around these developments.

Develop Organizational Choice Tools and Performance Measures (Fifth C)

Powerful internal tools can empower employees to make better decisions and keep up with empowered consumers who have more tools at their disposal.

As discussed in Chapter 7, better decisions tools have reduced the information asymmetries between companies and consumers. As consumers gain access to more powerful tools for gathering information, making decisions and managing their lives, companies need to expand the internal tools in the hands of employees so they can continue to add value. For example, if customers have access to basic investment tools, brokers need to have these tools and even more sophisticated tools so they can continue to add value. As consumers have direct access to information, physicians need access to the same information and more powerful information and decision support systems.

These internal tools include tools for gathering better information, such as increasingly sophisticated data mining technologies. Other tools help managers make better decisions, including decision support systems, just-in-time learning systems and simulations. Finally, employees need tools to manage the business more effectively across different channels.

For example, companies are developing sophisticated tools for multichannel marketing that help employees develop marketing strategies across different channels. If you buy a purse online at NeimanMarcus.com, you might be offered a coupon for a matching pair of shoes. As wireless technology develops, these multichannel tools could be sent to the cell phone or wireless appliance of a customer in a physical store.[16] These multichannel strategies are built upon increasingly sophisticated and integrated databases that provide the company with coherent customer information across different channels. A variety of companies, including IBM, Microsoft, Siebel and Oracle are offering database software to help integrate customer information across channels.

Real-Time Information
In addition to integration, companies are developing tools for faster information gathering to support decisions. Real-time information can change the way the organization responds to change and also gives managers the information they need to make quicker and better decisions. Cisco Systems is legendary for its ability to close its books on an hour's notice with a "virtual close." Unlike traditional accounting systems that take weeks or months, this system can close out books in real time

and give final numbers within a few days. This gives managers real-time information with which to guide the business and required a major redesign of the whole business processes. For example, the company's automation of expense accounting allows it to handle all the expense processing for a 38,000 employee organization with just two employees—and pay expenses within two days. (Of course, better tools don't automatically lead to better decisions. Cisco managers had real-time numbers about where they had been, but when the economy sank into a downturn, Cisco was slow to recognize it and ended up writing off $2.5 billion in excess inventory in early 2001.[17] It could be that they measured the wrong things, the virtual close provided the right information but managers ignored it, or the company did not have the flexibility in its supply chain to respond quickly enough.)

Trintech takes its metrics one step further. It populates its metrics with all the projects that are in the pipeline, tracking the revenue based on whether projects are in proposal, contracts are signed, or work is under way. Since its information is connected down to the contracts in the field, McGuire can see every move in the pipeline, giving him a window on where the business is headed. He tracks revenue and potential revenue by type of revenue and utilization rate, undelivered revenue and budgeted revenue, and days outstanding on receivables. He can also sort the information by product division.

Different managers in the organization have different windows on the data, showing the current snapshot on their part of the world. Managers can then click down for more detail on any part of the picture. "Because we are working off the same database of numbers, we can create data lenses, summary reports that can be constructed and then zoom down to various spots of data," McGuire said. "We can then manage by exception as opposed to detail."

To build different views of data, companies are creating customizable corporate portals. Companies such as Plumtree and Datachannel offer employees a "dashboard" with relevant information in an interface tailored to their own needs. Instead of being forced to extract meaning from standardized reports, the reports are tailored to the needs of the viewer.

Companies can use the same technologies they use to interact with customers to interact with their employees. These systems, such as Siebel's Employee Relationship Management software (ERM) can put more **How can you use technology to gather real-time, forward-looking metrics to guide your business?** real-time information and powerful tools in the hands of employees. These systems also can offer powerful online training tools to provide employees with just-in-time learning to help them better serve customers.

The choice of measures is also important. Although dot-com metrics clearly missed the importance of profitability, the reflexive cry to return to purely backward-looking metrics is also not appropriate. The convergent organization needs to combine traditional backward-looking metrics focused on ROI with more forward-looking measures for value creation. Current accounting metrics and organizational separations tend to make it difficult to focus on the potential hybrid consumer. Metrics focus on transactions while companies are increasingly focused on building relationships through communities or customerization.

Companies are finding new ways to measure the value they create. The rise of tools such as the Balanced Scorecard provides *broader* insights by integrating more "soft" measures such as customer satisfaction or what Siebel Systems called "relationship capital" into the model. Companies need to develop broader and deeper measures to assess lifetime value of customers across different channels. These measures should offer an integrated pictures of the actual costs of serving customers and potential value they contribute, both online and offline.

Create the Right Level of Transparency
Another aspect of online metrics is transparency. At Trintech, everyone can see what is happening, which parts of the organization are contributing to revenue and profit and which are lagging. They can also see the status of different R&D projects. This means that sales reps won't be sandbagged by product developers who are running behind but don't tell the sales rep.

Likewise, engineering won't be surprised by a sales promise that they can't deliver. It also means that any person in the company can see how they are performing relative to peers.

"It creates a culture of trust and transparency," McGuire said. "Trust is not retribution. We are not out to hang you if you are late, but there are cascading consequences of being late. The sooner you know, the better you are able to manage the expectations of the customer."

On the other hand, companies may be reluctant to create full transparency for customers. They do not want customers to necessarily be able to peer into their organization and see their internal structure and pricing. As they shape their tools and metrics, companies need to determine how much transparency they want to create.

How can you provide information and decision tools to employees to make better decisions and provide more value to customers?

RETHINKING THE ORGANIZATION

Applying the 5Cs within the company leads to a transformation across a wide range of aspects of organizational architecture. As summarized in Exhibit 10–4, these changes affect organizational culture and values, value-added processes, structure, customer interfaces, technology, organizational boundaries, metrics, and human resources. In each of these areas, the hybrid consumer is creating new challenges, and the 5Cs are offering new opportunities.

For example, consider how the traditional marketing organization is reshaped along each of these dimensions. Marketing needs new culture and values focused on a combination of execution and entrepreneurship. By creating modular processes for marketing, the marketing discipline can be more seamlessly integrated into the work of other parts of the organization and involve the customer as co-producer. By creating a structure based on a digital fabric, marketing can more easily offer access to its insights throughout the organization and

EXHIBIT 10–4 ILLUSTRATIVE ORGANIZATIONAL ARCHITECTURAL ISSUES

	Offline	**Online**	**Convergence**
Organizational Culture and Values	Bureaucratic, stable and executional focused	Entrepreneurial, constant change, chaotic	Entrepreneurial and executional excellence
Processes	Rigidly engineered from scratch	Fluid but not systematic	Modular "plug and play"
Structure	Functional, other silos, and matrix	Networked	Digital fabric, customizable
Customer interface	Physical interaction	Virtual interaction	Combination of physical and virtual interactions
Technology	Legacy and client server	Web browsers	Web services
Boundaries	Isolated organization	Boundaryless	Firm integrated into a larger community
Performance measures	Backward looking	Real time	Forward-looking
	ROI, Balanced Scorecard	Eyeballs and share	Value creation
People	People are here for life	People are fluid and "for purchase"	Grow people while they are here

create links with customers and suppliers. Marketing also has to create structures that integrate separate silos within marketing (between product development, advertising and other areas). Marketing needs to focus on breaking other organizational boundaries such as with R&D and across global operations. Marketing needs to manage physical and virtual customer interactions to create a coherent interface across channels. Marketing can use the technologies of web services, both in offering its own services to the organization and building services using outside vendors. Most of all, marketing managers need to rethink the boundaries between marketing and the larger organization, viewing the marketing function as a resource that can be drawn into a wide range of strategic decisions. Marketing managers need to develop creative performance metrics focusing on forward-looking measures and the lifetime value of the customer. These measures need to focus on share of wallet (the percentage of total customer spending in a category across companies) rather than just market share. Finally, marketing needs to identify and develop its people and keep them engaged, while at the same time offering marketing perspectives for attracting and retaining employees across the organization.

Given the sweeping nature of this impact, implementing a convergent organizational architecture can be daunting. In Chapter 11, we examine a variety of strategies for successful implementation of organizational change and a number of pathways to convergence.

NOTES

[1] Drucker, Peter, *The Practice of Management*, New York: Harper & Row, 1954; reissued paperback, 1993, HarperBusiness, p.37.

[2] Erik Brynjolfsson and Lorin M. Hitt, Beyond Computation: Information Technology, Organizational Transformation and Business Performance, *Journal of Economic Perspectives*, Fall 2000. http://ebusinesss.mit.edu/erik.

[3] Rick Rashid, presentation at Microsoft Faculty Summit, July 23, 2001.

[4] Remarks to the Wharton Fellows in e-Business program, Helsinki, June 8, 2001.

[5] Sawhney, Mohanbir, "Don't Homogenize, Synchronize," *Harvard Business Review* July-August 2001, pp. 101-108.

Action Memo

- Ask each of your stakeholders (managers and employees of key divisions, customers, suppliers) to sketch out their "ideal" interface with your organization. Take all these different views of the firm and begin to see if they can be connected to the company's existing systems.
- Draw your current organizational chart. Now challenge your top managers to come up with at least three different pictures of ways to view the organization.
- Imagine you don't have IT and marketing departments. What would you do if you were designing your systems and your IT and marketing organizations from scratch?
- What are the silos in your organization and how can you bridge them?
- Ask managers in your organization to inventory and categorize the core processes of their businesses. Which of these processes have significant overlap and duplication? Can they be standardized? As common processes are identified, create teams of managers who own similar processes to lead the design of standard, modular processes that can be tailored to the needs of individual business units.

We invite you to share the results of these activities and suggest other action memos at the Convergence Marketing Forum (www.convergencemarketingforum.com).

---

[6] Joseph Ripp, remarks to Wharton Fellows in e-Business Program, New York City, May 9, 2001.

[7] Michael Tushman and Charles A. O'Reilly III, *Winning Through Innovation: A Practical Guide to Leading Organizational Change and Renewal*, Boston, MA: Harvard Business School Press, 1997.

[8] The other types are managers who are performing and are consistent with the culture (the stars), managers who are not performing and are consistent with the culture (who are given a second chance) and managers who are not performing and not consistent with the culture (who are cycled out).

[9] General Electric, 2000 annual report, p. 5.

[10] Gulati, Ranjay and Jason Garino, "Get the Right Mix of Bricks & Clicks," *Harvard Business Review*, May-June 2000, pp. 107–114.

[11] This section draws upon insights from Peter Cappelli, "Making the Most of On-Line Recruiting, *Harvard Business Review*, March 2001, pp. 5-12.

[12] Reported by Kevin Marple, Director of Staffing, Motorola Broadband Solutions, at Wharton Fellows in e-Business, Philadelphia, December 1, 2000.

[13] Candice Carpenter, remarks to Wharton Fellows in e-Business program, Philadelphia, May 12, 2001.

[14] Himanen, Pekka. *The Hacker Ethic and the Spirit of the Information Age*, New York: Random House, 2001.

[15] Hagel, John III and John Seely Brown, "Your Next Internet Strategy," *Harvard Business Review*, 2001 forthcoming.

[16] Konrad, Rachel, "Marketing Tool May Be Right Mix for Store," *CNET News.com*, August 14, 2001.

[17] Mehta, Stephanie N. "Cisco Fractures Its Own Fairy Tales," *Fortune*, May 14, 2001.

11

C-CHANGE

PATHWAYS
TO CONVERGENCE

"It must be remembered that there is nothing more difficult to plan, more uncertain of success, nor more dangerous to manage than the creation of a new order of things. For the initiator has the enmity of all who would profit by the preservation of the old institutions, and merely lukewarm defenders in those who would gain by the new ones."

Machiavelli, The Prince

TRADITIONAL CONSUMER

"You have told a fascinating little fairy tale about this centaur. Perhaps in ten or twenty years, when the technology has advanced enough, this will actually come to pass. We've already been burned once by the hype. We have plenty of time, so we will wait and see. We'll be ready when and if this centaur emerges."

CYBERCONSUMER

"I'll admit that the centaur is the current reality but this is only because the technology is so limited now. When we have wireless, broadband access, and systems designed for online business—and it won't be long now—people will be doing everything but their laundry online. The centaur is only a temporary phenomenon. I'm still preparing for the cyberconsumer."

THE CENTAUR

"The technology is rapidly changing. In a few years, the Internet will look like a supersonic jet compared to the Wright Brother's plane. But while people will fly much faster and have the power to do much more, they will still be people. They will still expect to be able to ring the bell for a flight attendant and order drinks at 30,000 feet. The technology will change. We will not change as quickly. The reality today and in the future is the centaur. Are you ready?"

CONVERGENCE QUESTIONS

>>>*How can you move toward convergence strategies and a convergent organization to meet the challenge of the centaur?*

>>>*What are the pathways to convergence for new online startups and established offline firms?*

>>>*What are the obstacles to implementation and how can you overcome them?*

C-CHANGE: *Pathways to Convergence*

How can companies move toward the convergent organization? This chapter examines some strategies for the difficult process of creating a convergent organization.

Sandra James has been pulled out of her very successful role as marketing vice president of a Fortune 500 firm and asked by the CEO to lead a team in "e-transforming" the company. She sees her career flash before her eyes. There is little in her past experience that prepares her for this challenge. Yet the CEO has clearly stated it is one of the key priorities for the company to take advantage of the power offered by new technologies to better organize its systems and serve its customers. At a minimum, the company needs to have coherent systems to serve customers across multiple channels. There are also opportunities to transform the organization to better take advantage of the technology. But Sandra realizes this will require a fundamental organizational shift.

She is assigned a team drawn from across the organization and given broad aggressive goals and powers with the full backing of the CEO. The company is already online, with a small but effective online channel that is already delivering sales and cost savings to the company. But so far, these initiatives, which she had been involved in creating, were designed as small experiments. They were separate enough that they avoided direct conflict with the machinery of existing systems and channels.

Her current mandate is quite different. She faces the entrenched interests of the existing organization. Given the failure of many dot.coms, how can she convince managers that this transformation is still imperative? With the full support of the CEO, she has a lot of leverage, but she also knows that unless she can gain broad support, the organization will find ways to undermine the initiative.

As she accepts the assignment, with no small measure of reluctance, she still has fundamental questions. What does it mean to e-transform the company? How can they keep up with rapidly changing technologies and incorporate them into this vision? How can she learn about this area as quickly as possible and also bring the entire organization up to speed? And even if they can develop a clear sense of where they needed to go, what will they need to do to get this battleship to travel down this whitewater river?

THE CHALLENGE OF CONCURRENT CHANGE

Convergence requires a fundamental set of changes, and this type of deep change is difficult.[1] Incumbent offline companies and new online companies both have a difficult road as they face parallel challenges in moving toward convergence. Successful established organizations must overcome the inertia of systems that were designed for a traditional world. They have to find ways to integrate new perspectives and culture into a large and often resistant company without derailing its current business. But new online firms also face challenges in moving toward convergence. Their businesses were built in uncompromising opposition to the traditional world, making it harder to see the value of traditional approaches and to make the compromises needed in a hybrid world.

This chapter explores the challenges of implementing convergence strategies and organizational architecture, for implementing a c-change.

As the opening quote from Machiavelli suggests, the process of change runs into many obstacles from both the defenders of the status quo and the "lukewarm" supporters of the change. Any change in a large organization is difficult—and particularly a change that splits so deeply along technological and generational lines. The technology of convergence is threatening to many managers in the organization who have built their whole careers on fortifying a small piece of turf. The prospect of technology and processes that can bring these walls down is not always greeted with open arms. Even with the support of top management, such a transformation is often a painfully slow process.

There is a rich literature detailing the obstacles to the diffusion of new product innovations and resistance to organizational change. This is particularly true for the adoption of disruptive technologies. MIT professor Rebecca Henderson, drawing on research studies, identifies two broad sets of reasons for the failure of implementation of disruptive technologies. The first set of problems is strategic, including the genuine uncertainty involved, fear of cannibalization, fear of margin erosion because of the new approach, and concerns about the time horizon. The second set of problems is organizational, including lack of organizational competencies, interrelationships and complexity of change, the risk of jumping into the unknown, and initiative fatigue.[2] Convergence marketing initiatives, based upon disruptive mental models, face similar obstacles.

Given these challenges and the time compression of change, managers need to take a more concurrent approach to implementation. The process of change in organizations has sometimes been seen as a sequential process, but one of the challenges of disruptive change is that many changes need to move forward simultaneously. In contrast to a linear model in which managers create a convergence strategy, develop the organizational architecture to support it and then proceed to implementation, most change processes are quite a bit messier. The convergence strategy, architecture and implementation are overlapping and need to proceed simultaneously, as illustrated in Exhibit 11–1.

This is similar to the challenge of concurrent design in new product development and the more recent focus on concurrent development of new products, processes and supply chains, in which R&D, marketing, operations and other areas of the company work simultaneously in developing and launching new products. While it poses considerably more complexity than a more linear approach, it also tends to result in more seamless and innovative solutions. In contrast, the traditional

EXHIBIT 11–1 **SIMULTANEOUS CHALLENGES OF IMPLEMENTATION**

sequential model of new product development can lead to disconnects, as engineering throws the new product over the wall to marketing and then to operations. This often creates a mismatch between the goals of R&D, customer needs and manufacturing capabilities and constraints. An organization that proceeds to develop strategy, architecture and implementation simultaneously has a more complex process to manage, but will very often end up with a more coherent result.

Dual Strategy Processes

The process of developing strategy also needs to move on several fronts at once. Where companies in more stable environments might have been able to develop five-year plans, this time horizon is both too short and too long for disruptive innovations. In five years, dot-coms rose from obscurity and crashed to the ground. This is a lifetime in the short-cycled "dog years" of the Internet. By the time a five-year strategy is developed, it is often obsolete. On the other hand, companies that move forward only opportunistically, without a broader perspective, often find themselves swept away in fads or reactive maneuvers that move in no clearly discernable direction.

Author John Hagel contends that in an environment of increasing uncertainty companies need to pursue a dual strategy of rapid prototyping and visionary leadership.[3]

In a fast-moving technological environment, companies first need strategies for rapid prototyping and experiments based on 6- to 12-month cycles. Companies such as Cisco and Trintech have adopted policies of moving every project from concept to cash in six months. Large projects are broken up into smaller chunks. This discipline ensures that technology projects don't drag on forever. If a project goes for longer than six months, there is a high likelihood that it will be obsolete when it is developed. This also allows the company to quickly recognize success or failure before its commitments are too high.

At the same time the company engages in rapid prototyping, it needs to pursue the parallel approach of developing a broader strategic vision. A strategic vision of five to ten years or longer can define the general direction of the business, creating a framework for short-term initiatives. For example, Microsoft's early success was built on the basic vision that computing was moving from the mainframe to the desktop. The exact technology and strategies used to navigate that transition have changed radically since the firm was started, but the overall strategic vision remained the same. It gave the company a context for aligning its efforts and moving forward in an environment of high uncertainty.

Companies face the further challenge of changing the wheels of the car while they are driving. This means that while changes may be radical, they also need to follow a careful and consistent path from the current organization to the desired future, supporting the current business while moving to a new model.

Further, in complex and rapidly changing organizations, processes are not only centrally directed, but also self-organizing. Complexity theory offers insights into how such systems can evolve. Authors Susanne Kelly and Maryanne Allison point out that companies can use insights from complexity theory to gain advantage by using concepts such as nonlinear dynamics, open and closed systems, feedback loops, fractal (or nested) structures, co-evolution, and group behavior.[4]

THE CHALLENGE OF C-TRANSFORMATION

Most companies are just beginning to pursue their "c-transformation," changing their organizations to meet the challenge of the centaur, the SCs, and convergence. Some companies will initiate massive changes in their business, in the way that AOL and Time Warner are reshaping the boundaries of their industries; IBM moved from selling boxes to services; Enron moved from selling natural gas to providing a trading platform for electricity, natural gas, broadband and other commodities; Hewlett-Packard moved from instrumentation to computers; and Corning moved from glass to fiber optics. Some changes are within existing industries, others are across industries. While other companies such as eBay have created entirely new industries by understanding and responding to the hybrid consumer.

While the rise of the centaur creates opportunities for such sweeping changes in organizations and industries, the insights of convergence marketing can be applied on a smaller scale anywhere in the organization. Wherever you are in the organization, and wherever you are in the world, by focusing on the needs of the centaur and the opportunities of convergence marketing, you can transform your mindset and your approaches to marketing and business strategy. Look for ways to apply the 5Cs (customerization, community, channels, competitive value and choice tools) across your online and offline businesses.

Sun's e-Transformation

Like Sandra James in the opening example, Susane Berger, Vice President of Worldwide Sun Centers at Sun Microsystems, was pulled out of her job to lead a cross-organizational team created to spearhead the eSun initiative. She said it is very difficult "to take our old-world economy companies that have been around for 30 or 50 years and not just open stores but change the way you interact with everyone in the company."[5]

She offered the following advice for e-transformation during a presentation to the Wharton Fellows in e-Business program in Silicon Valley:

- *Don't make it an IT initiative:* "When we first went on our e-transformation, we took people and pulled them out of their jobs," she said. "We didn't make this an IT initiative. We didn't just bring in consultants. We wanted people involved who were going to be affected by it."

- *Anticipate resistance:* "Everybody loves change as long as it is not done to them," she said. "We underestimated how much resistance we were going to get."

- *Change business practices:* "A big rule was that you are not allowed to automate existing bad business practices," she said. "All you do is bad things faster."

- *Don't be limited by past experience:* "We didn't want people to dream in 'black and white,' but rather in 'Technicolor'. We want them to see the possibilities of change."

- *Make it temporary:* The goal was to put the team together and get back to their jobs in 18 months. It took 22 months, but now the eSun people are back in their original jobs or put into new roles around e-business. Continuously focus on transformation, but don't make it an institution.

- *Globalization is harder than it looks:* The original initiative was to be a global seamless system, but they quickly found they had to create many different versions of the site to address different markets. "We really underestimated the complexity of currency, language, and regulation," she said. "It is against the law to solicit business in Germany from the call center in Holland. The rule to follow is to follow the law of the land."

- *Expect to have all your dirty little secrets exposed:* "All of this stuff that used to happen behind the curtain is in front of the curtain," she said. "We had a lot of old business rules." For example, when they started doing auctions, they had to run a time-consuming credit check on cash payments. You must redefine business rules to work in web environments.

She said they are now focused on continuous transformation. "Every 90 days we relook at this," she said. "Projects are now short-term driven with long-term focus." Sun also has used its own experience to assist clients in transformation.

Initiatives such as its iForce project provide a hands-on lab where workers can draw together pieces of diverse legacy systems and new equipment to develop and test solutions.

The potential for cost savings can be large. Sun's 22-month project that launched its e-transformation has saved an estimated $574 million in operations in the first fiscal year. The economics of web sales are overwhelming: a face-to-face sales call costs companies about $150 per call, a branch office contact is about $12, a telephone call is about $6, while interaction on the Web goes down to about $1 per contact.[6] Sun also saved money on rationalizing and standardizing its product offerings (which once had as many as 1.8 million different configurations).

Sun's lessons should not be taken as a recipe for success in transforming the organization. These principles should be treated as possible hypotheses that you should test against your own experiences. There is no one-size-fits-all solution. The transformation of the company depends upon its distinctive past, present, and future, and the way its own hybrid consumers interact with the new technologies.

MANY PATHS TO CONVERGENCE

Looking back at her experiences leading the e-transformation at Sun, Berger commented, "I only wish I had been at Amazon.com. What a joy it would be to start with a blank slate." But online startups such as Amazon, designed for the cyberconsumer, face a different set of challenges in serving the centaur.

Established companies and online startups move from opposite ends of the spectrum toward convergence. The traditional, offline firm has to find ways to "c-transform" itself (change itself for convergence and to meet the challenge of the centaur). Its challenge is to keep what is best about its traditional organization and integrate new web-enabled consumer strategies and internal processes. It has to create the organizational equivalent of middleware that can tie its legacy organization into the new opportunities of the online world.

The opportunities are far deeper than adding clicks to bricks. The new technologies offer ways to fundamentally rethink the approach to the business and the company's connection to its customers.

For the online firm, the challenge is reversed. These companies have, in the words of Thoreau, "built their castles in the air" and now need to build solid foundations beneath them before they come crashing to the Earth. Amazon is busy shoring up relationships with bricks-and-mortar companies such as Toys 'R' Us, Borders, and Sotheby's. Online music industry pioneers and rebels CDNow and Napster were absorbed into the publishing empire of Bertelsmann. Even AOL, a powerhouse in its own right, saw the value of joining its online assets to the content-rich properties of Time Warner. Many organizations in both the physical and virtual worlds have already begun this journey toward convergence.

It is important to recognize that the goal is not coexistence of the channels but rather convergence. To take the analogy of food, the objective is not to create a mall "food court" where separate channels exist side by side but never overlap. Instead, the convergence model is to create a "fusion" of different cuisines, drawing together different channels to create something new. Too many online and offline initiatives have been envisioned as food courts. While this has spared organizations the challenge of truly changing themselves, it also has cost them the opportunity to build something fundamentally different through fusion.

Companies have taken different paths to transforming their organizations. Kmart, discussed in Chapter 5, started with a separate online organization, BlueLight.com, while WalMart initiated a more integrated approach. Procter & Gamble established the independent online beauty site, Reflect.com, to learn about the opportunities for new strategies online. Grocery retailer Tesco, discussed in Chapter 2, built a thriving online business upon the solid foundations of its existing grocery stores and logistics. At the same time, even well financed and managed stand-alone businesses have trouble surviving, as demonstrated by the closure of online grocery service Webvan in July 2001.

In the following sections, we consider two examples of the pathways to convergence from different ends of the spectrum: Charles Schwab and Amazon. These are not presented as exemplars of success, as both firms continue to face significant challenges. These examples are offered instead as illustrations of potential challenges and solutions, and the different paths online and offline firms need to take in moving toward convergence.

Charles Schwab: Crossing the Bridge to the Convergent Organization

In December 1997, Charles Schwab, which was one of the pioneers of online trading suddenly realized it had evolved into a company with a split personality. This split between its online and offline business was nowhere more evident than in the tiered pricing plans it offered to customers. At the low end, customers were presented with the radical online value proposition of $29.95 per trade through e.Schwab. But these low-end traders were given limited access to customer service, with a limit of only one free call per month to a live customer service representative. At the high end, customers who received full access to Schwab's customer service paid $64 per trade. Some low-end customers wanted access to service. Some high-end customers didn't like paying the higher fees. Still, most customers were not complaining, and Schwab's online and offline businesses were continuing to grow.

Yet it became clear to customer service representatives, and then to top leadership, that the company needed to make a change. Schwab needed a more integrated strategy, and the best way to create this strategy was to move to uniform pricing. But when founder Charles Schwab and co-CEO David Pottruck sat down and looked at the numbers, only one thing was fairly certain: it would cost the company about $100 million in lost revenue in the first quarter alone. A single price of $29.95 would knock the wind out of their very profitable company and create fear and uncertainty on Wall Street. What happened after that was uncertain. The hope was that the move would attract many new customers, encourage more trading, and lead to increased revenues and profits. It was clearly a "bet the company" move, and not the first such move the company would make in its pace-setting history.[7]

Schwab had had a great year. Schwab's net income had been growing at annual rates of 23% for the past four years. Its number of online accounts had doubled in the past year, despite the growing competition from steep discounters such as E*Trade and Ameritrade that offered commissions as low as $8 per trade. Profits were up. The stock was soaring. This would be a time when many leaders would leave a proven formula alone. But Schwab and Pottruck saw that their old model would no longer hold in the age of the centaur. They knew they needed to reshape their organization to move ahead. They created the single pricing with value-added services. They took a stand in the battle between online and offline trading. If the pure online view won, E*Trade might be the future of the industry. If the Internet proved to be a fad, the cautious oldline firms like Merrill Lynch would rule the day. But Schwab placed a bet that the centaur was the future. It risked its entire firm on a belief in the power of convergence.

It was a leap from one business paradigm to another, yet entirely consistent with Schwab's strong focus on the customer. As a symbolic demonstration of this move from the old business to the new business, Pottruck and Schwab led the top 150 managers on a march across the Golden Gate Bridge. They walked from one side to another, from the old business to the new, from the split business models of its past to the convergent model of the future. Schwab recognized that this was more than a change in its pricing or marketing strategy. This was a change in its organization, and the bridge walk ensured that everyone in the organization fully recognized what a significant step this was.

As they had anticipated, the new pricing model led to a sharp drop in revenues and the company's share price was punished. But then, the business took off in ways that outstripped the company's projections. By the end of 1998, Schwab made headlines when its market cap climbed past Merrill Lynch for the first time. The wisdom of this convergent model has continued to be proven. The majority of Schwab's customers set up their accounts offline, where they can turn their money over to someone they can see, but then they conduct most of their trading online. A company without a convergent business model would never have been able to respond to this need, or even see this pattern.

The Charles Schwab story, as noted in Chapter 2, also illustrates the perils of dramatic, large-scale change. In committing its organization to a bold online strategy, Schwab was a pioneer, rapidly growing its base of online customers and extending its leadership. But its fortunes were tied so closely to the booming Internet and equally booming bull market that it was also drawn down quickly when the bottom fell out. With a downturn in the dot-coms and general economy, Merrill Lynch's more conservative strategy allowed it to once again regain its leadership position for the time being. In the face of these challenges, Schwab had to rethink its business model to leverage its network of independent financial advisors, its acquisition of U.S Trust and other assets. In a fast-moving environment, the model that works today will not necessarily work tomorrow. Companies need to continue to respond dynamically and flexibly to changes in the environment and consumer behavior.

Amazon:
Building a Road Out of the Digital Jungles

Amazon faces the opposite challenge of established firms. It needs to transform its cyberbusiness into a convergent model to compete with rivals such as Barnes & Noble and WalMart. As Amazon rapidly built its online business, it came face-to-face with several harsh realities of e-tailing. First, it is very expensive to bring new customers in and they can leave again easily (although recommendations, one-click purchasing and other features make the sites stickier than most people initially thought). The cost of acquiring new customers was very high, particularly as companies raced to gain a share in what was considered a winner-takes-all game. Second, while the costs of processing an order online are low, the costs of fulfillment are high. Amazon sank money into warehouses and logistics that eroded its bottom line. In contrast, the oldline retailers who moved online could leverage their existing stores and distribution facilities. They could combine their advertising for their online stores with their existing advertising for their offline stores. And they offered customers multiple channels. This, in itself, offered a tremendous advantage.

Amazon invested in building market share and made what CEO Jeff Bezos called "bold bets" in cyberbusinesses such as pets.com and living.com, which crashed in the burst of the dot-com bubble. At the beginning of 2001, Amazon announced it was laying off 15 percent of its staff, after a brutal year in which 80 percent of its market value evaporated.

Amazon has continued to strengthen its connections to the offline world. Amazon began creating a series of online partnerships with oldline retailers. In August 2000, Amazon announced plans to partner with Toys 'R' Us to create a single online toy store. Toys 'R' Us would choose and buy toys and Amazon would take orders and deliver them. After a successful holiday season in December 2000—in which Toysrus.com posted holiday sales of $124 million and on-time delivery was above 99 percent —the two partners extended the relationship into a new Babiesrus.com site and the educational toy site Imaginarium.com.

In April 2001, Amazon and Borders Group announced that they would be joining forces to turn Borders.com into a co-branded site. The partnership would join Amazon's online inventory, fulfillment and customer service platform with Borders' network of 335 U.S. stores and 14 overseas superstores. The web site is also promoted in Borders' 869 WaldenBooks stores. In May 2001, Amazon launched an "In Theaters" service on the Amazon site, creating partnerships with major movie studios to promote new films in theaters. Amazon uses recommendation software (collaborative filtering) to suggest movies and also offers local showtimes and ticketing. Among the first initiatives in this area, Amazon teamed up with Buena Vista Pictures Marketing to promote the release of *Pearl Harbor*, to help it drive some of it 32 million customers into physical theaters.

It remains an open question whether the maturing of the e-business market and the advance of technology for accessing the Internet will make an online-only model viable. But, given the reality of the hybrid consumer, there seem to be advantages for companies that can move their offerings across multiple channels as Amazon and others appear to be recognizing. The Boston Consulting Group reported that in 2000, pure-play e-tailers spent $82 to acquire each new customer, compared with just $12 by bricks-and-clicks retailers.[8]

The transformation here is not merely, as some analysts have claimed, the new economy firms coming under the discipline of old economy economics. It is the recognition of the centaur. A company that only interacts with customers online will only have a part of the rich interactions of their lives. The pure play by definition only sees one side of the total revenue potential of the hybrid consumer.

WHERE THE HOOVES HIT THE ROAD: THE PROCESS OF IMPLEMENTATION

How do you c-transform your organization to meet the challenge of the hybrid consumer? The advance of the Internet among consumers can offer a useful model for the process of change within the organization. The Internet spread not because it was forcefully imposed upon users, but because people were offered the opportunity to use it, given compelling applications such as email that made them want to do so, drawn in by attractive content and community, and encouraged to play and experiment. The youthful early adopters became mentors to those who followed. In the end, the consumer market was transformed and many people who never imagined they would be online were actively participating.

This sweeping change in the structure and behavior of consumer mindsets and markets in a very short period of time is the opposite of the scientific approach that is usually taken in organizational change initiatives. How can organizations drive the process of c-change, to meet the challenge of convergence? Among the strategies:

- *Create a sense of urgency and focus on idealized design:* Wharton Professor Emeritus Russell Ackoff tells how the head of Bell Labs in 1951 assembled all his top researchers one morning and told them the entire telephone system in the United States had been destroyed the night before. He said: We have to design it from scratch right now. He also pointed out that all the significant technological innovations in the industry had been made before the people in the room had been born. "What have you been doing?" he asked. He challenged them to identify new needs and plans for meeting them. Out of that challenge came the ideas for Touch-Tone phone, Caller ID, cordless phones, and many other innovations. In addition to creating a sense of urgency, he encouraged the researchers to engage in a process of "idealized design."[9] Instead of planning by looking backward at the past, this approach creates a vision for an idealized solution and then works backward to create a plan for arriving there. How can you use idealized design to create a new vision of a convergent business and then develop a strategy for getting there?

- *Provide exposure to technology:* Companies such as Ford and Enron are giving home computers and Internet access to all their employees worldwide. This step will be far more effective than formal training programs in exposing workers at all levels to the possibility of online business. It encourages employees to play with the technology and integrate it into their lives. This also gives them the direct experience as hybrid consumers that they need to understand new convergence strategies for their businesses. Companies can also develop reverse mentoring programs, pioneered by General Electric and expanded in the Wharton Fellows in eBusiness program, to share insights and experience of younger, more tech-savvy employees or students.

- *Develop a strategic understanding of technology:* Gone are the days when CEOs could talk about the importance of technology while never having logged onto a PC. To understand the technology, managers have to use it. Moving organizational processes such as expense reporting, benefits, and travel online can help force this transition. Top leaders also need to actively seek out and learn about emerging technologies. They don't need a detailed knowledge of every technology or know how to write code, but they do need to understand the capabilities and limitations of technology and how they can be applied to their business. For example, Stephen Andriole, former CTO of Safeguard Scientifics, has developed a screen for investing in technology ventures (see box) that combines a strategic and technological assessment of the business.

- *Learn from experience:* Managers need to learn from the mistakes and successes of others. After a strategy has failed, managers often are too quick to dismiss it. ("We tried that. It didn't work.") Instead, by conducting a more careful post mortem, they can learn why the initiative didn't work and perhaps separate the good ideas from the causes of failure.

  Many useful ideas and businesses are buried in the wreckage of the dot-com upheaval. Many of these bold experiments, as might be expected, failed. And some rather unlikely ones succeeded. If we had never had Pets.com, we would never have had eBay. There was no way to separate the winners from the losers at the outset, as so many intelligent investors proved dramatically. And both the successes and failures—often the failures more than the successes—have taught us lessons about what works and what doesn't. Astute managers will learn from the mistakes and successes of these experiments before making their own bold experiments.

- *Create bold experiments:* The hybrid consumers and the best models for businesses to serve them continue to emerge from a process of experimentation. To transform the organization, you need to bring this process of experimentation inside your organization. Most managers are too timid to indulge in experimentation. They tweak and extend, but these experiments usually produce little value and even less knowledge. The key is to create experiments that are bold enough and creative enough—even if they are conducted on

---

15 Things That Should Be True For Technology Investments

1. Products & services that are on the right technology/market trends trajectory.
2. Products & services that have the right infrastructure story.
3. Products & services that sell clearly into budget cycles and lines.
4. Products & services whose impact can be measured quantitatively.
5. Products and services that do not require fundamental changes in how people behave or major changes in organizational or corporate "culture."
6. Products & services that represent total, end-to-end "solutions."
7. Products & services with multiple "default" exits.
8. Products, services & companies that have clear horizontal & vertical strategies.
9. Products & services that have high industry awareness.
10. Products, services & companies that have the right technology development, marketing & channel alliances & partnerships.
11. Products and services that are "politically correct."
12. Serious people recruitment & retention strategies in place or in the queue.
13. Products, services & companies that have compelling "differentiation" stories.
14. Executives who have been there/done that.
15. Persuasive products/services "packaging" & communications: A damn good "elevator story."

Stephen Andriole, Presentation to Wharton Fellows in e-Business, 2001

---

a small scale—to provide insights that could transform the organization. You also need to create a balanced portfolio of experiments and continuously assess the knowledge gained to create new experiments. This process of adaptive experimentation allows you to rapidly generate and test new hypotheses about the future business.

The online world facilitates experimentation. Companies can vary strategies, approaches and product offerings in almost endless variations through virtual sites. For example, one online retailer experimented with different ways to position a box for entering coupons on its checkout page, finding a way to produce an immediate, sustained jump in sales. Other companies have reported increases of three times or more in converting browsers to buyers from fairly small changes in their web sites or marketing strategies.

- *Create a learning organization:* These experiments will not have much impact if the learning from them is not captured and shared widely. To engage in a c-transformation, companies need to strengthen their emphasis on learning. In contrast to the organizations that focus on doing the same things more efficiently and effectively, the learning organization is focused on continuous improvement and innovation through the development of creative new insights. In an environment of rapid change and transformation, organizations need to develop frameworks for capturing and sharing learning. Technology can help in creating the organizational interaction and memory to facilitate learning.

Companies also have to capitalize on the opportunities offered by e-learning to provide just-in-time education to both consumers and employees. However, in designing such a learning organization, we have to keep in mind that the "learners," whether consumers or employees, are centaurs. Therefore, you want to create a hybrid design that combines some face-to-face interaction and online, customizable systems that allow students to customize the education to their learning style. You also need to look for opportunities to apply the 5Cs to create customized educational programs, learning communities, and multi-channel approaches.

- *Use a market-driven approach to implementation:* By thinking about stakeholders in the change process as "customers," managers can use market-based approaches to design change processes that achieve organizational objectives while addressing the needs of stakeholders. To do this, we first need to identify the stakeholders who are key to implementing the change and understand their needs and likely objections. Then we can develop strategies to meet these needs and overcome their objections.

- *Align incentives:* Incentives can make or break a c-change. Incentives that reward employees for the progress of their own small silos will work against convergence. If the progress of your offline and online businesses is treated separately, it is unlikely the two sides will cooperate. On the other hand, reshaping your incentive structure can lead to changes in the behavior of managers and the future direction of the organization. The challenge is that it is far easier to reward progress within the existing organization than to create incentives to reward creativity in redesigning the business.

- *Stimulate the generation of creative and innovative implementation plans:* To generate creative options, GE pioneered the "destroy your business" approach in which each business unit appointed a team to develop strategies to destroy the current business. This helped to encourage the development of creative strategies. There is a need to use creative approaches to generate innovative ideas for implementation.

- *Select the "right" champions:* Find champions who have the passion for the needed changes. It is particularly important to have one of the key top executives protect the champion and have strong top executive support for the needed changes. Research on new product development and innovation finds that the key determinant of new product success is the presence of a strong champion and protector.

- *Create a culture of change:* Above all, to be effective at implementing change, the organization has to develop a number of competencies and values for change that span various change initiatives. Companies need the courage to be able to make bold experiments and accept failure. They need *systems thinking*, to take a holistic, interactive approach to challenges. They need *entrepreneurial energy*, with a focus on adaptive experimentation and learning.

Beginning the c-Change

What began as the revolution of e-commerce has now been transmuted into the challenge of creating a c-change to meet the hybrid consumer. How do you carry the transformation forward in your organization? How do you make people feel comfortable with discontinuous change? How do you overcome the objections of the naysayers who believe that the collapse of the Internet bubble means a return to business as usual?

The key is to use the principles of convergence in making changes in your own organization. Create a community around these ideas. Share the ideas or the book with others and create physical and virtual discussion groups to explore what these concepts mean for your business. Get in touch with managers outside your industry to understand their experiences and experiments. One way to do this is through the Convergence Marketing Forum (convergencemarketingforum.com), an online community to continue to explore these concepts with managers around the world.

There is no last word in this area. Knowledge is not fixed but fluid. In this book, we identified some enduring characteristics of consumers, examined some of the fundamental changes and explored deeper implications of convergence. But every day in businesses around the world, there are fresh experiments taking place. New business models are tested in the crucible of commerce and proven true or rejected. In this environment, there is a need for a close collaboration between researchers and practitioners. There is a need for ongoing learning within a community.

One example of such a learning community is the Wharton Fellows in e-Business program. In contrast to traditional degree programs, the Fellows program is based on the principle that learning should be continuous and lifelong rather than something you take in at one point and apply throughout your career. The program is also based on a collaborative model, in which the students and faculty, along with an extensive array of outside experts and practicing executives, work together to develop programs and explore new knowledge. The program is designed to combine learning across different channels, with face-to-face sessions as well as online programs and a continuing virtual community. It is customizable to the needs of the community and to the needs of individual students who direct the design of future programs. The program also challenges the traditional value proposition of education and takes advantage of research, collaboration and decision tools. It provides a lifelong network of peers from diverse industries and regions of the world.

There are, therefore, many opportunities for continuing your learning about convergence marketing. You can create an informal community in your own organization or join in the cross-company discussions of an online forum such as the Convergence Marketing Forum. Or you could make a commitment to a more formal learning community such as the Wharton Fellows program.

RUNNING WITH THE CENTAURS

We are just at the beginning of understanding the implications of the hybrid consumer for transforming the organization. Leaders of established companies cannot afford to ignore the Internet or view it superficially. They need to look at the new technologies for opportunities to transform their relationships with customers and their entire organizations. Leaders of new e-business organizations also need to raise their sights, to move from focusing on the new technologies and cyberconsumers to address the hybrid reality of the centaurs. This is one of the most significant changes in the history of modern organizations, and the revolution is just beginning.

As noted in the opening of this book, the consumer is already changing. The genie of the Internet is out of the bottle. It cannot be put back. The centaurs will continue to expand and these new hybrid consumers will demand levels of interaction and value that can only be delivered by more convergent organizations. Those organizations that fail to transform themselves for this environment will be left behind. Those that succeed will have the opportunity to "run with the centaurs."

Action Memo

- Consider the chart below of the balance between online and offline revenue. If the balance between your online and offline business shifts how do you need to change your organization in response at each point?

  Percentage of Revenue

Offline	90	50	10
Online	10	50	90

- Take a guided tour of a modern art gallery and consider how the artist was able to build upon tradition to rethink the approach to the artwork. By analogy, how can you take the traditional parts of your business and reframe and reshape them into something different? How do you think your customers will react to this "modern art"?

- Ask all your employees to spend one week experimenting with a set of online sites drawn from those mentioned throughout the book. Then ask them to report insights from these experiments that could be applied to your business.

- Imagine a world in which online access is fast, easy and always on. What will this mean for your business? What potential threats and opportunities will it create?

- Create a reverse mentoring project where students or younger members of the organization work with more experienced managers to understand the new technology.

- Go out to hunt the centaur. Send managers to parts of the world at the leading edge of the changing technology and behavior, such as Helsinki and Tokyo or emerging online markets such as Korea and China. Talk with teenagers in these areas to see the future of your markets. (If the price of such expeditions is prohibitive, then create online research and connections with these regions.)

We invite you to share the results of these activities and suggest other action memos at the Convergence Marketing Forum (www.convergencemarketingforum.com).

NOTES

[1] Wind, Yoram (Jerry) and Jeremy Main. *Driving Change.* New York: The Free Press, 1998.

[2] Rebecca Henderson, MIT, presentation at IBM Global Services Academic Conference, August 2001.

[3] John Hagel, presentation to Wharton Fellows in e-Business Program, San Jose, July 13, 2001.

[4] Kelly, Susanne and Mary Ann Allison. *The Complexity Advantage: How the Science of Complexity Can Help Your Business Achieve Peak Performance*, New York: Business Week Books, 1999.

[5] Susane Berger, presentation to Wharton Fellows in e-Business program, The Wharton School, January 2001.

[6] "e-business Strategies for Enhanced Customer Service," IBM, 2001; while other studies have somewhat different numbers, the ratio of costs of contacts through different channels is consistent. See for example Penton Research Service, 1997, reported in *Marketing Journal*, June 1998, p.13.

[7] From presentations by Neal Goldstein as well as Harvard Business School case 9-300-024, "Charles Schwab Corporation (A)," Harvard Business School Publishing.

[8] Hunt, J. Timothy. "Beyond Point and Click," *Financial Post—Canada*, May 1, 2001.

[9] Ackoff, Russell. *Re-Creating the Corporation : A Design of Organizations for the 21st Century.* New York: Oxford University Press, 1999.

12

CONCLUSION
THE WISDOM OF CHIRON

"Do not seek to follow in the footsteps
of the men of old; seek what they sought."

Matsuo Basho, Japanese poet

CONCLUSION: *The Wisdom of Chiron*

What do you need to do today to run with the centaurs? What do you need to do to prepare for the even faster pace of the next generation of centaurs who will be interacting with ever more powerful technologies?

It is four years later. Sally Anderson, whom we met in Chapter 1, is driving to the party store to pick up some additional balloons for her daughter's sixteenth birthday. On the way, Sally tells her car to call her son, Peter, in France. It seems like only yesterday, she was driving Mary to soccer practice. Now Mary is 16 and Peter, after graduating from the University of Chicago and working briefly for McKinsey, is studying at INSEAD in France.

Peter answers his cell phone from the train as he is heading to meet some friends in Paris. She reminds Peter that his sister's sweet 16 party will be taking place this afternoon and invites him to join them. He says he'll be visiting friends at the time, but will patch in through his cell phone to join them by video. He wouldn't miss it for the world, and he double checks to make sure his mother has the package he sent through MyGiftBuyer,[1] a personalized online gift recommendation service that helps him keep track of birthdays, interests and past purchases of his family and friends. (Of course he had received a confirmation on his cell phone at the moment the package was delivered to the door, but he wanted the personal satisfaction of his mother acknowledging his thoughtfulness.)

Peter thanks his mother for sending him the dinner that was delivered from Americanpie.com last week, a customized catering service that delivers home-cooked food to him in Paris, using his mother's own recipes. He reassures her that as much as he enjoyed this taste of home, it could never compare with her own cooking. Peter tells his mother he has been taking a marketing course over the Internet with a Wharton professor in Philadelphia who taught him at INSEAD as a visiting professor last year. The professor has created a virtual community of former students and invites them to join his current students and visiting executives from around the world virtually in the classroom. Using Internet 2 technology at INSEAD and Wharton, Peter and other peers on both sides of the Atlantic can actually interact in real time with a realistic, three-dimensional classroom at Wharton.

Peter also tells his mother about a great new piece of world music he's downloaded from a group in a tiny African village that he's been listening to on the train. As he's talking, he plays her a short clip and then with a touch of the button sends her the link to download the music by email through the MusicNet site that pays the artists. Sally hangs up as she walks into the party store, shaking her head at how much the world has changed in such a short time. She never thought the day her daughter turned 16 would come so soon, and she never imagined the world would look anything like this.

THE NEXT GENERATION OF CENTAURS

The next generation of centaurs is already at your doorstep and the strategic decisions you make today will determine whether you are positioned to meet them. In a few years, the centaurs will be traveling even more quickly on the hooves of technology. The Internet will be faster and more fully developed. Technology will emerge in ways that we cannot even anticipate at this time.

But while consumers will be changed in some ways by these new technologies, and they will be more empowered to do new things, they will continue to have human characteristics that make them resistant to change. The advances of technology in the future will only bring our human needs into sharper relief and make the demand for convergence marketing strategies all the more urgent. To understand and prepare for these new convergence challenges, we need to listen to the lessons that the centaurs are teaching us today.

The Wisdom of Chiron

In Greek mythology, Chiron was one of the wisest and most famous of the centaurs, who helped train the warrior Achilles for battle. Today, business leaders face a battle for the future that will not be won by tradition or current strengths alone, but by learning from the centaurs. We need creativity and wisdom about where industries and consumer markets are headed. It is our contention that the hybrid consumer, the centaur, will play a central role in how the markets of the future unfold. So this centaur, like Chiron, may have much to teach us. What lessons can we learn from the centaur that will make us better prepared for the emerging technologies and competitive battles ahead?

Among the lessons of the centaur highlighted in this book:

- *Focus on the centaur:* Focusing your marketing strategy on either the cyberconsumer or the traditional consumer alone is a mistake. The hybrid consumer is neither a cyberconsumer nor traditional consumer, but a new mixture. As more consumers are introduced to the technology, the centaur is where the action is.

- *Capitalize on the new drivers of marketing:* As we examined, the technology allows consumers to meet their needs in ways they never could before. As discussed in Part II of the book, this has helped create new drivers of marketing: customerization and personalization, community, multiple channels, new competitive value, and choice tools. How can you use these new drivers to rethink your approaches to marketing? What is the next generation of drivers that will be drawn from the interaction of consumers with emerging technology? Although some managers will continue to contend that traditional marketing principles hold in the new environment, there are fundamentally new marketing dynamics presented by these interactive technologies, and these dynamics create the need for new marketing strategies.

- *Don't stop with marketing, but change the organization:* The modern organization is not designed for the new convergent marketing and marketing-driven business strategy. To meet the interaction and rapid-change demanded by the centaur, you need to redesign your organization. As your company's systems become more transparent to employees, suppliers and customers, it is not enough to put up a fancy web page façade over an old organization. You have to change the underlying architecture utilizing the 5Cs to make it more customer-centric, more flexible, and more wired. You also need to create a culture that is comfortable with experimentation.

- *Continue to listen to the centaurs:* Both the technology and how consumers relate to it are changing. Broadband access and mobile telephony are just the tip of the iceberg. The generation that has grown up with computers, cell phones, and the Internet has a different relationship to the technology. But these next generation centaurs still have the same human needs, and the most interesting questions in marketing are centered on how these consumers balance the new technology against enduring human needs. Create panels of consumers online and offline across diverse demographic and cultural groups—including kids—and across levels of experience with the technology. Look at what they do and listen to what they say about their relationship to the technology.

Their comments may surprise you. For example, a Helsinki teenager on a Wharton panel on mobile culture in June 2001 commented on the difference between voice communication and short messaging (SMS): "When you get a phone call, it is totally the opposite of SMS. SMS represents the joy of communicating, while phone calls are the burden of communicating." How many developers of phone systems and mobile services could have possibly anticipated such a statement? Most assumed that voice would be the most attractive mode of communication, while text would be difficult and uninteresting. They failed to recognize the intimacy and privacy of the written word, something that only consumers using the devices would fully reveal. What an unpredictable thing is the emerging consumer. The only way to really know what consumers will do is to watch them.

- *Creativity is the capital for the future:* Creativity and innovation are vital to the future success of the enterprise. In an environment in which many things are changing, sticking to the same strategies and principles is the road to decline and death. One way to develop creative perspectives for the future and creative solutions is to use scenario planning to explore the possibilities of the future. The challenge is to develop organizations that can use the forces that Joseph Schumpeter called "creative destruction" to drive innovation and organizational creativity. This is the source of long-term value.

- *Change your mental model:* We have to change the way we see the world to be able to see the possibilities in the new technologies. Research in neuroscience and complexity theory indicates that we use less than 20 percent of the information around us to make sense of visual images.[2] The remaining part is provided by the models in our brains. In other words, we very often see what we expect to see. The mental models of traditional marketing limited the ability of managers to see the potential of the new technology. The mental models built around the cyberconsumer focused too much attention on the technology. Both limit our ability to understand the centaur. We need to change our mental models and experiment with new models to understand the opportunities created at the intersection of the consumer, technology, and company.

- *Transformation, transformation, transformation:* Today the secret to marketing success in an interactive, networked world is transformation, transformation, transformation. How can the company change itself to meet the ever shifting competitive environment and the ever escalating demands of consumers? How can you continuously transform your organization into the type of company customers will want to come to, become your co-producers and stay?

- *Ask the right questions:* There are a number of diagnostic tools, such as Cisco's Net Readiness instrument, to help assess your level of competency in addressing the challenges of the Internet. Throughout the book, we've raised a series of questions related to the content of each chapter. What are the right questions for your company? What are the answers today? How would you like to be able to answer them?

- *Identify and reexamine your assumptions:* Explicitly examine the assumptions you have made in your current mental model and how these assumptions need to be challenged in the light of the centaur. Consider the diverse aspects of your company strategy and architecture as summarized in the rows of Exhibit 12–1. Fill out this table. For each row, answer three questions: What are your assumptions about each area? How are these assumptions challenged by the centaur? How do you need to redesign to reflect these changed assumptions?

- *Experiment:* Since the future is not knowable, and the certainty is that very intelligent and well-informed managers will get it wrong tomorrow as they have in the past, we have no choice but to experiment. Design a number of bold experiments to test new directions and confirm or disprove your assumptions and hypotheses. Throughout the book, we have offered a few suggestions for experiments in a series of "Action Memos." These might serve as a starting point for your own experiments.

EXHIBIT 12–1 A STRATEGY PROCESS

	I. Identify Assumptions	II. Challenge Them in Light of the Centaur	III. Redesign
Vision			
Business Paradigm			
Value Proposition			
Stretch Objectives			
Business and Revenue Models			
Strategies			
Organizational Architecture			
Implementation Plan			

THE COMPLEX IMPLEMENTATION CHALLENGE WITH A SIMPLE FOCUS

To meet the challenge of the centaur, you face a complex challenge. You need to transform your company along multiple dimensions simultaneously, as illustrated in Exhibit 12–2. You need to transform your view of the consumer from either a traditional or cyber consumer to the hybrid centaur. You need to understand the nature of the centaurs and their needs. You also need to explore how the 5Cs (community, customerization, channel options, competitive value and choice tools) offer new ways to meet these needs.

The ripple effects of this focus on the centaur extend out across the entire organization. To serve this centaur, you need to develop convergent business and marketing strategies. And to do this effectively, you need to transform the organizational architecture to create a convergent organization and develop an implementation plan. Since all these changes reinforce one another, you need to pursue them simultaneously.

EXHIBIT 12-2 THE COMPLEX CHALLENGE OF CONVERGENCE

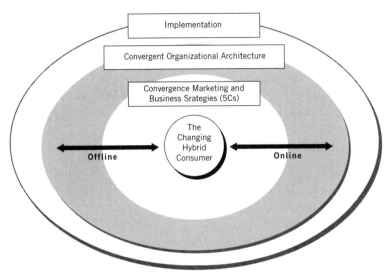

This may seem like a very ambitious challenge. But at the heart of this complex picture, there is a simple center. Keep your eye on the centaur and where the centaur is headed. As long as you don't lose sight of the centaur, the strategies and architecture you need to succeed will follow. As long as you continue to follow the centaur as new behaviors and technologies emerge, you will have insights into where you need to position your organization for the future.

Responding to the Challenge of the Centaurs

Listen carefully as we enter this future. With each new wave of technology, you will hear some people arguing that it means the end of the marketing and business strategy approaches that we have known in the past. Others will argue that each new change can be seen as an incremental move through the lenses of the past. To succeed, you need to sail between these two extremes to focus on the centaur. With every new revolution in technology or processes, ask: How will the consumer change as a result? How will the consumer remain the same?

Two years ago, the cyberconsumer was king and the dot-coms where changing the world. Today, the landscape has been radically altered. We cannot let the headlines or NSADAQ dictate our corporate strategies. We need be able to step back from the headlines and take a broader view. We cannot focus exclusively on the technology—as exciting as it may be—or on the company, or on the consumer in isolation. We need to focus on the interactions among all three.

The time to prepare for Peter Anderson and other centaurs is now. The experiments you conduct, the investments you make today will determine the offerings you'll be able to provide to young consumers like Peter four years from now. These children of the centaurs will be quite different. It will be easier for them to integrate these diverse technologies. They will have more technological savvy and expectations, but will be humans nonetheless at heart. Peter is even more wired than his mother, yet he is still his mother's son. Are you ready for the c-change ahead?

The challenges presented in this book are not theoretical. They will mean the future of your business. Incumbent firms have a tremendous opportunity in today's environment. They have the relationships and the resources to build effective online businesses that are truly integrated with their existing organizations. Internet startups also have tremendous opportunity in learning from the lessons of the dot-com failures and using their technology expertise to integrate their operations with established firms or built their own offline expertise. But will you seize this opportunity? How can you apply the concepts discussed in this book to your own organization? Are you ready to change your mental models and business paradigms? Will you be prepared to run with the centaurs?

NOTES

[1] Note that most of sites listed in this section are fictitious. Any resemblance to existing sites is purely coincidental.

[2] Crook, Colin, remarks to the Wharton Fellows in e-Business Program, The Wharton School, May 7, 2001.

INDEX

M

Malleable digital environment, 241–242
Managers
  sharing
    decision-making tools, 184
Manufacturing
  moving toward customerization, 69–74
Market-driven approach
  implementation, 309–310
Marketing
  adapting to change in, 305
  approach
    for hybrid consumer, 11
  boundary changing, 199
  broadening capabilities, 251–252
  capitalize on drivers, 318
  changing interactions, 200
  convergence questions, 202
  convergence strategies, 38
  customization, 69–70
  decision-making tools
    convergence challenges, 184–185
  disintermediation, 206
  Internet evolution, 123
  messages
    focus, 196
    recognize limits, 195
  metaphors, 231
  moving toward customerization, 69–74
  network, 239
  new rules, 121–124
  personal example, 204–205
  personalize messages, 86
  reaching forgotten areas, 212
  redefining, 208–209
  research
    augmented with modeling, 250–251
  shifts
    consumer interaction, 209
  target overlooked areas, 241
  transforming, 201–222
Marketing and business strategies
  convergence, 219–221
Marketing strategies
  convergence, 225–252
    personal experience, 228–230
  economic targets, 210
  examination, 252
  focus on whole, 239
  four P's, 231–239
  implications, 220–221
  other, 240–251
Mass customization
  benefits, 69

Mass production
  combining with customer
    configuration, 82
  to customerization, 67–68
Mental model
  change, 320
Mergers
  cross-industry, 208
Messages
  company
    third party information, 185–186
  marketing
    focus, 196
    recognize limits, 195
  tailor to consumer, 86
Metaphors
  marketing, 231
Metcalfe's Law, 37
Metrics, 282
  focuses on, 283
Metrics centered culture, 219
Mexico
  Internet connections, 33
Military metaphors, 231
Mobile Internet, 33–34
Modeling
  on demand with marketing research,
    250–251
Modular organization creation
  customizable, 268–271
Moore's Law, 37
Motivations, 51–53
Multichannel solutions
  for customers, 267
Multiple pricing options, 165–166

N

Name-your-own price, 163
NetMeeting, 276
Novelty
  new value source, 218
  offline vs. online, 153
  value
    equation, 150
    offering and experience
      convergence, 157–158

O

Offering
  convergence value, 156
Offline
  needs met, 127

The *Financial Times* delivers a world of business news.

Use the Risk-Free Trial Voucher below!

To stay ahead in today's business world you need to be well-informed on a daily basis. And not just on the national level. You need a news source that closely monitors the entire world of business, and then delivers it in a concise, quick-read format.

With the *Financial Times* you get the major stories from every region of the world. Reports found nowhere else. You get business, management, politics, economics, technology and more.

Now you can try the *Financial Times* for 4 weeks, absolutely risk free. And better yet, if you wish to continue receiving the *Financial Times* you'll get great savings off the regular subscription rate. Just use the voucher below.

8 reasons why you should read the Financial Times for 4 weeks RISK-FREE!

To help you stay current with significant
developments in the world economy ...
and to assist you to make informed business
decisions — the Financial Times brings you:

❶ Fast, meaningful overviews of international affairs ... plus daily briefings on major world news.

❷ Perceptive coverage of economic, business, financial and political developments with special focus on emerging markets.

❸ More international business news than any other publication.

❹ Sophisticated financial analysis and commentary on world market activity plus stock quotes from over 30 countries.

❺ Reports on international companies and a section on global investing.

❻ Specialized pages on management, marketing, advertising and technological innovations from all parts of the world.

❼ Highly valued single-topic special reports (over 200 annually) on countries, industries, investment opportunities, technology and more.

❽ The Saturday Weekend FT section — a globetrotter's guide to leisure-time activities around the world: the arts, fine dining, travel, sports and more.

For Special Offer See Over

FT FINANCIAL TIMES
World business newspaper

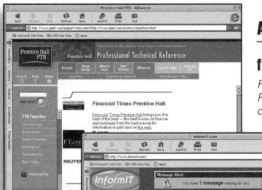